What People Ai
Country Are S

D0208878

Without a doubt Peter Lalonde is a leader in providing solid documentation of the prophetic significance of current news events.

—Dave Hunt,
author, researcher

Like no one else I've met, Peter Lalonde has the ability to take the prophecies of the Bible and make them completely understandable to those that hear him. Now I know exactly what to be watching for on the evening news.

—Pat Matrisciana
Jeremiah Films

Peter Lalonde's clear message not only helps us to understand that these are indeed the very last days, he also encourages us to live every day in that light.

—Arno Froese
Midnight Call Ministries

I believe that God is using Peter Lalonde's ministry in very special ways in these last moments before Jesus' return.

—John Wesley White,
Associate Evangelist,
Billy Graham Crusades

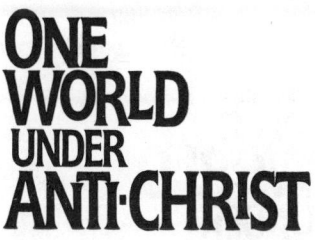

ONE WORLD UNDER ANTI-CHRIST

I thoroughly enjoy Peter's writings and find them a constant source of information and inspiration.

—Tim LaHaye, author
Understanding Bible Prophecy

Today our world is being seduced by a message so powerful and deceptive that if it were possible even the very elect would be deceived. Peter Lalonde explains this deception as few others can.

—David Webber

If you want to know what is happening in the world of Bible prophecy you should be reading Peter Lalonde.

—David Breese
Christian Destiny Ministries

I believe that the insights you will gain from Peter Lalonde's writings will thrill and amaze you.

—Ray Brubaker
God's News Behind the News

Peter Lalonde's ministry has a vital role to play in awakening the Church to the rapidly unfolding signs of the soon coming of the Messiah.

—Grant Jeffrey, author,
Armageddon: Appointment with Destiny

Peter Lalonde presents the clearest and most insightful descriptions of the New Age movement that I've ever heard.

—Bob Souer
CBN Radio

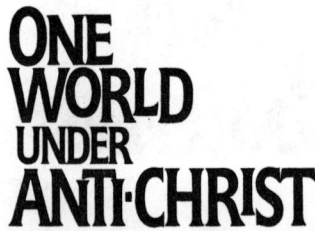

ONE WORLD UNDER ANTI-CHRIST

ONE WORLD UNDER ANTI-CHRIST

Peter Lalonde

HARVEST HOUSE PUBLISHERS
Eugene, Oregon 97402

ONE WORLD UNDER ANTICHRIST

Copyright © 1991 by Harvest House Publishers
Eugene, Oregon 97402

Library of Congress Cataloging-in-Publication Data

Lalonde, Peter.
    One world under Antichrist / Peter Lalonde.
    ISBN 0-89081-931-9
      1. Bible—Prophecies—International organization.   2. Antichrist.
I. Title.
BS649.I56L34   1991   91-3314
236'.9—dc20   CIP

Printed in the United States of America.

To Patti,
My co-laborer and best friend.

Contents

Section I

The Prophetic Players

Chapter 1

A Way That Seems Right

We stand at the edge of history. Dramatic changes in Europe, the Middle East, and the Soviet Union make this inevitable. The world as we know it is being changed forever. Even more exciting is the fact that today's news was actually foretold thousands of years ago in the Bible!

Longtime students of Bible prophecy stand in awe. Skeptics are taking a second look. Even the casual observer is shaking his head in amazement. The evidence is clear: A simple analysis of the facts makes the conclusion almost inescapable that we live at the most expectant moment of history. As citizens of the 1990's we have front row seats to those very events that will culminate with the return of Jesus Christ to this planet and the establishment of His kingdom!

Unfortunately, by believing that Bible prophecy is just a confusing mix of heads, horns, and beasts, many people have been missing out on some of the most exciting, fascinating, and faith-building events in the entire history of mankind. Others have heard about some of the pieces of the prophetic puzzle but have failed in their effort to bring the big picture into focus. Most people, however, just have no idea how unbelievably accurate the Bible is in describing these very days.

By reading this book you will not only learn how accurate the prophecies have been, but you will come away with an understanding of what lies ahead, who the major actors in this final drama are, and what to watch for as history builds to the climax that only God Himself could have envisioned!

Why Study Prophecy?

There is no question that Bible prophecy is fascinating. Aside from that, however, many people ask why we should study and seek to understand Bible prophecy. After all, they protest, so much of it seems so "negative." Some argue, "If it's all going to happen anyway, and there's nothing we can do to stop it, why bother worrying about it?" One national alliance of 26 evangelical denominations declares that an expectant waiting for the soon return of Jesus Christ is actually a "bogus theology" which is "paralyzing" the efforts of *Christians to reform this world.*[1] They argue that we should go on with life as usual, and if the Lord comes, He comes; and if He doesn't come, we won't have wasted any time "foolishly gazing into the heavens."[2]

Such logic is inconsistent with the words of our Lord. If Jesus did not want us to watch for His coming, He would not have taken so much time to clearly describe hundreds of signs that would precede His coming, and He would not have promised a special blessing to those who make the effort to read and understand the prophecies of the Bible.[3] Furthermore, when the disciples asked Jesus, "What shall be the sign of thy coming, and of the end of the world?" He did not tell them it would be a waste of valuable time to be watching for these things. Conversely, from both the detailed answer that Jesus gave and the tremendous amount of space given to these signs in the Scriptures it would seem that God thought it important for believers to keep a close watch on the signs of the times. Why?

Perhaps the best way to help us to understand the reasons is with a brief illustration. Imagine a lazy summer day. Floating down a peaceful river is a Christian man in a fishing boat. As he relaxes the Lord speaks to him and says, "My son, I need to warn you about what lies ahead on this river. You see, one day you will come around a bend and suddenly the water will become very rough. Treacherous rocks will loom in the water and the waves will begin to crash over the bow of your boat. As you look around you will see some very specific things on the shoreline that will pinpoint for you exactly where you are on this river. Then you will look up, and as your boat begins to take on water, you will see a waterfall lying ahead more frightening than Niagara Falls. You will realize that your boat is about to go over the falls."

"Why are you telling me this?" we might expect our terrified Christian brother in the boat to ask. "Because I want you to know," the Lord answers, "that before that boat goes over the falls I will reach down from heaven and in a moment, in the twinkling of an eye, pull you out of that boat, that where I am you may be also! I want you to remember that your hope is not in that boat but in *me*."

A More Sure Word

Of course, this short story is a very simplistic illustration of the message of Bible prophecy. However, it does allow us to put into focus some of the reasons that make a clear understanding of Bible prophecy so very important.

The Bible is a message to all mankind and a promise of hope to those who place their trust in God's Messiah, Jesus. The prophetic portions of the Scriptures are for the consolation and instruction of those believers in the face of the present predicted turmoil. Some of the signs of the times are very troubling, but by telling us beforehand specifically what will happen in the last days, God has given us the assurance that He is in control. No turn of events will take Him by surprise. Likewise, no turn of events need take *us* by surprise either. All these things are allowed and used by God to bring about His purposes. They can be seen as signs that we are getting close to the Lord's imminent return, first to catch away all His followers and later to rescue Israel and reign from Jerusalem for a thousand years.

When we see these signs of the times we know how to respond. First, if our trust is in our Savior, Jesus Christ, we know not to fear. Surely this is the most beautiful message of the prophetic Word. While the rest of the world shakes in fear "at those things coming upon the earth,"[4] we as believers can rest in great hope and assurance. That is why Jesus told us that in these last days "ye shall hear of wars and rumors of wars; see that ye be not troubled, for all these things must come to pass."[5]

Secondly, prophecy serves as a reminder to the believer that true hope will not be found in this world. Like the man in the boat, we know that we are not to focus on the seaworthiness of our "boat," since God has already told us that this world system in which we live is destined for destruction.

Another purpose of prophecy is to wake people up, shake people up, and cause them to examine their lives and get on with righteous living. As the apostle Peter put it:

> The day of the Lord will come as a thief in the night, in which the heavens shall pass away with a great noise and the elements shall melt with fervent heat; the earth also and the works therein shall be burned up. Seeing then that all these things shall be dissolved, what manner of persons ought ye to be in all holy conversation and godliness, looking for and hastening the coming of the day of God, wherein the heavens being on fire shall be dissolved and the elements shall melt with fervent heat? Nevertheless we, according to his promise, look for new heavens and a new earth, wherein dwelleth righteousness (2 Peter 3:10-13).

The point is very clear: If we accept the truth of the prophetic Word of God, then our life's focus will not be primarily on this world's problems but on the coming of the Lord. Our concerns will be shifted from the cares of daily living to concern for the spiritually lost and dying.

Directly related to the prophetic call to take our eyes off this world is the call to set our sights on the skies. Luke 21:28 states very plainly what we are to do as we see the fulfillment of Bible prophecy:

> When these things begin to come to pass, then look up and lift up your heads, for your redemption draweth nigh.

The predominant message for the believer is not the *bad news*, but the *good news it foreshadows*. And that good news is the soon return of our Lord and Savior Jesus Christ.

I Didn't Hear That!

However, let's build upon our fishing boat story for just a moment. Let's imagine that in this boat of life there is not only the Christian man but an unbeliever as well. Though they are both in the same boat, the unbeliever did not hear God speak. When the boat hits the rough water they both see the same fearful outlook—the rocks, the water-filled hull, and the waterfall looming ahead—but the unbeliever, unlike the Christian, has no hope of rescue and no promise that Christ will take him to heaven.

These two men both see the same events, but they have two very different reactions. The Christian sees these signs and reacts with peace and joyous anticipation, while the unbeliever, having no assurance of the future and no hope of rescue, places his faith in his own efforts to preserve his life. If we understand this crucially important principle, we can move toward a fuller understanding of the times we live in.

The Great Fear

Today much of the world believes that we could well be approaching a climactic ending to this planet. The nuclear and chemical "sword of Damocles," reborn in the Persian Gulf crisis, is one clear indication that it is not just students of Bible prophecy who recognize that Armageddon looms just over the horizon. Every man, woman, and child on this planet is aware of the signs of the times. Where people differ is in *their understanding of what this means*: The child of God who understands Bible prophecy responds with peace and hope, while those who do not trust in God's assurances are overcome with distress and perplexity, their very hearts "failing them for fear."

The humanist, the atheist, the agnostic, the scientist, the politician, and all who do not know God's Messiah, Jesus Christ, obviously cannot take their eyes off this world; they are not awaiting the return of Jesus. And because they do not possess this true hope, they find that their only remaining hope is in personally saving this world from destruction.

Unlike the Christian, they are not looking to the Savior to lead them to the skies; instead, they are looking to their own strength to turn their boat around by rebuilding their planet and creating a New Age of peace. They are not looking for the biblical new heavens and new earth in which God reigns. Instead they are determined to build their own New Age of peace and prosperity right here on planet Earth.

Indeed, it is this earth-based hope that has become the foundation stone of the New Age movement. The heart of the movement is not about crystals, trance channelers, holistic healers, or reincarnationists, although they are all a part of it. It is not even primarily about the rapidly spreading teachings of "human potential" and the belief that we are gods, although these are also becoming central New Age tenets. Instead, the heart of the New Age movement is *the rejection of hope in Jesus Christ* in the face of these planet-threatening crises. The determination to solve man's problems without God forms the basis of this new humanism called the New Age movement. Under this definition the New Age movement, far from being an oddball assortment of hippies and eccentrics, is becoming a collection of everyone trying to create global peace without the Prince of Peace, Jesus Christ.

We're in This Boat Together

In the late 1980's and early 1990's we witnessed the emergence of terms like "global village," "spaceship earth," and "one world." These phrases, which were once uttered only by hard-core globalists and New Agers, have now reached the mainstream. They are the language of the consciousness-raising campaign to convince us that planetary crises will only be solved through planetary action. As a result the Christian hope of new heavens and a new earth is under a barrage of heavy artillery from virtually every flank. The message of biblical, individual salvation has been placed in opposition to planetary salvation. Adherents of biblically defined salvation are now being viewed as selfish, dangerous outsiders. New Agers make their rejection of the Christian's "blessed hope" very clear. John Randolph Price, the organizer of the World Peace Day, writes:

> [I see] images of a new heaven and a new earth. . . . This world will be saved. The planet will be healed and harmonized. We can let the kingdom come . . . which means that this world can be transformed into a heaven right now. . . . This is no fantasy. This is not scientific or religious fiction. This is the main event of our individual lives.[6]

Likewise the organization "Planetary Citizens" complains:

> Someone is always trying to summon us back to a dead allegiance: Back to God, the simple-minded religion of an earlier day. . . . Back to simple-minded patriotism . . . [we must] take the future into our own hands.[7]

New Age leader and Catholic theologian Thomas Berry argues that the time has come for a new theology which better understands these signs of the times: "All human institutions, professions, programs and activities must be judged primarily according to the extent they either obstruct and ignore or foster a mutually enhancing human-earth relationship. That is how good and evil will be judged in the coming years."[8] Psychiatrist and bestselling author M. Scott Peck agrees:

> ... the most extraordinary result of nuclear technology is that it has brought the human race as a whole to the point at which physical and spiritual salvation are no longer separable.[9]

The unity of perception is incredible. Sun Myung Moon claims, "Our globe today is like a boat sailing on a stormy ocean. If the boat weathers the storm, we will all be saved, and clearly we must save ourselves. To do that, we must learn to live together in brotherhood as part of one common family. Then we will not only survive but prosper."[10] Dennis Weaver, TV's "McCloud" and a New Age convert, is a frequent participant in consciousness-raising events and an evangelist of this same New Age gospel. He claims, "Nothing will be accomplished by ourselves, but together there's nothing we can't do. We are the architects of our destiny because we have the power of thought and the power of choice. We are the only ones who can save this Earth. . . ."[11]

The American Humanist Association took a full-page advertisement in the *New York Times* with the headline "Humanism is the best way of life, creating joy and beauty in the here and now."[12] It boldly proclaims that "there is no pie in the sky awaiting us" and offers the hope of Edwin Markham's poem "Earth Is Enough":

> We men of earth have here the stuff
> Of Paradise—we have enough!
> We need no other stones to build
> The Temple of the Unfulfilled—
> No other ivory for the doors—
> No other marble for the floors—

> No other cedar for the beam
> And dome of man's immortal dream.[13]

Peace and Safety and the New World Order

Today the chorus of voices calling for unified human action has extended far beyond the New Age and humanist subculture. The voices are now being heard in the corridors of political and ecclesiastical power as well.

In his book *Perestroika* Mikhail Gorbachev echoes the same call for world community. He even directly warns against some "false" biblical hope of escape:

> In short, we in the Soviet leadership have come to the conclusion, and are reiterating it, that there is a need for new political thinking. Furthermore, Soviet leaders are vigorously seeking to translate this new thinking into action, primarily in the field of disarmament. This is what prompted the foreign policy initiatives we have honestly offered the world. As regards the scope of new historical thinking, it really embraces all the basic problems of our time. For all the contradictions of the present-day world, for all the diversity of social and political systems in it, and for all the different choices made by the nations in different times, this world is nevertheless one whole. We are all passengers aboard one ship, the Earth, and we must not allow it to be wrecked. There will be no second Noah's Ark.[14]

Gorbachev is not alone. In a nationwide address following the 1990 Iraqi invasion of Kuwait, the leader of the world's other superpower outlined his new vision. According to George Bush:

> A new partnership of nations has begun. And we stand today at a unique and extraordinary moment.

The crisis in the Persian Gulf, as grave as it is, also offers a rare opportunity to move toward an historic period of cooperation. Out of these troubled times, our fifth objective, a new world order, can emerge: a new era, freer from the threat of terror, stronger in the pursuit of justice, and more secure in the quest for peace. An era in which the nations of the world, east and west, north and south, can prosper and live in harmony.

A hundred generations have searched for this elusive path to peace, while a thousand wars have raged across the span of human endeavor. And today that new world is struggling to be born. A world quite different from the one we've known. A world where the rule of law supplants the rule of the jungle. A world in which the nations recognize and share responsibility for freedom and justice. A world where the strong respect the rights of the weak.... This crisis is the first assault on the new world that we seek.[15]

The Gospel of This Earth

Meanwhile, liberal church groups join in the same call. The Reverend W. Franklyn Richardson, a member of the Central Committee of the World Council of Churches (WCC), was recently asked what role the council would play in the future. His response was:

The WCC...I guess it's similar to the United Nations of the Church...I think that the future for the world is that we are becoming more of a village, that this is a "global village" and that everything that happens in the world is related...we are in one world, one community, and we're going to have to learn how to live together in it, or else we're going to destroy each other. And that is going to be the hardest lesson.

> The church is going to have to aid the world in under-
> standing that. . . .[16]

An association of Oriental and Eastern Orthodox churches on creation goes even further and says our ultimate goal is to "become a transfigured world, a new world." Since human beings are part of the "material side of created reality," the group says, "the salvation of humanity necessarily involves the salvation and deification of the cosmos."[17] The World Council of Churches has now gone as far as to make environmental consciousness a test for orthodoxy.

These sentiments are at the very heart of the religious mainstream. In fact, it is precisely this assimilation of the world's fears and concerns that has the present Pope leading the way in several interfaith efforts in the name of world peace. For example, the Global Day of Peace in the mid-eighties has moved the ecumenical movement well beyond Christian denominational unity onto the fast lane of interfaith unity efforts. All of this is being done, of course, in the name of saving the earth.

The Pastoral Letter of the National Conference of Catholic Bishops (May 1988) has no problem identifying the solution:

> Just as the nation-state was a step in the evolution of
> government . . . we are now entering an era of new
> global interdependence requiring global systems of
> governance to manage the resulting conflicts . . . these
> growing tensions cannot be remedied by a single
> nation-state approach. They shall require the con-
> certed effort of the whole world community.

It is becoming ever more apparent that religious unity has become the basis for this world community. One example is this observation by a Buddhist Monk:

> The unity of religion promoted by the Holy Father
> Pope John Paul II and approved by his holiness the

> Dalai Lama is not a goal to be achieved immediately, but a day may come when the love and compassion which both Buddha and Christ preached so eloquently will unite the world in a common effort to save humanity from senseless destruction, by leading it toward the light in which we all believe.[18]

The globalist arguments are so persuasive, the cause so noble, and the stakes so high that a Christian has a difficult time justifying opposition to such efforts to construct an era of "peace and safety." How can a Christian politician stand against the creation of global institutions to protect the environment? How can he counter the convincing argument that the World Court must be given more power to enforce environmental laws for "the common good" of mankind?

To say that Christians should set their focus on eternal matters in the face of immediate temporal dangers seems so simpleminded that many evangelical leaders deride such thinking as "defeatist" and "escapist." Likewise, the world grows angry at such thinking. We are warned not to stand in the way of global progress. In fact, in one important area, the environment, prominent unbelievers charge that it is the Judeo-Christian tradition's rejection of the deity of the cosmos that got us into this mess in the first place.

A Way That Seems Right

The preceding thumbnail sketch demonstrates society's widespread desire to build a New World Order consisting of a world government, world economy, and world religion. It is with this understanding that we can begin to discern one of the most important purposes of Bible prophecy. It is God's warning that because the world will not understand the signs of the times they will try to build a man-centered kingdom of peace. In Revelation 13 we are given an incredibly clear picture of this prophesied world system. Furthermore, the Bible indicates that in man's most brilliant attempt to build this kingdom of peace he will run headlong into the greatest villain in history. The Word of God points out the three central pillars of the Antichrist's system:

1. World government: "Power was given him [the Antichrist] over all kindreds and tongues and nations" (Revelation 13:7; cf. Daniel 7:23).

2. World economy: "He [the False Prophet] causeth all, both small and great, rich and poor, free and bond, to receive a mark in their right hand or in their foreheads, and that no man might buy or sell except he that had the mark or the name of the beast or the number of his name" (Revelation 13:16,17).

3. World religion: "All the world wondered after the beast. And they worshiped the dragon which gave power unto the beast; and they worshiped the beast, saying, Who is like the beast? Who is able to make war with him? . . . And all that dwell upon the earth shall worship him, whose names are not written in the book of life of the Lamb slain from the foundation of the world" (Revelation 13:3,4,8).

It is breathtaking to realize that what we are witnessing today in the emergence of the "New World Order" may well be the fulfillment of Revelation 13! In the world's rejection of the true Prince of Peace and in their rush to build their own earthly kingdom, the Antichrist's government is being prefabricated for him! And just as the "anti"-Christ is a fraudulent messiah, this "anti"-kingdom will be a cheap but convincing imitation of Jesus' millennial kingdom.

When the Bible speaks of this final New World Order it is always completely intertwined with the emperor who will one day rule it. This emperor is, of course, the one whom the Bible calls the Antichrist or the Man of Sin. Since the Bible indicates that the emergence of the prophesied New World Order is simultaneous with the rise of the Antichrist, we need to take a look at this coming world leader and see how he will burst onto the world scene. Once we understand that scenario, and know who the key players in the last-days coalition are, we will be able to understand the nature of this coming false kingdom of peace.

Chapter 2

The Fake Messiah

It was late 1990. The world's attention was riveted on the nation of Kuwait. The largest multinational force in world history stood poised to do battle with Saddam Hussein and his occupying troops. Newscasts carried little news except that from the Persian Gulf. Nothing, it seemed—not even the increasing Soviet brutalities in the Baltic States—could pull the world's attention away from the looming Gulf War. The one exception centered around a tiny piece of real estate known as the Temple Mount.

Here in the city of Jerusalem, some 1920 years after the last Jewish temple had been destroyed by the Roman armies, the world's focus was snapped back to this very location when Arabs began to hail fist-sized rocks down onto the Jewish worshipers at the Wailing Wall. This Western Wall, as it is also called, is the last existing part of the wall which surrounded the ancient Temple of Solomon. The earth inside that wall comes up to the top of the wall and forms what is known as the Temple Mount. The level of the ground outside the wall is about 60 feet lower. It is here that Orthodox Jews gather for prayers. Today, on the inside of the wall, the Temple Mount is Arab-controlled. In place of the Jewish Temple the Dome of the Rock now stands.

It was from their positions at the top of the 60-foot wall that the

Arabs began to shower Jewish worshipers with their deadly weapons. The cause of the riot and ensuing clash, which ended in the death of 21 people and the shifting of worldwide attention to the tiny nation of Israel, was the rumor that a Jewish group was planning to march up onto the Temple Mount and lay the cornerstone for the building of the third temple! However, it wasn't the size or nature of the clash that attracted worldwide attention. The reason is simple: *Jerusalem and the small country of Israel are at the very center of God's plans in these last days.* All remaining history will in one way or another revolve directly around the descendants of Abraham, Isaac, and Jacob. Furthermore, as the recent uprising foreshadowed, the Temple Mount itself will be center stage for much of the prophetic drama that lies ahead.

The Promised Land

If one thing is paramount in having a correct biblical view of prophecy, it is understanding this central role that Israel plays in all the last-days events. The fact that the Jewish people are back in their land after having been scattered to every corner of the globe for almost 2000 years is a miracle in itself. But it is much more than that. Israel's return to her homeland in 1948 is one of the most significant prophetic fulfillments in all of world history. This rebirth of the State of Israel confirmed the truth of God's Word in two dramatic ways. First, it completed God's promise to both scatter and then regather His chosen people. Although they were driven from their land on several occasions because of their sin and unbelief, God promised Israel that He would ultimately regather them. Countless prophecies in both the Old and New Testaments detail what the Hebrew prophet Ezekiel told us thousands of years ago would happen:

> I will take you from among the heathen, and gather you out of all countries, and will bring you into your own land (Ezekiel 36:24).

Ezekiel was even so specific as to tell us that Israel would at first return to their land in unbelief, as they are today, but that God would then begin to spiritually revive them (Ezekiel 37). But that is not all the Hebrew prophets have told us. They foretold that this final regathering would take place only after the land had been laid waste for centuries,[1] after the Jews had been scattered to every nation under the sun,[2] and after the Jews had been persecuted and afflicted in every country in which they dwelt.[3]

Of course, we know that this is exactly what happened to Israel and her people. However, that was only the beginning. Jesus Himself told us that once the Jews were back in their homeland they would regain control of the city of Jerusalem. In 1967, when Israel was attacked by several Arab nations with many times her military might, she not only successfully defended herself but also recaptured the City of Jerusalem. It was the first time that Jerusalem was back in Jewish hands since 70 A.D. The fact that these things are happening in this generation has great significance for us because the prophets have told us that these things would come to pass at a very specific time—namely, the time of the end (Ezekiel 38:8).

Next: The Temple

There are still other prophecies about Israel which have yet to be fulfilled. One of the most dramatic of these is the one stating that the Jews will rebuild their temple on the Temple Mount. Today all that stands in the way are millions of Arabs, the United Nations, and the fact that the Arabs control the Temple Mount, which is now the home of the Dome of the Rock, the second-holiest site in the Islamic faith. If Israel ever took concrete steps in the direction of rebuilding, there would immediately be a Holy War! The riots that erupted at the Western Wall when the idea was even rumored would be a picnic in comparison.

How the rebuilding of the temple will come about is unclear. Many students of Bible prophecy believe that the Dome of the Rock must be destroyed before the temple can be rebuilt. Others point to the studies of Dr. Asher Kaufman, whose surveys have found that the temple could actually be rebuilt in its original location, right alongside the Dome of the Rock, without the Islamic mosque having to be moved.

With individual Arabs and Jews barely being able to live next door to each other, it is hard to conceive of them sharing holy sites. Yet this is exactly what could happen in the days ahead. Far from being an isolated prophecy, the rebuilding of the temple, peace between Arabs and Jews, and a solution to the "Palestinian problem" are at the very heart of Bible prophecy and the birth of the New World Order. It is not too much to say, in fact, that one of the central pillars of the New World Order will be a peace treaty between Israel and her enemies. To understand the connection of all these events we need to recall a little of Israel's history.

The Seventy Weeks

The Word of God is very clear in stating that the reason the temple was destroyed, Jerusalem burned, and Israel scattered in 70 A.D. was because the Jewish people rejected and killed Jesus. Just as He had promised, God sent them their Messiah. However, because they were looking for a conquering hero to subdue all their enemies, to bring them peace and to sit on David's throne, they did not recognize Jesus' fulfillment of the role of the suffering Servant. They could not see that He had to come *twice*.

Hundreds of years before the time of Jesus, the prophet Daniel was given an overview of God's upcoming dealings with His chosen people. While he was in captivity in Babylon he was praying for God's mercy upon the children of Israel. As he prayed, the angel Gabriel appeared to him. He told Daniel that God had heard his prayer and wanted to give him understanding of what would happen to Israel in the future. What followed in that dramatic chapter of the Bible is a prophetic overview of what lay ahead for the descendants of Abraham, Isaac, and Jacob. It is that overview which helps us to understand the role of Israel, the Temple Mount, and the coming false messiah in these last days.

In what is known as "the prophecy of the seventy weeks," Daniel was told that 490 years had been given to the nation of Israel (Daniel 9). Daniel was told that by the end of these 490 years Israel would make an end of her sins, enter the age of everlasting righteousness, and accept her Messiah. However, the prophecy was broken down into several parts. The first 483 years, Daniel was told, were to be measured from the time of "the going forth of the commandment to restore and to build Jerusalem" until the coming of the Messiah. Archaeological discoveries and extensive research by Sir Robert Anderson, the one-time head of the criminal investigation division of Scotland Yard, have conclusively proved the pinpoint accuracy of the prophetic Word of God. They show that it was exactly 483 years to the day from the time that Nehemiah was given permission to rebuild Jerusalem (Nehemiah 2:4-8) until what we now know as Palm Sunday! It was on this day that Jesus was presented to Israel as their long-awaited Messiah and King. In order to comply with Old Testament prophecies Jesus sent two of His disciples to get a colt upon which He would ride into Jerusalem:

> All this was done that it might be fulfilled which was written by the prophets, saying, Tell ye the daughter of Sion, Behold, thy king cometh unto thee, meek and sitting upon an ass, and a colt the foal of an ass (Matthew 21:4,5).

The Scriptures tell us that multitudes cast their garments and palm leaves on the path as He rode down the Mount of Olives and into Jerusalem.

> They that went before and they that followed cried, saying, Hosanna! Blessed is he that cometh in the name of the Lord; blessed be the kingdom of our father David, that cometh in the name of the Lord; hosanna in the highest! (Mark 11:9,10).

However, we know that ultimately Jesus was not received by Israel as her Messiah. Indeed, as Jesus had said, they declared, "We will not have this man to reign over us" (Luke 19:14). It was then that Jesus wept at the slowness of their hearts:

> If thou hadst known, even thou, at least in this thy day, the things which belong unto thy peace! But now are they hid from thine eyes. For the days shall come upon thee that thine enemies shall cast a trench about thee... because thou knewest not the time of thy visitation (Luke 19:42-44).

Exactly 483 years after the day when the commandment to rebuild Jerusalem had been given, Israel failed to recognize her day of visitation and rejected her Messiah. At that exact moment the prophetic clock of God's dealing with Israel stopped, seven years short of the 490 years that had been given to Israel. Why did the clock stop? It stopped because Israel had spurned her Messiah and because, as the prophecy indicated, the Messiah had to be "cut off, but not for Himself." What a beautiful picture of the plan of God! Indeed the Messiah was cut off (killed), but it was not for Himself; it was for us. As we know, God gave His own Son to die for the sins of all who would simply believe in Him. Now God's attention was no longer focused upon Israel but upon a new entity called the church, the group of people all over the world who would accept Jesus Christ as their Savior.

Did this mean that Israel was forever cast off? Of course not. As the Word of God makes plain, the world which had previously been divided into Jews and Gentiles was now made up of three different groups: the Jews, the Gentiles, and the church of God. (1 Corinthians 10:32). Furthermore, the prophecy of the 70 weeks is a constant reminder that there are still seven years on the prophetic clock, interrupted by the church age, when God's focus will once again be directed toward Israel.

When will this seven-year period come about? It would seem to make sense that if the prophetic clock stopped with the birth of the church, it could not begin again until the church is gone. Such an idea fits perfectly with the biblical teaching of what is known as "the rapture." The rapture is the great hope that Jesus has given to all believers that in the last days there will be a generation of Christians who would never know death. These believers will suddenly be "caught up" to meet the Lord in the clouds.

> The Lord himself shall descend from heaven with a shout . . . and the dead in Christ shall rise first. Then we which are alive and remain shall be caught up together with them in the clouds to meet the Lord in the air; and so shall we ever be with the Lord (1 Thessalonians 4:16,17).

The biblical teaching of this "catching away" is that it will occur at the beginning of a period of time known as "the tribulation period" or "the time of Jacob's trouble" (Jeremiah 30:7). As you might expect, the Scriptures teach that this "tribulation period" will last seven years! With the church gone to heaven to be with the Lord before this seven-year tribulation period begins, the way is paved for God's focus to return to Israel for the last seven years on the prophetic time clock.

The Counterfeit Messiah

When the Jews rejected Jesus as their long-awaited Messiah, He uttered an incredible pronouncement upon the Jewish people. Of the blindness of their hearts He said:

> I have come in my Father's name and ye receive me not; if another shall come in his own name, him ye will receive (John 5:43).

The true Messiah was warning the spiritually blind children of Israel that a counterfeit messiah would come in the future and that they would receive him with open arms. This Antichrist, the prophet Daniel tells us, will arise at the beginning of the tribulation period, the last seven years on God's 490-year "timepiece." Author Dave Hunt points out:

> Many prophecy students have this picture of the Antichrist as some obviously evil ogre who will directly oppose Christ. However, the meaning of antichrist also means "in the place of." Thus the Antichrist will rise to power brilliantly. He will oppose the Messiah by pretending to be Him![4]

If the Antichrist will arise at the beginning of the tribulation period and pretend to be the true Christ, the true Messiah of Israel, then in order to understand this counterfeit we need to understand exactly who and what he will be impersonating. To do that we need to jump ahead to the end of the tribulation period, when the real Messiah, Jesus Christ, will return to this world.

The Second Coming of the True Messiah

When Israel rejected Him on that day so many years ago, Jesus wept at the hardness of their hearts:

> O Jerusalem, Jerusalem, thou that killest the prophets and stonest them which are sent unto thee, how often would I have gathered thy children together, even as a hen gathereth her chickens under her wings, and ye would not! Behold your house is left unto you desolate. For I say unto you, Ye shall not see me henceforth till ye shall say, Blessed is he that cometh in the name of the Lord (Matthew 23:37-39).

According to Jesus there is a day coming when His chosen people will finally recognize and accept Him. They will then cry out, "Blessed is he that cometh in the name of the Lord." According to the prophet Zechariah, however, that won't happen until Israel is on the verge of being destroyed at the battle of Armageddon and Jesus Himself comes to rescue Israel.

> Then shall the Lord go forth and fight against those nations, as when he fought in the day of battle.
>
> And his feet shall stand in that day upon the mount of Olives, which is before Jerusalem on the east, and the mount of Olives shall cleave in the midst thereof toward the east and toward the west, and there shall be a very great valley; and half of the mountain shall remove toward the north and half of it toward the south. . . . And the Lord shall be king over all the earth. . . . And it shall come to pass in that day that I will seek to destroy all the nations that come against Jerusalem.
>
> And I will pour out upon the house of David and upon the inhabitants of Jerusalem the spirit of grace and of supplications; and they shall look upon me whom they have pierced, and they shall mourn for him as one mourneth for his only son, and shall be in bitterness for him as one that is in bitterness for his firstborn (Zechariah 14:3,4,9; 12:9,10).

Two thousand years ago the nation of Israel rejected Jesus as He came down from the Mount of Olives. This time Israel will receive Him as He once again stands on the very same mount. This time, however, far from being the suffering Messiah who came to bear the sins of the world, He is coming in power and glory to set up His everlasting kingdom, the first thousand years of which will be right here on this earth. The prophets tell us that all of this doesn't happen until the battle of Armageddon, at the end of the final seven-year countdown. At that time of judgment, sin and transgression come to an end as the new kingdom is established. Only those people whose faith is in Christ are allowed to enter. Finally all the purposes of the 490 years will be fulfilled: Israel will have recognized her Messiah, sin will have come to an end, and everlasting righteousness will have begun.

With this understanding of the second coming of the true Messiah in mind, we can now turn the clock back seven years to the coming of the impostor. We now know the circumstances that he will be trying to counterfeit. The Bible tells us that his masquerade will be almost flawless.

Fake Armageddon for a Fake Messiah

There is a famous saying that in a group of three Jews there are four opinions. When it comes to the ideas about what the coming of the Messiah will be like, the same holds true. However, there are a couple of predominant themes worth noting. To the average Jew, the coming of the Messiah will somehow bring about the redemption of Israel and the world, although how or when this will happen is poorly understood. To the Orthodox Jew the ideas are a little clearer. He understands that the Messiah will come at some point in time to save Israel from their Gentile enemies. He will come to the Mount of Olives and, along with the Jews, rebuild the temple.

This understanding comes largely from passages in the book of Zechariah. In vivid detail, as we have just quoted, the prophet shows a scene of the whole world gathered against Israel. They have gathered for only one purpose—to wipe Israel from the face of the earth forever. But as Jerusalem stands on the edge of destruction the Messiah Himself will return to defend and fight for Israel. He will put a stop to the war that if continued would "destroy all flesh." Then shall Israel mourn as they look upon "Him whom they have pierced" and recognize that Jesus is truly the Messiah. He will finally bring peace to Israel, and He will then establish His reign on the throne of David for 1000 years.

However, before this happens, the impostor is coming. It would seem that if he is to convince Israel that he is the Messiah he will have to somehow convince them that he is fulfilling this prophecy. Therefore the possibility exists that there may be an uprising in the Middle East with all the nations of the world in attendance. The War in the Persian Gulf may have been the shadow of such an event. The world will fear that the brink of Armageddon has come. The Antichrist may dramatically arise with "all power and signs and lying wonders." He may appear to Israel to be the fulfillment of Zechariah's prophecies. He may intervene to "save" Israel. Most importantly, he will seem to establish peace. Such a scenario does mesh with the implication of Scripture that the Antichrist will burst onto the world scene by establishing a guarantee of protection for Israel.

Of course, this may not be exactly the way it happens. Regardless of the actual Mideastern scenario, the rise of this Antichrist at the beginning of the seven-year tribulation period will coincide very closely with the rapture of the church. Thus the whole world, and not just the Middle East, will be in complete turmoil. What a time for the Antichrist to rise! He will be a great statesman whose "look is more stout than his fellows" (Daniel 7:20). He will be a great orator with "a mouth speaking great things" (Daniel 7:8; Revelation 13:5). Such a description of this dramatic rise to power would hold little meaning if there were not massive fear and chaos. Great charismatic leaders and orators do not arise in a sea of calm; they arise in a time of great fear and uncertainty.

A Fake Peace and the Fake Messiah

Regardless of the events that propel the Antichrist to power, we do know that once there he will finally seem to settle the problems of the Middle East and the whole world. And this false peace will be one of his primary credentials for his claim to be the Messiah. As one author notes, "When asked why he doesn't believe that Jesus was the Messiah, the average Jewish person will most likely reply, 'Because he didn't bring peace.'" As we have seen, Christ will bring peace when He comes again at the end of the tribulation period. However, one of the central ways that the counterfeit messiah will impersonate the real Messiah will be by bringing a *false* peace to the world as a whole and Israel in particular.

The prophet Daniel tells us that under the terms of that coming peace covenant, Israel will be allowed to reinstitute Old Testament sacrifice (Daniel 9:27). This means that the deal will almost certainly include Israel's right to rebuild her temple. It would also seem that through this covenant Israel will give up some of her land, because Daniel 11:39 tells us that the Antichrist will "divide the land for gain." In Scripture "the land" always refers to Israel.

Many authorities today tell us that the temple could be rebuilt right alongside the Dome of the Rock on the Temple Mount. Only recently did it occur to me just how powerful a symbol to the world this will be. It will be a monument to a man who has succeeded in doing what Carter, Kissinger, Habib, and Baker have all failed to do: *He will have brought peace between Israel and her enemies*. In all probability, the Antichrist will actually have Isaac and Ishmael living side-by-side in peace; the temple and mosque will be the most dramatic symbol imaginable. Maybe even a "Christian" cathedral will join the two somewhere on the Mount, representing the religious unity of the New World Order! The final remaining hindrance to the establishment of a worldwide New Age of peace and prosperity will have been removed, and the Antichrist will have achieved what the Jews think only the Messiah can do: He will have brought peace.

No wonder, with this case of mistaken identity, Israel will lay down their mighty arsenal and become a land of "unwalled villages" as the prophet Ezekiel foretold (Ezekiel 38:11). They will think the Messiah Himself is there to defend them!

However, the covenant of peace will probably be much more far-reaching than a simple Mideast Peace Treaty. Although the treaty centers around the nation of Israel, we know that as a result of the rapture the whole world will be in turmoil. The prophet Daniel tells us that this peace covenant will be signed by the Antichrist and the "many." The word "many" used here in the Hebrew means "abundant in quantity, size, age, number, and rank." This covenant may well turn out to be a peace treaty for planet Earth. It could be "the Constitution of the New World

Order"! As such, not just Israel but the whole world could be equally deceived in thinking that under the leadership of "the Christ" the millennium has actually begun. This gives us a great insight into God's warning that "by peace [the Antichrist] shall destroy many" (Daniel 8:25).

The Mideast and the New World Order

No one can doubt that we are on the way to such a New World Order today. When Saddam Hussein marched 120,000 of his battle-hardened troops into Kuwait in the summer of 1990, a clear message was sent to the rest of the world: Even with the collapse of Communism, the destruction of the Berlin Wall, and the emergence of the post-Cold-War era, world peace would not be possible until the Middle East caught up with the times. President Bush sent massive forces to the region, claiming that the Persian Gulf crisis was the final great threat to the emerging new era. Other nations followed suit until the largest multinational force in history was gathered to battle in the world's most volatile region.

Recognizing that most of the problems in the world revolve around the Arab-Israeli conflict, the call has gone forth to seek a comprehensive solution to the entire regional problem. President Bush has claimed that the end of the Persian Gulf crisis must lead to regional peace. U.S. State Department spokeswoman Margaret Tutwiler makes the administration's view clear when she says, "The invasion underscores the need for all countries in the Middle East to achieve peace."[5] The Soviet Union, now a recognized member of the "community of nations," is likewise using its newfound Mideastern influence to press Israel to agree to the convening of an international peace conference. As former Soviet Foreign Minister Eduard Shevardnadze noted in 1990 to the UN General Assembly, the Iraq-Kuwait crisis did help pave the way for the broader Middle East settlement that Saddam Hussein claimed to be championing:

> We hope that at this time of grave trial the Arab states will live up to the expectations of mankind and help to find a way out of the Persian Gulf crisis. This would make it possible to deal with other hotbeds of conflict in the Middle East, and at last to find an equitable solution to the Palestinian problem. Some may find that Iraq is being judged by a different, higher standard than applied to other countries.... These days are trying times, a test for organization. If it passes this test it will immeasurably enhance prestige, gain in experience and new capabilities. There is no doubt it will use them to restore peace and justice in other conflict situations, and to insure the implementation of its resolutions.

The call for the convening of some form of international peace conference in the Middle East is virtually universal. U.N. Secretary General Perez de Cuellar has declared that such a conference has to be on the agenda sooner or later. French President Francois Mitterand claims that "at the end of the road, one finds oneself with the idea of an international peace conference which would guarantee the implementation of the agreement..." (Francois Mitterand to the UN General Assembly, September 24, 1990). Similarly, the European Economic Community promises that the emerging United States of Europe is willing to put its full power into resolving "all the problems of the Middle East."[6]

It is not hard to imagine the position that Israel will be put in at such a gathering. You may recall that before Iraq invaded Kuwait the U.S. blamed Israel for the lack of peace in the region. Ironically, just before the Iraqi aggression, Secretary of State James Baker even went so far as to go on national television and give Israel the White House telephone number. He told them that when they were serious about peace they should give him a call! Even now, after Israel's restraint under the heavy SCUD missile bombardments, the pressure is building on Israel to sit down at an international peace table with those sworn to her destruction. It is at that very peace table, whether in an initial gathering or in one well down the road, that Israel may well come face-to-face with the one who comes "in his own name"—the Antichrist!

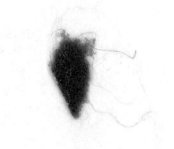

Chapter 3

The Democratic Kingdom of Antichrist

There is another prophetic pillar of the last days that calls for our attention. As we have seen, the Antichrist will make his entrance onto the world stage by arranging a miraculous peace treaty centering largely around Israel. The treaty will not only guarantee their protection but will also allow them the right to rebuild their temple and reinstitute the Old Testament sacrifices. However, this treaty will not be confined to the Middle East. The document signed may actually be "the Constitution of the New World Order"! The peace between Jacob and Esau, Isaac and Ishmael will seem to be the signal to the whole world that the New Age has finally begun.

However, the Bible tells us that the Antichrist will rise to power out of an alliance of nations with its center in Western Europe. If we are indeed living in the last moments of time before the rapture of the church and the revelation of the Antichrist, we would expect to see that alliance coming onto the world stage as well. And in fact that very thing is happening.

For the first time since the fall of the Holy Roman Empire over 1500 years ago, the countries of Europe are once again banding together. By the end of 1992 the European Economic Community plans to erase all borders and truly begin to become the United States of Europe. What Charlemagne, Napoleon, and Hitler could not do through force is now happening on a democratic basis, with each nation freely giving up huge chunks of sover-eignty in the name of the "New Europe." No one believed such a thing was possible. In fact, the children's rhyme "Humpty Dumpty" is a story based on the belief that a reunification of Europe was impossible.

> Humpty Dumpty sat on the wall. Humpty Dumpty had a great fall. All the king's horses and all the king's men couldn't put Humpty back together again.[1]

However, what all the king's horses and all the king's men couldn't do through the use of force is today happening through treaties and negotiation, precisely as the Word of God said it would. But this is only the beginning. The prophets have told us that in the near future this New Europe will rule the world and be the springboard of power for someone whom the Bible calls "the Man of Sin." In order to understand how all of this will come about, we need to go back to the prophecies themselves and take a look at what they say about this Revived Roman Empire.

The Case for a Revived Roman Empire

In the second chapter of the book of Daniel we read the account of a startling dream had by Nebuchadnezzar, the king of Babylon. The king claimed that he could not remember the dream, so he called together all the magicians, sorcerers, and "New Agers" of his day. He wanted them to tell him his dream and its interpreta-tion. When they could not, he commanded that they be put to death. However, when Daniel, the Hebrew prophet, who was in captivity in Babylon, heard all the uproar he asked the king to give him time to pray. He discerned that his God, the God of Israel, would reveal Nebuchadnezzar's dream to him and that he in turn would tell the king what the New Agers of the day could not.

What the king had seen, Daniel explained, was a great image that resembled a man (Daniel 2:31-45). This "man" had a head of gold. His breast and arms were made of silver. His belly and thighs were made of brass. His legs were made of iron and his feet were partly iron and partly clay. Since the king couldn't figure out what this meant, he was greatly pleased when Daniel was able to interpret the dream for him. Imagine his surprise when the Hebrew prophet told the king that what he had seen was an outline of the future, from Nebuchadnezzar's day until the end of world history!

The image was made of various metals in order to represent four different kingdoms in history that would rule over the entire earth, Daniel revealed. The first of these was Nebuchadnezzar's Babylon. Daniel simply said, "You are this head of gold." This was the perfect symbol for the empire, since Babylon was known as the Golden City. However, the king then learned that "after you will arise another kingdom inferior to you." This kingdom was represented by the silver chest and arms. In 539 b.c., just as prophesied, the Medo-Persian armies conquered Babylon and became the new superpower of the day (Daniel 5:30,31).

After that the prophet spoke of "another third kingdom of brass, which shall bear rule over all the earth." History tells us that the Greek Empire, under the leadership of Alexander the Great, defeated Persia in 331 b.c. His kingdom extended from India to Egypt and Europe. Alexander even decreed that he be called "King of the World." That empire was symbolized by the abdomen and thighs (cf. Daniel 8:20,21).

Finally, Daniel spoke of a fourth kingdom that would be as strong as iron. The two iron legs of the statue represented the power which succeeded Greece—the Roman Empire. In 63 b.c. the Romans conquered all the lands surrounding the Mediterranean and ruled for over 500 years. They imposed Pax Romana— the Roman Peace—a peace enforced by the iron heel of Rome. However, that is where the historical record matching Nebuchadnezzar's dream comes to an end. There has been no empire in history so far that corresponds to the description of the feet, which were partly iron and partly clay.

Why Rome Must Rise Again

The fact that the historical record has not yet fulfilled this last portion of the dream indicates that there will have to be a fifth or last-days kingdom represented by the feet and toes of the image. However, according to Daniel's interpretation of the dream, there simply is no separate fifth kingdom. Although the image that Nebuchadnezzar saw was broken down into five empires, the fourth and fifth empires are combined into one—"the fourth kingdom"—in the description Daniel gives. Therefore this fifth kingdom will have to be a revived form of the Holy Roman Empire.

The connection of these last two world powers is further shown by the fact that in the image that Nebuchadnezzar saw, they both contained iron. In the previous instances the substance of the kingdoms changed completely between empires. This shows that much of what existed in the original Roman Empire will also exist in this final empire. Also, God told Daniel that in the days of these toes (kings), "the God of heaven [shall] set up a kingdom which shall never be destroyed" (Daniel 2:44). Since this clearly did not happen in the first phase of the Roman Empire, this fourth empire will have to be revived in the last days at the time when Jesus comes to set up His kingdom.

We also know that the Roman Empire must come back together because Daniel tells us that it is out of this empire that the Antichrist will arise in the last days. Speaking a full 500 years before the birth of Jesus, Daniel revealed that right after the Messiah was killed, Jerusalem and the temple would be destroyed by the people of the Antichrist.[2] Did this happen? In 70 A.D., a few short years after the death [and resurrection!] of the Messiah, the Roman armies destroyed Jerusalem and the temple. Since the coming Antichrist's people are of the Roman Empire, then it means that they will have to be reunited in the last days. But what is this Revived Roman Empire? What will it be like and where will it be? Are there any signs of its emergence today?

Identifying the Revived Roman Empire

Some students of Bible prophecy think that what we should be watching for is the emergence of a kingdom with the exact same boundaries as the original Roman Empire. This teaching overlooks the fact that the prophecy tells us that this stage is an outgrowth and an evolution of the fourth beast, not just a duplication. The ten toes (or the ten horns, as they are identified in the seventh chapter of Daniel) represent an entirely new phase. As J. Dwight Pentecost notes, "This beast is seen to be the successor to the three preceding empires. This may suggest not only the idea of power, but also geographical extent, so that this final form of Gentile power may encompass all the territory held by all the predecessors."[3]

Many more believe that the Revived Roman Empire will take the form of a ten-nation confederacy rising in the heart of what was once the Holy Roman Empire. The 12-membered European Economic Community has been seen as the temporarily oversized fulfillment of that prophecy. This belief centers on the belief that the ten toes (or horns in Daniel 7) represent ten nations. After this confederacy of ten nations is in place an eleventh nation may join the first ten. The head of that nation will be none other than the Antichrist himself.

This idea comes from the prophecy recorded in the seventh chapter of Daniel. Actually, this prophecy is a parallel to the dream that Nebuchadnezzar had. However, this time the four great kingdoms that Nebuchadnezzar saw are seen through the eyes of God. Instead of being seen as a great image, the four kingdoms are seen for what they truly are—four great hideous beasts. The fourth beast has ten horns, and these ten horns are the same as the ten toes in Nebuchadnezzar's dream. However, this time we are given a greater picture of what will occur in the "days of these kings." Daniel tells us:

> I considered the horns, and behold, there came up
> among them another little horn, before whom there

> were three of the first horns plucked up by the roots;
> and behold, in this horn were eyes like the eyes of man,
> and a mouth speaking great things (Daniel 7:8).

This little horn is the Antichrist. Those who hold the view that these ten horns represent ten nations joined in a last-days confederacy have watched with mounting excitement as the European Economic Community has burst on the scene. In fact, when Greece joined the EEC in 1981, bringing the number of members to ten, there was great expectancy. After all, all we had to do now, we were told, was to watch for the eleventh nation to join the Community. The head of that nation would be the "little horn" of Daniel's prophecy. Can you guess what happened? In 1986 Spain and Portugal both joined the EEC at exactly the same time. The number went from ten to twelve, and there was no number eleven.

In answer to this, many of the proponents of the "ten-nation" theory now argue that the Antichrist will rise after 13 nations are in place. This, they say, would make it possible for the Antichrist to subdue three horns, as Daniel states he will, and still leave us with ten nations. It is further pointed out that Austria is waiting to join the EEC right now, which would bring the number of members to 13. The problem with this theory is that it overlooks the clear wording of Scripture:

> I considered the [ten] horns, and behold, there came up among them [the ten horns] another little horn, before whom were three of the FIRST [ten] horns plucked up by the roots (Daniel 7:8).

> The TEN horns out of this kingdom are TEN kings that shall arise; and another shall arise after them [the ten]; and he shall be diverse from the first [ten], and he shall subdue three kings (Daniel 7:24).

Therefore if the EEC is to be the ultimate fulfillment of the Revived Roman Empire, there will eventually have to be ten members, after which the Antichrist will rise. This doesn't seem likely for a number of reasons. In the first place, as we shall see, Austria is not the only nation which seems to be knocking at the door for EEC membership. With their recent moves toward freedom, the entire East Bloc wants desperately to be included in the EEC. Even the Soviet Union, in its call for a "Common European House," is trying to insure its own inclusion. The idea that the EEC will shrink in size in the face of this explosion of applicants seems rather improbable.

From a biblical point of view we must also note that the ten horns are always identified clearly as ten kings who reign in the last days. Nowhere are these horns identified as nations. So maybe we are looking for something larger than the present European Economic Community. I believe that Daniel gives us the clue we need in order to determine just how large this Revived Roman Empire may be.

The Democratic Kingdom of Antichrist

One thing that seems certain from the Scriptures is that this Revived Roman Empire will not be a totalitarian system imposed by force. Instead, it seems evident that it will be a willing alliance of nations. As the prophet Daniel explained it to Nebuchadnezzar:

> Whereas thou sawest the feet and toes, part of potters' clay and part of iron, the kingdom shall be divided; but there shall be in it the strength of iron, forasmuch as thou sawest the iron mixed with miry clay. And as the toes of the feet were part of iron and part of clay, so the kingdom shall be partly strong and partly broken (Daniel 2:41,42).

Just what do the iron and the clay most likely represent? This is important because these are the two defining characteristics of this last-days form of the Roman Empire. J. Dwight Pentecost notes:

> The final form of the Gentile power is marked by a federation of that which is weak and that which is strong, autocracy and democracy, the iron and the clay. . . .[4]

Since the decline and fall of the Roman Empire in 476 A.D., Charlemagne, Napoleon, Hitler, and others have all tried to reunite Europe by force. But it never worked. Yet now, exactly as the Bible has prophesied, Europe is coming together not through the iron of force but through the clay of democracy. The European Economic Community, which is undoubtedly at least the hub of this new empire, is today a willing association of nations.

However, the prophets give us another important clue about the nature of this coming empire. The Bible indicates that not only will the alliance of nations that make up the Empire be democratic, but the nations within the alliance will be democratic as well. This is important because it helps us to begin to determine who will, and who will not, be a part of the Revived Roman Empire.

There are many reasons for believing that the empire will be made up of democratic nations. First, the presence of the clay, representing democracy, in the feet and toes could well represent democracy within the nations as well as within the alliance. Also, although the rise to power of the Antichrist does appear to be a coup d'etat of some type ("subdues three kings"), the primary focus of his rise to power is his immense acceptance by the people of his empire and the world. His entrance onto the world scene is characterized by "a mouth speaking great things" and "a look more stout than his fellows." So great is his charisma that all the world will greatly admire him and eventually worship him.

This does not seem to indicate the rise of an appointed totalitarian leader but of the ultimate Western democratic politician. Indeed, the Bible tells us that "by peace [not war] he shall destroy many" (Daniel 8:25). As opposed to a military consolidation, it appears that he may ride a wave of peace, democracy, human rights, and religious freedom to power. Such a wave does exist today. In what now sounds like archaic language, *The World Press Review* observed in early 1990 that "west of the Iron Curtain— for the first time in history—every European state is a parliamentary democracy." Today that could be expanded to include the East Bloc nations and the Baltics, which were until recently ruled by the iron fist of Communism.

All of this is staggering. Who would have thought, just a few short years ago, that democracy and not Communism would begin to sweep the world? Who could have imagined that instead of Communism sweeping west, democracy and freedom of conscience would begin to surge into the void left by a rapidly retreating totalitarianism? The clay and the iron are beginning to mingle. And, although the iron of military might will be involved in this revived version of the Roman Empire, it will be primarily united by democracy, symbolized by the clay.

The New EEC

There is little doubt that the European Common Market is the nucleus of what will become the Revived Roman Empire. Indeed, the secular *Europe Magazine*[5] explained that the first ECU (European Currency Unit) silver coins have imprinted on them the 12 stars of the EEC and the bust of Emperor Charles V. The reason for this, according to the report, is "because of the striking geographical similarity between the Common Market and the Holy Roman Empire." However, as we have pointed out, we believe that the Revived Roman Empire will build on this ancient foundation and grow much larger than just ten or twelve nations in western Europe.

Just as Daniel foresaw, the EEC had its beginnings as a democratic alliance of nations—Belgium, France, Italy, Luxembourg, the Netherlands, and West Germany—in 1957. The goal of this group was the consolidation of the coal, steel, and iron industries in these nations. Interestingly, the treaty beginning the EEC was called the Treaty of Rome. By 1973 the EEC grew to include

Denmark, Ireland, and Great Britain, thereby bringing the total number of members to nine. Greece joined in 1981, bringing the number to ten, and Spain and Portugal brought the membership to the present 12 in 1986.

Of course, the talk now centers on Europe's plan for complete monetary union by late 1992. This has been seen as the point in time when the EEC will truly become "the United States of Europe." However, while that plan has continued to steam along, developments in Eastern Europe and the Soviet Union have dramatically expanded the vision and scope of the proposed union of these new "United States."

Mikhail Gorbachev is calling for a "common European house." George Bush sees a "Europe whole and free." Francois Mitterrand envisions a "broad confederation." Jacques Delors, the head of the EEC, wants to create "three concentric circles" centered around the existing EEC. Germany's Helmut Kohl is pushing for the complete integration of the entire Eastern Bloc:

> I am firmly determined that this federation should not be an exclusive club confined to the present members of the European Community . . . federation should be as open to Poles, Czechs, Slovaks, or Hungarians as well as to countries like Austria, Sweden, Norway, and Finland that want to join.[6]

All of these models foresee the European Community becoming a virtual superpower in the midst of Europe, and everyone wants a piece of the action.

The New Europe and the New Democracies

With the Eastern European nations throwing off Communism and embracing democracy, there is no question that they are on the fast track toward their European roots. EEC leaders are fully aware that there will be no denying them their place in the "European House." The new president of Czechoslovakia,

Vaclav Havel, has called for Poland, Hungary, and other Eastern European countries to join Czechoslovakia in a coordinated bid to "return to Europe." "Before us is a historic opportunity to fill a large political vacuum created in Central Europe after the fall of the Hapsburgs," he says.

However, as Paul Johnson notes in *The World Press Review*, this is only the beginning:

> If Austria joins the community, it will not be easy to resist the demands not only of Czechs and Slovaks but also of Slovenes, Croatians and Dalmatians, who still share the important if ghostly bond of having belonged to the Hapsburg empire. If Poles and Prussians [from East Germany] come in—as well as free Baltic states such as Sweden and Finland—how can we deny entry to Estonians, Latvians, and Lithuanians?[7]

There is no question that this is the way things are moving. Like Poland, Czechoslovakia, and the others, Latvia, Lithuania, the Ukraine, and Estonia are being drawn by their European roots, their desire for freedom, and their common Catholic ties squarely back into the European fold. Of course, the symbolic certificate of membership that these nations are holding out is their democratic reform. In fact, the Warsaw Pact itself has thrown in the towel and its members now pledge to move forward on a solely "democratic basis."[8]

The New Europe and the European Free Trade Organization

Furthermore, according to *Newsweek* magazine, the EEC has "opened exploratory talks with the six small but highly developed countries that form the European Free Trade Association: Switzerland, Sweden, Norway, Finland, Iceland and Austria. The odds are good that the EFTA nations will accept close association with the community by the end of 1992."[9] This would add another six democratic nations and 370 million people to the new superstate. The democratic empire, out of which the Antichrist will rise, is growing. And the new coalition spans a far greater area than continental Europe.

The New Europe and the United States

Like the Soviets, the Americans have also taken note of the leading role that Europe is beginning to play in world affairs. In a speech in Berlin last December, U.S. Secretary of State James Baker called for an expansion of the vision of the new Europe until it included a "New Atlanticism." This was his way of reminding the Europeans that, although they were separated by an ocean, any new empire would also have to include the United States. Democracy, he claims, must be one of the central keys to membership:

> Free men and free governments are the building blocks of a Europe whole and free.... Working together, we must design and gradually put into place a new architecture for a new era.... The charge for us all then is to work together toward the New Europe and the New Atlanticism.... We propose that the United States and the European Community work together to achieve, whether in treaty or some other form, a significantly strengthened set of institutional and consultative links.... As we adapt, as we update and expand our cooperation with each other and with the nations of the East, we will create a new Europe on the basis of a new Atlanticism.[10]

Baker's call for this "new" Atlanticism is not really new, he says. After all, the United States argues, our roots are as European as anyone's! Already, "The Association to Unite the Democracies" has kicked its advertising and publicity machine into high gear. Jacques Delors, the President of the EEC, meeting with U.S. President George Bush, endorsed an American role in the New Europe. Delors called for "a new and profound partnership with the USA":

> We have embarked on an exciting journey toward political union in Europe. What we are doing will have a profound effect on shaping the world of the next century, in which member nation-states will increasingly have to share sovereignty with each other as our world becomes more interdependent. . . . It is time to reassess the [U.S.–E.E.C.] relationship. . . . Both partners now have to think about a wider political dialogue, leading possibly to joint action over issues of mutual interest. [11]

By late 1990, that wider dialogue took on the form of what the EEC's Andreas van Agt called a "Love Letter" [12] of cooperation between the U.S. and the European Community. According to a German official it was not set up as a full treaty, but was prepared in the form of a declaration because—

> A declaration rather than a treaty would give the right political signals without offending national political sensibilities or aggravating fears. . . . [13]

The New Europe and Canada

Canada is also very much involved in forming new democratic alliances with the New Europe. Prime Minister Brian Mulroney stresses that Canada wants "to be involved in that definition of the new architecture of Europe." [14] In explaining Canada's efforts to make sure that it is not left out of this huge emerging alliance of Western democracies, External Affairs Minister Joe Clark explains:

> You have almost a renaissance in Europe, in its sense of its role in the world. . . . If there was a time when Europe may have felt it was secondary to the United States or Japan, that time has passed. There's a sense that they are where the action is.[15]

The New Europe and the Soviet Union?

There is little doubt in the minds of careful observers that Mikhail Gorbachev's policies of "perestroika" and "glasnost" have been largely motivated by his desire to gain an entrance for his country into this New Europe. His call for a "Common European Home" is designed specifically to try to mold a view of Europe which includes his own country. He knows that without such membership his country is doomed to the ash heap of economic history.

Gorbachev now proclaims to be building a democratic society that would be qualified for membership in this great alliance of free nations. In his dramatic U.N. address in 1988 he acknowledged the new force in world affairs:

> A new world is emerging; man, his concerns, rights and freedoms, are [being] placed at the center of things. . . . The idea of democratizing the entire world has grown into a powerful surge and political force.[16]

Not long after Gorbachev called for a new unity based on democratic principles, he said that "it is time to recognize that the world of today does not consist of two mutually exclusive civilizations. It is one common civilization in which human values and freedom of choice have primacy."[17] What association the Soviets will have with this New Europe is not clear. However, their efforts to at least appear to be moving toward democracy show that they also understand that democracy will be one of the foundation stones of this "new" empire.

Democracy and Deception

The prophet Daniel, after seeing all that God revealed to him, was utterly confused by it all. However, the Lord told him to "seal the book, even to the time of the end" (Daniel 12:4) because it was only then that the prophecies could begin to be fully understood. Thus, while we must be careful not to bend the Scriptures to fit current events, the Lord is indeed telling us, through His words to Daniel, that current events can most definitely give us more light on the prophetic Scriptures. The light shed by today's headlines certainly seems to confirm exactly what the prophet Daniel saw over 2600 years ago. One of the common denominators of the Revived Roman Empire, which will eventually hold sway over all the earth, will be democracy. The power base from which the Antichrist rises to power could well be an alliance of Western democracies not limited to ten nations in Western Europe but stretching from Eastern Europe to the shores of California. As George Bush has put it:

> We now see before us a growing community of democracies anchoring international peace and stability and a dynamic free-market system generating prosperity and progress on a global scale.[18]

This is an incredible indication of exactly how accurate and up-to-date Bible prophecy really is. Just a few years ago no one foresaw the complete collapse of Communism. No one would have guessed that democracy and religious freedom would spread into the former enclaves of the bastions of official atheism. Yet here was this Hebrew prophet, captive in the ancient city of Babylon, who described the empire of the last days as being built on the foundations of democracy despite the fact that the very concept of democracy had not yet been invented!

It is also a firm indication of just how important a proper understanding of Bible prophecy actually is. To most of the world the spread of human rights, freedom of conscience, and freedom of religion seems like a great move of God. All over the globe statesmen and church leaders alike extol the near-miraculous spread of democratic principles and ideals. To the natural mind of man it literally seems as dramatic as the victory of good over evil. However, while this breakdown of Communism is indeed giving a temporary open door to the gospel, the Bible warns that the result of this "way that seems right" will be the establishment of the empire that will pave the way for the rise of the Antichrist. Compounding the deception is the other common denominator that will, along with democracy, define the Revived Roman Empire.

Chapter 4

The Great Whore

While the prophet Daniel told us that the Revived Roman Empire would be an alliance of democracies, the apostle John revealed the other central defining characteristic of this last-days empire. John, seeing a panorama of events still far into the future, saw this same beast that Daniel had seen, but now he saw something that Daniel had not. Riding atop this beast was a woman arrayed in scarlet and purple robes. She wore gold, precious stones, and pearls, and she had a name written on her head. It was "Mystery Babylon the Great, The Mother of Harlots and Abominations of the Earth."

John was given a number of clues as to the identity of this Mystery Woman. Her close relationship with the beast is an important clue. From this we can deduce that if the beast is representative of the Western democracies, we must find this whore dwelling in and representing a prime characteristic of those same nations as well. John F. Walvoord describes the first thing we know about this symbolic woman:

> The picture of the woman as utterly evil signifies spiritual adultery, portraying those who outwardly and religiously seem to be joined to the true God but who are untrue to this relationship. The symbolism of spiritual adultery is not ordinarily used of heathen

> nations who know not God, but always of people who outwardly carry the name of God while actually worshipping and serving other gods. . . . In the New Testament the church is viewed as a virgin destined to be joined to her husband in the future, but she is warned against spiritual adultery.[1]

This religious whore is principally made up of those who profess to be Christians but who are actually not true believers at all. They are all those who will be left behind after the rapture and who will join in a coalition with the Antichrist, believing that he is the true Christ. Therefore the whore is not made up of any particular denomination but of all those who do not truly love the Lord. Eventually, as the Revived Roman Empire grows to include the whole world, this whore will likewise grow to include all religions, beliefs, and ideologies. Indeed, all religions will follow her lead until this great whore is composed of everyone whose name is not written in the Lamb's book of life. Initially, however, she will claim to be a great ecumenical Christian church.

This leads us to the next point. Since this whore and this beast ride together and represent the coalition that will form the Revived Roman Empire, prophetic student F.C. Jennings could see as far back as 1940:

> . . . the boundaries of the [Revived Roman] Empire will be the boundaries of the professed but utterly apostate Christianity; and vice versa the boundaries of the apostate Church will be exactly coterminous with those of the Empire . . . [which] will include . . . every country everywhere in which there is any claim to apostate Christianity at all, and so will include North and South America.[2]

Today we are witnessing this precise phenomenon. With all of the newly elected governments in Eastern Europe, and with their rush to join the new Europe, we now have the makings of an empire sharing both democracy and professing Christianity as defining characteristics. Thus Jennings' understanding that the Revived Roman Empire would include all of the "Christian democracies" who share a common religious system (the whore) and a common political system (the beast) seems amazingly accurate. This is really the scope of the New Europe that we are looking for today. The vivid picture of the whore riding herd over the beast, emphasizing as it does the predominantly spiritual dimensions of this coalition, is a much better picture of the scope of the Revived Roman Empire than one assuming that the size of the empire is limited to ten nations in Western Europe.

The Mother of Harlots

Although the great whore is initially made up of all false Christians and then eventually grows to include everyone who has rejected Christ, this does not mean that we cannot identify the leader of this apostate world church. In fact, the apostle John gives us so many clues that identification is unmistakable.

The first thing we should remember is that if this is a revived form of the Holy Roman Empire, we would expect the religion to be the same. From its early days the religion of the Roman Empire was built on Babylonian, pagan beliefs. However, as time continued, these beliefs were woven into the new religion of the Roman Empire, the Roman Catholic Church. Indeed, the Catholic Church, with the paganism of Babylon incorporated into its practices, formed the heart of the Roman Empire. And by quietly incorporating all of the Babylonian practices into a church that claimed to be the true bride of Christ, there arose a church perfectly fitting the description of "Mystery Babylon," the great harlot. As noted historian Will Durant observes in *The Story of Civilization*:

> Paganism survived . . . in the form of ancient rites
> and customs condoned, or accepted and transformed,

by an often indulgent Church. An intimate and trustful worship of saints replaced the cult of pagan gods. . . . Statues of Isis and Horus were renamed Mary and Jesus; the Roman Lupercalia and the feast of purification of Isis became the feast of Nativity; the Saturnalia were replaced by Christmas celebration . . . and ancient festival of the dead by All Souls Day, rededicated to Christian heroes; incense, lights, flowers, processions, vestments, hymns which had pleased the people in older cults were domesticated and cleansed in the ritual of the Church . . . soon people and priests would use the sign of the cross as a magic incantation to expel or drive away demons.

A perfect example of how the Roman Catholic Church Christianized and then incorporated pure Babylonianism into its bosom is the way that it elevated Mary to the position of "Queen of Heaven." This teaching is a direct transfer of title from the Babylonian goddess Ashtoreth. Not only that, but this is the same goddess who appears in other pagan religions under other names. She is the Babylonian "Semiramis," the Assyrian "Astarte," the Egyptian "Isis," the Greek "Aphrodite," and the Roman "Venus." Each was worshiped as the Queen of Heaven in her respective land. Catholicism's Mary is just the latest in a long line of pagan "queens of heaven." This is in spite of the fact the Bible itself clearly condemns the idea of a "queen of heaven" (Jeremiah 7:18; 44:17-26).

Catholic writers themselves are clear in their teachings: They unabashedly elevate Mary above Jesus Himself. Cardinal Alphonsus de Liguori, for example, in his book *The Glories of Mary*, plainly states that "he falls and is lost who has not recourse to Mary."[3] He also explains the Catholic teaching that "we shall be heard more quickly if we have recourse to Mary and call on her holy name, than we should be if we called on the name of Jesus our Saviour."[4] He continues, "Many things . . . are asked from God, and are not granted; they are asked from Mary, and are obtained [for] she is even Queen of Hell."[5] The full flavor of Catholic teaching is spelled out by the Cardinal:

> All power is given to Thee in heaven and on earth [so that] at the command of Mary all obey, even God. Thus . . . God has placed the whole church . . . under the dominion of Mary.[6]

This is Babylonianism, pure and simple. The Catholic Church has lifted the Babylonian "Queen of Heaven" above God! And this is no misrepresentation of Catholic teachings. When I was at the Vatican recently I was amazed as I walked through the Vatican Museum. Priceless treasures collected over 2000 years documented the history of this institution. Most revealing were the beautiful tapestries and murals that hung on every wall. A stereotype in these murals began to emerge from the very oldest to the most recent. You would see the light of God shining down onto Mary; from her it was reflected onto the Pope; from the Pope the light of God was reflected down onto the people. Where was Jesus? Almost invariably He was pictured as a helpless little child or as a boy off to the side in no position of importance. This is in complete opposition to the teachings of Scripture:

> . . . there is one God, and one mediator between God and men, the man Christ Jesus (1 Timothy 2:5).

When Jesus died upon the cross for our sins, the Bible tells us that the veil of the temple was miraculously torn in two. The tear went from the top to the bottom, symbolizing the fact that this was an act of God alone. What was so significant about this act? In Old Testament times only the high priest was allowed into the holy of holies because that was where the presence of God resided. When Jesus, who was God, died for our sins, He made it possible for anyone who would put his or her trust in Him to have full and free access to the very presence of God. Jesus Himself had bridged the gap. Believers no longer needed a high priest to intercede for them. Yet to this very day the Catholic Church places priests, the Pope, and Mary between the individual and God.

Rome and the New Europe

There are still more indications which the apostle John gave to us to prove that the Roman Catholic Church is indeed at the core of Mystery Babylon. As we already mentioned, since the religion of the Holy Roman Empire was Catholicism, and since that empire is being revived, we would expect Catholicism to be central to that revival. A clear indication of just how pivotal the Catholic Church is in the efforts to build the "new Europe" was given by the former Archbishop of Canterbury in late 1990. In his much-publicized call for Anglicans to return to Rome, Robert Runcie set the role of religious unity right in the center of all European unity efforts:

> We cannot discover European unity without reap-propriating Europe's Christian roots. In the past Christian faith gave unity and coherence to culture and society. . . . Christian disunity has also largely contrib-uted to the disunity of Europe and the wider world. In my own country I long for Anglicans and Roman Catholics, together with other Christians, to work together much more closely. . . . Could not all Chris-tians come to reconsider the kind of Primacy the bishop of Rome exercised within the early church, a "presiding in love" for the sake of unity . . . ?[7]

The archbishop backtracked on his statement somewhat when he was sharply criticized for the suggestion, claiming that he meant that the role should be largely symbolic. However, the Pope was quick to correct the perception. He wanted no back-tracking and firmly clarified that "the office of the papacy could not be merely symbolic" but had to be the recognized leader "in action and initiative." Malachi Martin, believed by many to be the unofficial voice of the current Pope (and the author of the book *The Keys of This Blood: The Struggle for World Domination between Pope John Paul II, Mikhail Gorbachev and the Capitalist West*), recalls the unity that Catholicism once provided Europe:

> During the centuries when European unity was at its height and vibrant, Europeans housed their hopes and found their believing trust beneath the domes and Gothic spires of the churches they built. They called the whole territory by a kind of family name: Christendom. . . . Europe's protection was centered on its faith. Its identity was provided in the papacy. The unifying principle of its civilization lay in its common acknowledgment of the primacy of the pope.[8]

The present Pope himself argues that there is no unity possible for men and women other than by an "exercise of the human and Christian solidarity to which the [Roman Catholic] church calls. . . ."[9] He further explains:

> Europe . . . despite its . . . divisions . . . cannot cease to seek its fundamental unity, must turn to Christianity. . . . Despite the different traditions that exist in the territory of Europe between eastern and western parts, there lives in each the same Christianity. Christianity must commit itself anew to the formation of the spiritual unity of Europe.[10]

In a February 26, 1990, *U.S. News* article, Vaclav Havel takes it a step further. He directly links the two prophesied characteristics of the Revived Roman Empire—democracy and professing Christianity—together into one vision of the New Europe:

> The spiritual impulses of Antiquity, Judaism and Christianity, merged into a force that has forged the

> world as we know it.... In fact, individual rights together with individual responsibility for the common good may constitute the very idea of Europe that we are looking for.

Maltese Prime Minister Eddie Fenec Adami also recognizes the coalition which forms the basis of the new Europe. Speaking of Malta's bid for EEC membership, he claimed that "the EEC we want to join is the Europe of Christian values, of liberty, of spirituality."[11]

Havel and Adami are right on the mark: They realize the role that "Christianity" plays in the current reforms of Europe. They know that Catholicism has been at the very heart of the democratization of Eastern Europe. Solidarity was only the first example of how the Catholic Church was deeply involved in the freedom movements, not only in Poland but in Czechoslovakia, Lithuania, Latvia, the Ukraine, and many other places.

As John Paul II has made it clear, the Roman Catholic position is that "no human activity escapes the religious dimension.... The hard intractable problems of the world—hunger, violation of human dignity and human rights, war and violence, economic oppression, political persecution—any and all of these can be solved only by acceptance and implementation of the message of Christ's revelation announced by the papacy and the Roman Catholic Church."[12]

A Common European House

But the Pope, Havel, and Adami are not the only ones to realize the arm-in-arm relationship that religion and democracy will play in bringing forth this new Europe. When Mikhail Gorbachev speaks of a "common European home" which stretches "from the Atlantic to the Urals," there is no doubt that he longs for even the Soviet Union to be a part of the New Europe. As such, he claims to be reforming the Soviet Union in such a way as to regain its status as a European power. To do this he recognizes that he must meet the two requirements of European citizenship—democracy and Christianity.

When he was asked a few years ago how the Berlin Wall could be compatible with his new democratic emphasis, Gorbachev answered "nothing is eternal." True to his word, the Berlin Wall fell within the year. At least in the minds of the Western world, "Gorby" was molding the Soviet Union in our very own image. "A new world is emerging," the world's newest hero promised; "man, his concerns, rights and freedoms, are [being] placed at the center of things. . . . The idea of democratizing the entire world has grown into a powerful surge and political force."[13]

At the same time Gorbachev knew that mere democratic reform was not enough to put the Soviet Union into the heart of this "common house." He had to satisfy the second condition of true European citizenship. As a result he went to the highest religious authority in the world. After his historic 1989 meeting with the Pope he announced:

> We need spiritual values. We need a revolution of the mind. This is the only way towards a new culture and new politics that can meet the challenge of our time.

It was this acknowledgment that gave the Soviets the only opportunity they have to join the European Community. In the March 1990 *World Press Review*, Paul Johnson explains the importance of the visit Gorbachev paid to the Roman pontiff:

> For Russia to be ready to join the community, it will have to recover its European past. This can be done in a number of ways, but if one is paramount, it is allowing the Christian religion once more to occupy the forefront of life. For Russia is at heart a profoundly Christian country, and that is its chief title deed to European status.

Today, in a complete turn of events unimaginable just a few short years ago, the cornerstone of worldwide atheism is claiming to be *Christian*! More staggering still is the fact that no one seems to see the clear opportunism that motivates the current Soviet leader. Gorbachev wants to get the Soviet Union incorporated into the New Europe. Any moves the Soviet leader makes must be seen in that light. At the same time the Catholic Church wants to reestablish its connections with millions of followers behind the disintegrated Iron Curtain. Therefore, as the December 4, 1989, issue of *Newsweek* magazine notes:

> But now, for the sake of European civilization—and their own parochial needs—the papacy and the party are searching for ways to cooperate. John Paul II speaks of Christianity as the common culture of a divided Europe while Gorbachev talks enigmatically of "a common European home."

Ruling over the Kings of the Earth

The fact that the heart of European unity is Catholicism and that the Roman Catholic Church has been a major player in the recent changes in Europe begins to show how the Church of Rome is different from every other religious institution in the world. This difference is simply that the Roman Church is as powerful a political force as it is a religious force. Indeed, the Church of Rome believes itself to be such a powerful political force that it argues, with good cause, that it can outmaneuver the Marxists and the capitalists, and bring forth its own vision of the New World Order! As Vatican insider Malachi Martin reveals:

> It is not too much to say, in fact, that the chosen purpose of John Paul's pontificate—the engine that drives his papal grand policy . . . is to the victor in the competition . . . [to determine] who will establish the

first one-world system that has ever existed in the society of nations.[14]

Understanding this part of the Catholic Church is crucial to understanding the vision that John saw of the great whore. The fact that the harlot was riding the beast is extremely significant. For this religious power to be in control shows that the harlot is also very powerful in the political realm. John makes this point expressly clear:

> The woman which thou sawest is that great city which reigneth over the kings of the earth (Revelation 17:18).

There is only one religious body with a corresponding city that truly reigns over the kings of the earth: the Roman Catholic Church and Vatican City. John even goes so far as to point out that the prophetic city sits on seven hills. The first thing our guide reminded us on our recent visit to Rome was that this was the city of seven hills! While there may be other cities that claim to sit on seven hills, none of those are a professing Christian city that commits fornication with the kings of the earth. Malachi Martin proudly describes the way the Roman Church served as the ruler of Europe in the past. His description is astonishingly similar to that of the apostle John:

> The centerpiece of [Europe] was the man who sat on the throne of Simon Peter in that Holy See of Rome. Among the major players at the Round Table of international politics, no ruler could take command, no government could govern, no commerce could function, without the spiritual blessing and the imperial nod of the Roman Pope.[15]

That power remains to this very day. No other religious institution in the world possesses the political clout that the Vatican does. With 116 full-fledged embassies in Vatican City, it has been described by a multitude of sources as the best intelligence-gathering location on the face of the earth. Not recognizing the geopolitical power of Vatican City would be a grave error, warns Malachi Martin:

> . . . any world leader who takes the Roman Pontiff as possessing only spiritual weapons . . . with which to deal in practical, this-worldly matters is making a strategic error of grave proportions.[16]

In fact, when it was revealed in *Newsweek* magazine in late 1990 that both U.S. President George Bush and Soviet Premier Mikhail Gorbachev consulted on a weekly basis with the Pope, any doubt of Rome's political clout was dispelled. After his first meeting with this present Pope the surprised Soviet Foreign Minister Gromyko exclaimed, "This is a man with a worldview!" Martin concludes that "Karol Wojtyla was one man who came to the papacy with a full understanding and a sophisticated appreciation of the geopolitical power of the Holy See."[17] He intends to use that power to once again fully reign over the kings of this earth.

The Whore That Sits on Many Waters

There is yet another clue that God, through the vision that He showed the apostle John, gave us as to the identity of this Mystery Woman. This is the fact that her influence is worldwide and her power spans the globe:

> Come hither; I will show unto thee the judgment of the great whore that sitteth upon many waters. . . . And he saith unto me, The waters which thou sawest, where the whore sitteth, are peoples and multitudes and nations and tongues (Revelation 17:1,15).

With its almost one billion adherents, the Roman Catholic Church accounts for about 18 percent of the world population. The global reach of this institution is unparalleled. Its number of priests is equivalent to the number of troops that the U.S. sent to the Persian Gulf to liberate Kuwait. It has over 3000 Bishops, 211,156 parishes, 1920 dioceses, and 513 archdioceses. But that's not all. The Catholic portfolio includes multitudes of schools, universities, research institutes, medical and social science centers, hospitals, convents, churches, cathedrals, chapels, monasteries, religious centers, embassies, legations, archives, libraries, museums, newspapers, magazines, publishing houses, and radio and television stations. Furthermore, the Vatican Bank, often the center of scandal, admits to massive investments "in virtually every sector of the world's commercial and industrial activity."[18] Truly, as Soviet Ambassador Maksim Litinov realized, the Church of Rome's "terrain is the world of nations."

Once again Malachi Martin describes the reach of this global institution:

> What captures the unwavering attention of the secular leaders of the world in this remarkable network of the Roman Catholic Church is precisely the fact that it places at the personal disposal of the Pope a supranational, supra-trade-bloc structure that is so built and oriented that if tomorrow or next week, by a sudden miracle, a one-world government were established, the Church would not have to undergo any essential structural changes in order to retain its dominant position and to further its globalist aims. . . . There is tacit agreement among the great international political and financial leaders that the very attributes that give the Holy See its georeligious power and capability provide it, as well, with everything essential for the same power and capability on the political plane.[19]

Applauding the Antichrist System

Just as the Word of God predicted, the Revived Roman Empire as the new Europe—the very hub of power out of which the Antichrist will rise—is currently being formed. And, exactly as foretold, it is being forged out of two corresponding and intermingling components—the democratic feet of clay and the deceptive harlotry of false faith. The deception is astounding. In fact, it is so intense that the erection of this system is being applauded not only by conservative politicians but by church leaders and mainline evangelicals as well.

Once again we see why a clear understanding of Bible prophecy is so important. Without the light it casts, man's natural intellect is applauding the very system that the Antichrist will rule over! Natural man will believe that the system promising human rights and freedom of religion is leading to greater godliness and what one evangelical leader calls "a new millennium."[20] No wonder the Bible warns that if it were possible even the very elect would be deceived! If church leaders are so deceived by the basis and ideology of the Antichrist system, how deceived will the world be by the masquerading "angel of light" himself?

Such deception is possible because doctrine has been pushed so far off center stage that most people can't discern that the spread of "religious" freedom translates to the spread of Catholicism and not the spread of the true gospel! It seems that we can't even differentiate between the "whore of Babylon" and the pure teachings of Christ.

Despite Rome's unmistakable apostasy, many of evangelical Christianity's most visible leaders are beating a path to the Pope's door. Robert Schuller says, "It's time for Protestants to go to the shepherd [Pope] and say, 'What do we have to do to come home?' "[21] Pat Robertson in his book *The New Millennium* speaks glowingly of the great unity that was evident under the leadership of Rome before the Reformation, and anticipates its return. Trinity Broadcast Network's Paul Crouch claims, "I [am] eradicating the word Protestant even out of my vocabulary. . . .

I'm not protesting anything anymore. . . . It is . . . time for Catholics and non-Catholics to come together as one in the Spirit and one in the Lord."[22]

However, this new unity is not to be a two-way street. The Pope himself is very clear on that matter. On a recent trip to Bolivia the Pope "warned Roman Catholic bishops to protect their congregations from evangelical preachers . . . [who] are sowing confusion in the people . . . [which] can very quickly dilute the coherence and unity of the Gospel message."[23] The Pope makes no bones about it—the gospel of this new ecumenical coalition is the *gospel of Rome.*

Pointing out these developments is not meant to be an indictment of anyone. Instead, it should be seen as a warning of how far the deception has gone. The whore of Babylon is forming right before our very eyes. Initially she will gather deceived multitudes who claim to be Christians under her wings. That is why God cries out, "Come out of her, my people, that ye be not partakers of her sins" (Revelation 18:4).

As her dominion spreads beyond the Revived Roman Empire she will begin to draw together all religions under her leadership. Ultimately every single person on the planet whose name is not written in the Lamb's Book of Life will succumb to her enchantments. She promises human rights, prosperity, freedom of religion, and freedom of choice, but in the end she will share deception, judgment, and hell itself with her converts.

That's how serious the issues really are, and that's why we must not hold our peace for the sake of unity.

Chapter 5

The Whore and the Beast

> I have come to believe firmly today that our future peace, justice, and fulfillment, happiness and harmony on this planet will not depend on world government but on divine or cosmic government . . . my great personal dream is to get a tremendous alliance between all major religions and the U.N.
>
> —Robert Muller, former Assistant
> Secretary General of the United Nations
> in *The New Genesis*

Under the leadership of the Antichrist and the False Prophet, the alliance of "Christian" democracies that makes up the Revived Roman Empire will quickly expand its sphere of influence until it reigns over the whole world. This does not mean that the whole world will convert to democracy; it just means that *the New Europe will be the core of the New World Order*. Nor does it mean that all will convert to Catholicism or any form of false faith that claims to be Christian. The great "Mother of Harlots" that John saw has many children, and Rome is simply the chief of these. Nonetheless, we do know that under the guidance of the False Prophet (who will almost undoubtedly be the head of the Roman Church) the followers of every religion and no religion will actually worship "the christ" who has arisen out of the New Europe.

This idea of a worldwide system is completely in keeping with the vision that Nebuchadnezzar had showing the four empires that would rule the entire known world of their day. In today's global age such an empire would have to span the whole globe. The apostle John makes it clear that this is exactly the degree of power that the Antichrist and his False Prophet will achieve. In Revelation 13 he gives the three central pillars of power in this New World Order:

> Power was given him [Antichrist] over all kindreds and tongues and nations (Revelation 13:7).

> All that dwell upon the earth shall worship him (Revelation 13:8).

> He [the False Prophet] causeth all . . . to receive a mark (Revelation 13:16).

The Unification of Church and State

This close association between the whore and the beast, and the Antichrist and False Prophet, reveals to us that we could expect to see an amazing similarity in the goals and aspirations of the two. As we saw earlier, in addressing the mounting problems which the world faces today, the solutions offered by political and religious leaders are virtually interchangable.

The cry in the world today is for the separation of church and state. In the very near future that cry will change. Why? Because the emerging world church will not be an offense to the world. The world will not be convicted by its preaching. It will share the same ambitions, desires, and goals. Already we see this happening. The evolving world church no longer preaches "a new heaven and a new earth" but a "new age on this earth." The world church has become so infected with social issues and a social gospel that it is virtually indiscernible from the emerging global political philosophies. While political leaders call for a New World Order, apostate church leaders cling to the same earthly hope. This position was openly taken by the Roman Catholic Church at the time of Vatican II, when Pope John Paul VI told the departing bishops that their Church—

> had decided to opt for man; to serve man, to help him build his home on this earth. Man with his ideas and his aims, man with his hopes and his fears, man in his difficulties and sufferings—that was the centerpiece of the Church's interest.[1]

Likewise the present Pope's first encyclical promised that the "preoccupation" of his papacy was to be with "man in all his works and ambitions to build a secure home on this earth." In confirmation of this thrust, "The Challenge of Peace," a Pastoral Letter of the National Conference of Catholic Bishops, argues that—

> Just as the nation-state was a step in the evolution of the government at a time . . . we are now entering an era of new global interdependencies requiring global systems of governance to manage the resulting conflicts. . . . These growing tensions can not be remedied by a single-nation-state approach. They shall require the concerted effort of the whole world community.

Meanwhile, a letter entitled "In Defense of Creation" from the United Methodist Church offers virtually the identical solution:

> The transformation of our conflict-ridden nation-state system into a new world order of common security and independent institutions offers the only practical hope for enduring peace.

Tom Hugdens, the head of the Rocky Mountain delegation to the conference (which spawned the letter), remarked that "it is obvious that the United Methodist Bishops and others have the same goal as World Federalists [and] . . . the same solution as how to get there." Now, with environmental concerns surpassing military concerns on the collective human psyche, the World Council of Churches has added environmental consciousness to the "essentials" of the Christian faith. In the new test for orthodoxy these "Christian" leaders not only place environmental consciousness on an equal level with belief in the resurrection, but they actually claim that it supersedes it! In the gospel of this earth it is better to let Muslims and Hindus go to hell than to chance harming the environmental movement! That's how far the earth-based theology of the world church has come.

However, it is not just the apostate World Council of Churches who are buying into this deception. Richard Land, the director of Southern Baptist Convention's Christian Life Commission, also feels that "Christians need to embrace a broader sense of salvation: salvation of humankind and redemption of creation."[2]

It is an amazing parallel and return to the biblical account of the Tower of Babel. You will recall that the whole world was united as one in building their tower. They needed to do this, they argued, "lest we be scattered abroad upon the face of the whole earth." The Hebrew word for "scattered" comes from a primary root which means "to dash in pieces . . . to break in pieces." Likewise the builders of today's global society are coming together to build a tower, in the form of a New World Order, for the exact same reason—lest they be destroyed off the face of the earth. It comes as no surprise, therefore, that the official poster put out by The Council of Europe shows the Tower of Babel surrounded by the 12 stars of the European Economic Community.

The New Liberation Theology

Make no mistake about it—the emerging world church and world order are fitting together like a hand in a glove. The leaders of this drive to a new world are fully aware of the critical role that a properly guided religion can play. During the 1980's this type of coalition was most obvious in the mixture of Catholicism and Marxism, under the banner of Liberation Theology in Latin and South America. In the nineties the worldwide coalition will be defined by a mixture of "religious freedom" and "human rights."

The same thing that made Liberation Theology possible in Latin and South America will make the "Christian"-Democratic foundation acceptable globally. George Orwell's *1984* pictured a world of doublespeak. In that world one word would sound like it meant one thing while it really meant just the opposite. We have entered that world in "Christian civilization" today. By manipulating the meaning of words that the faithful assume to have a certain religious significance until they begin to mean something slightly different, a political agenda can be infused into a religious vocabulary. This is happening at a breathtaking pace in mainline denominations and even among evangelicals. Unfortunately, this is made possible because of the low emphasis placed on doctrine in most churches today.

Consider the word "peace," for example. Recently religious leaders all over the world have hailed the beginning of a great period of peace. "Peace among men," it is proclaimed, is the divine will of God. They urge us to enhance this peace by forgetting the foolish barriers of doctrine and embracing as equals all religions and philosophical persuasions. But the sad truth of the matter is that this kind of peace is not of Christ but of Antichrist. It is a false peace based on the desires of men and bound by circumstance. It is this peace which the Bible speaks of when it proclaims, "When they shall say peace and safety, then sudden destruction cometh upon them..." (1 Thessalonians 5:3).

The peace of Christ is totally different from this false peace. The peace of Christ is not primarily peace *between men* but peace *between God and man*. Only when that form of peace comes about—in the millennium, with the Prince of Peace in the midst—can "peace among men" be achieved. Until that time Jesus Himself said:

> Think not that I am come to send peace on earth; I came not to send peace but a sword. For I am come to set a man at variance against his father, and the daughter against her mother, and the daughter-in-law against her mother-in-law. And a man's foes shall be they of his own household. He that loveth father or mother more than me is not worthy of me, and he that loveth son or daughter more than me is not worthy of me. And he that taketh not his cross and followeth after me is not worthy of me (Matthew 10:34-38).

This sounds so harsh. Can you imagine a pastor preaching that verse to his carnal congregation? But to the spiritual person Christ promises a different kind of peace:

> Peace I leave with you; my peace give I unto you; not as the world giveth give I unto you. Let not your heart be troubled, neither let it be afraid (John 14:27).

What is this peace that is different from the world's? It is the peace of knowing that God loves you and that your well-being is not determined by circumstance, treaties, or war. It is the peace of knowing that "you, being dead in your sins and the uncircumcision of your flesh, hath he quickened together with him, having forgiven you all trespasses, blotting out the handwriting of ordinances that was against us, and took it out of the way, nailing it to his cross" (Colossians 2:13,14). It is the peace of being able to say, "I know whom I have believed and am persuaded that he is able to keep that which I have committed unto him against that day" (2 Timothy 1:12).

Human Rights and the Rise of the Antichrist

Perhaps the key phrase of the nineties will be *human rights*. All over the world, especially with the seeming collapse of the

Communist world, glowing speeches are being given in the name of human rights. This spread of rights of the people is being referred to as a "resurgence of biblical truth."[3] Church leaders are rushing to implant the ideals of American rights into the freed lands. But what are we giving these people? While government based on liberty and freedom of choice may be the best hope that man has to offer, basic rights in the United States are now being pushed to such extents that they include abortion on demand, quick and easy divorce, immunity from parental discipline, full homosexual rights, storefront pornography shops, and the freedom to be free of any public display of Christianity.

Suddenly the human rights campaign has become nothing short of a do-as-you-wish banner seeking to throw off the shackles of sin and conviction. Are these the rights the church should be holding up so proudly? One observer makes a much-needed point when he warns us not to confuse "of the people, by the people, and for the people" with "of God, by God, and for God."[4]

The truth of the matter is that a Christian has given up his rights. We are dead. When we were buried in baptism we were buried in the likeness of Christ's death.

> I am crucified with Christ; nevertheless I live, yet not I, but Christ liveth in me; and the life which I now live in the flesh I live by faith of the son of God, who loved me and gave himself for me (Galatians 2:20,21).

The apostle Paul referred to himself as a prisoner of Christ, dead to his will but alive to that of Christ. Has that been forgotten in the church today? It certainly seems to have been by the multitudes who preach that we have to learn to claim and profess our rights in Christ! They speak glowingly of our rights to be given respect and of our rights to political power and monetary gain. They tell us that we are dishonoring God if we do not heap our rightful rewards upon ourselves.

Building a Moral Society

I happened to hear George Bush's Christmas message one year. My ears perked up when I heard him say something like this: "Let us not forget in the midst of the materialism and hype what the true meaning of Christmas is. The true meaning of Christmas is family. Let us this Christmas join with our loved ones and share a blessed time together." As I listened to this self-professed Christian I was amazed. It was the first time that I had seen family values so clearly replace Christ as the true message of Christmas in this way. In a like way the call for family values, a moral society, and conservative politics is slowly becoming accepted as the goal of the Great Commission. Instead of the Great Commission being the call to go into all the world and preach the gospel to the unsaved, it is subtly being transformed into the call to go into all the world and make it a Christian society. This is the heart of the rapidly spreading Reconstruction message, which teaches that Christians are to take over and rule over society.

The problem is that, according to the Bible, hell will be full of good, clean-living, moral people! Good, clean-living, moral people do not go to heaven; people who have invited Jesus into their hearts do. The finest Buddhist, the best singer in the Mormon Tabernacle Choir, and the most charitable Muslim in the world will land in hell unless he or she is reached with and accepts the gospel of Jesus Christ. This is a divisive message seldom heard today, but that fact does not make it any less true.

These few examples of how political agendas are being woven into and rewriting the true meaning of the Christian faith show how a merger with other faiths and political philosophies will be possible as we move toward a "Gospel of this earth." Ultimately that great ecumenical coalition will willingly line up under the Antichrist and his False Prophet. As the apostle John makes clear, "All that dwell upon the earth shall worship him [Antichrist] whose names are not written in the book of life of the Lamb" (Revelation 13:8).

The Gospel of This Earth

It is under the pull of the gospel of this earth that Rome is pulling many mainline denominations and even many professed evangelical groups and ministries under her wings. As John F. Walvoord writes, "It is a sad commentary on contemporary Christendom that it shows an overwhelming desire to return to Rome in spite of Rome's evident apostasy from the true biblical Christianity."[5]

However, Protestants are not the only ones whom the Church of Rome is courting. The ecumenical movement, which received serious criticism a decade ago because it was based on a watering down of religious differences between denominations, has today grown to the point where the goal is now the merger of different religions! The Pope's Global Day of Peace was only the first display of Rome's attempt to bring together all faiths under its leadership. In a recent Apostolic Letter on Lebanon the Pope wrote:

> The tragedy that the people of Lebanon are suffering prompts me to write to you. I do so with confidence, not in the name of any particular group or school of thought, but in the name of the same God whom we adore and whom we seek to serve.... May God find us, both Muslims and Christians, together... who... have known how to be worshippers in spirit and in truth!

Likewise in a recent message to Hindus, Muslims, and Protestants, the Pope noted how "their efforts were unleashing profound spiritual energies in the world and bringing about a new climate of peace." He has also recently urged "all religions to work together against political, ideological, and economic tensions." Even the secular *International Herald Tribune* joins in the call:

> If the security council can bring together the United States, the Soviet Union and the People's Republic of

China for a common expression of commitment to international law, surely religious leaders can devise a forum for a common commitment to religious peace. The pope should issue an invitation to an interfaith selection of widely recognized religious leaders. He should present a draft document stating that violence in the name of religion is contrary to the word of God. He should seek the active support of as many leaders as will join with him for such a document.[6]

Former United Nations Assistant Secretary General Robert Muller also hopes that "religions will get together and define . . . the cosmic laws which are common to all faiths."[7]

. . . the pope will come before the year 2000 to the United Nations, speak for all the religions and spiritualities on the planet and give the world the religious view of how the third millennium should be a spiritual millennium.[8]

There is no question that the present Pope has gone a long way in establishing himself as both the leader of the mainline denominations and the moral voice of the world's religions. I believe that after the rapture those who professed to be Christians but were not saved will rally around "the whore" headed by the Catholic Church. I also believe that in the name of peace on this earth all the world's religions will cooperate with this whore in a great ecumenical coalition. The World Council of Churches figures to be front-and-center in this compact. According to its own press service:

The WCC promotes church unity and unity of the human family. . . . Ecumenicism in the Middle East is a process of making the churches more open to society. It is also an attempt to bring the church, the synagogue, and the mosque closer to one another. It is a vision of one God for all the faithful, be they Christians, Muslims, or Jews.[9]

Almost immediately, however, this religious compact will join with the political beast in an alliance with the goal of inaugurating the New World Order. Far from being a distant and unlikely scenario, recent pioneering meetings between world political and religious leaders indicate that such a merger is now in the works.

The Shared Vision

In the fall of 1985 a meeting was held between parliamentarians from five continents and spiritual leaders from Buddhism, Hinduism, Islam, Judaism, and Christianity. The purpose of the meeting was to "initiate a dialogue on issues of global survival." The meeting, which was jointly sponsored by the Global Committee of Parliamentarians on Population and Development and The Temple of Understanding, issued a joint call "for a world conference of spiritual and parliamentary leaders to be held in the spring of 1988 that would carry the dialogue to new and wider dimensions."

The new coalition named itself "The Global Forum of Spiritual and Parliamentary Leaders on Human Survival." Its manifesto boasted that its members had found "great stimulus in a fruitful exchange and exploration, transcending barriers in a spirit of harmony." Furthermore, based exclusively on the gospel of this earth, they concluded that all religions and political philosophies must work together because "the fate of the human community is inseparable from the fate of this earth."[10]

> We are entering an era of global citizenship.... This new consciousness transcends all barriers of race and religion, ideology and nationality, linking humanity into an extended family.... This family cares for itself... and must draw upon all achievements of the

> human spirit—on the universal principles embodied in the great world religions, on the great secular philosophies, and on the astounding insights of science.... We hold up the vision of a new community, where the long and tragic history of human violence gives way to an age of mutually assured welfare and peace... in this conviction, spiritual and parliamentary leaders from all parts of the world will meet at Oxford to forge a new partnership in response to our global crisis.

Many years ago Professor Hans Kung argued that there could be "no world peace without peace among the religions." It is the recognition of the political reality of this statement by political leaders that has spawned a new coalition with religious leaders thought impossible only a few years ago. This coalition of religious and political leaders is an unmistakable sign of a growing effort to unite all faiths and political systems into the exact New World Order prophesied in the Bible. Global Forum executive coordinator Akio Matsumura explains how far this process has come:

> Even as recently as five years ago, our Oxford conference would not have worked. But now, suddenly, interfaith initiatives have gathered strength, with, for example, both the Vatican and the World Wildlife Federation bringing people of all beliefs together at Assisi. In our Initiative, with our conference, we hope to go a little further—and join all faiths with all political attitudes.

Global Forum participant U.S. Congressman James H. Sheuer contended more directly that "we must merge the ethical and the practical, the politician and the priest, the sacred and the secular." The 1988 gathering was hosted by the Archbishop of Canterbury, Robert Runcie, and attended by such notables as

Mother Teresa, the Dalai Lama, U.N. Secretary General Javier Perez de Cuellar, former Peruvian Prime Minister Manuel Ulloa, and many others. The then-head of the world's Anglicans, Robert Runcie, used the occasion to reinforce his stance that—

> ...we are learning that we are interdependent in spiritual matters too...that there is a certain incompleteness in each of our traditions...that some claims about exclusiveness of the church have to be renounced...[in the name of] a new and larger vision of unity.

Indeed, in this conference (which included shamans, medicine men, and rain forest rituals) the Archbishop's only complaint was against those fundamentalist, narrow-minded Christians who believe that the current global situation is a fulfillment of Bible prophecy.

> ...nor can we accept the despair of those who interpret the various crises we face today in the political, economic and ecological areas as the harbingers of the end of the world. The fatalism inherent in such a philosophy has no part in authentic religious awareness.

This preoccupation with solving the problems of this world despite any "external" differences is an exact carbon copy of the Roman Catholic stance. As Malachi Martin notes in *The Keys of This Blood*, when world leaders meet with the Pope, "the context of these conversations, of course, is never a pie-in-the-sky exchange of religious or philosophical views....The context is always the growing interdependence of modern nations."

By the time the Global Forum gathered in Moscow for its second conference in 1989, the wheels were well in motion for a political and religious merger. Now some real political heavyweights were becoming involved. Mr. Peace himself, Mikhail

Gorbachev, gave the closing address. Other speakers included Javier Perez de Cuellar; former Norwegian Prime Minister Gro Harlem Brundtland; U.S. Senators Claiborne Pell, Al Gore, Dave Durenberger, and Tim Wirth; Zimbabwe's Natural Resources Minister Victoria Chitepo; Soviet parliamentarians and scientists Evguenij Velikhov and Alexey Yablokov; astronomer Carl Sagan; oceanographer Jacques Cousteau; Nobel laureate Elie Wiesel; Dr. Jose Goldemberg, Rector of the University of Sao Paulo; and Lester Brown, founder-president of the Worldwatch Institute of Washington D.C. In all, 700 spiritual and parliamentary leaders gathered together for an event that culminated in a live global broadcast beamed by satellite into over 100 countries with a potential viewing audience of over two billion people. According to Global Forum organizers, it was the first time in history that both the Intelsat and the Intersputnik satellite systems, with 129 member countries, granted free access to such a project.

These conferences are only the beginning; an irreversible prophetic coalition is forming. Speaking of the first gathering in April 1988, Global Forum cochairman James Parks Morton explained:

> The purpose of the conference was not just to have a conference. I mean it was to inaugurate a process. . . . We're going to get a whole series of conferences, meetings, strategy sessions at the grassroots level, at the national level and at the regional level. And those are going to start right away.

This coalition is the only one that can truly begin to influence the direction of change which the organizers of the Global Forum believe in. According to *Shared Vision*, 1989:

> The two groups of leaders are central to the process of change because they are the opinionmakers and policymakers who work most closely with people at all

levels, from the local to the global. Through dialogue and interaction, the Global Forum gives them the opportunity to influence not only each other—ethically, morally and practically—but to extend this influence to the communities they serve worldwide.

The Deceptive Logic of Man

These summits of political and religious leaders are significant in two ways. In the first place, they provide a platform to show the world how religious unity must work together with political unity if world peace is to be achieved. They have begun a process of placing religious leaders on an equal level with political leaders in the concrete effort to solve the world's problems—which is, of course, a major step toward the combined political/religious system which the Bible prophesies that the Antichrist will rule over. Secondly, the Dalai Lama's argument that this new "spiritual energy and power can be purposefully used to bring about spiritual conditions necessary for world peace" reinforces a growing view, even within the evangelical church, that sees cooperation with other faiths as acceptable as long as the cause is good. Thus these meetings will serve to build on the tone set by Pope John Paul II's Global Day of Peace. The meetings will thereby pull more Christian denominations into the Catholic-led ecumenical movement, which far from signifying interdenominational compromise now promises a full-scale interfaith merger. In a day when many evangelical Christian leaders have no qualms about aligning themselves with the likes of Rev. Moon or the Mormons if it is "for good cause," the results will be disastrous.

"The Global Forum of Spiritual and Parliamentary Leaders on Human Survival" is only one indication of how the merger of the whore and the beast is coming about. However, their logo—a religious leader and a political leader together holding the planet in their hands—is certainly the correct symbol of the coming coalition that the Antichrist and the False Prophet will bring forth as the New World Order.

Chapter 6

Toward the New World Order

There is much talk today of a coming New World Order. Although there are differing visions of what this new order will be like, almost all observers agree that it will be an outgrowth of the alliance of Christian democracies that make up the New Europe. As one Europe-watcher notes:

> In the very long term, the European structure will be considered the prototype for something much more ambitious. Talk of world government is at least a century old and has gone nowhere. But an ever-widening association, based on shared cultural values, is a more promising idea. The European cultural concept is not a conventional idea. It is a global one. We are taking the first steps toward an ecumenical community that will ultimately spread to all corners of our planet.[1]

Jean Monnet, considered by many to be the father of the European Economic Community, always saw the EEC as no more than an intermediate step. It was his conviction that "the sovereign nations of the past can no longer solve the problems of the present . . . or control their own future. And the community itself is only a stage on the way to the organized world of tomorrow."[2]

Incredibly, this is exactly what the Bible prophesied: that the Antichrist would arise out of a Revived Roman Empire and from that power base exert his dominion worldwide! Compounding the coming deception is the fact that many people, including German Chancellor Helmut Kohl, seem to have this new world order confused with the biblical millennium.

> The United States of Europe will form the core of a peaceful order . . . the age prophesied of old, when all shall dwell secure and none shall make them afraid.[3]

Architects of the New World Order

Today the call for this global age is coming from all corners. George Bush used the hope of this new order as an explanation for his massive and unexpected reaction to the Iraqi invasion of Kuwait. But the American president is not the one who truly brought this idea into the mainstream. The credit for that goes to the leader of the world's other superpower: It was Mikhail Gorbachev who stunned the world with his "new thinking" in the late eighties.

In December 1988 he took the podium at the United Nations and set the world on a course of dramatic change. He declared that closed societies had failed. He called for a "democratization" of the world and absolute freedom of choice for all its people. He unilaterally cut Soviet troops in Europe by a half-million and then called for the formation of a New World Order as the only solution to the multitude of global problems facing the community of nations.

It was with that speech that the drive toward the New World Order truly kicked into high gear. Commenting on that startling turn of events, Pope John Paul II claimed that the world was at a "very special moment . . . as if awakened from a nightmare and opened up to a better hope."[4]

However, as the leader of the world's most powerful religious organization, Pope John Paul II is far from being just an observer.

Like Mikhail Gorbachev and George Bush, he too has a vision of the shape that the New World Order should take. In fact, the present Pope claims to believe that he is in a winner-take-all competition with the Soviets and the capitalist West to determine "who will establish the first one-world system of government that has ever existed in the society of nations."[5] As we already noted:

> It is not too much to say, in fact, that the chosen purpose of John Paul's ponticate—the engine that drives his papal grand policy and that determines his day-to-day, year-by-year strategies—is to be the victor in that competition, now well under way.[6]

Catholic writer Malachi Martin reveals the importance that John Paul II places on this effort:

> John Paul has a clear vision of our near-future world. . . . All of the Pontiff's papal actions . . . are dictated by that vision. Moreover, everything he did, even in the earliest days of his pontificate, was undertaken according to a timetable linked to that vision. . . .[7] He was and is gambling . . . on the objective he had chosen for his papacy—that he could play an integral part in the geopolitical formation of the society of nations.[8]

Regionalism and the New World Order

Minor details aside, all agree that the New Europe will be the hub of the New World Order. Likewise, no one envisions a world where all borders and nationalities have completely vanished and the world has truly become one global nation. Instead, in the New World Order one powerful world government will rule over various regional groupings of nations and alliances. Globalist George Ball argues:

> ...sooner or later we are going to have to face restructuring our institutions so that they are not confined merely to the nation-states. Start first on a regional basis and ultimately you could move to a world basis.[9]

Zbigniew Brzezinski, the organizer of David Rockefeller's Trilateral Commission, agreed in *Between Two Ages* (1970) that:

> ...the movement toward a large community of the developed nations will necessarily have to be piecemeal.... Such a community cannot be achieved by fusing existing states into one larger entity.... It makes more sense to attempt to associate existing states through a variety of indirect ties and already developing limitations on national sovereignty.

These various regions, which would answer ultimately to a world government, would be based not only on geographic location but also on cultural uniformity. Thus while one region might consist of the Western "Christian" democracies, all born out of European culture, another may be formed by the Arab states, another by black African states, perhaps another by Orientals, etc. Using the New Europe as an example, Paul Johnson shows in *World Press Review* (1990), how cultural similarities must be the defining factor of each region:

> ...Europe is essentially a cultural concept.... The flow of European colonists all over the world was a...cultural expansion.... [think] of Europe not as much in geographical, political and economic terms as in cultural terms.... [and] we begin to see how impossible it is to set geographical limits.

This regional concept, with each region being defined by the distinct cultural and religious histories of the area, is to be the cornerstone of the New World Order. It also will give the meaning to the slogan of the New World Order: "Unity in Diversity." Although each region will maintain its cultural diversity (according to the planners of this new age), there will be overall unity in the name of saving this earth.

This idea of global regions, each a grouping of nations, is a perfect fit with the way the Bible describes this last-days kingdom. While the Bible states clearly that the Antichrist will rule over the whole world (Daniel 7:23), it is also very clear that his rule will be over distinct "kindreds and tongues and nations" (Revelation 13:7). Even at the point of Armageddon, the prophet Zechariah tells us that it is *the nations of the world* that will be united against Jerusalem, making it evident that individual countries will not be wiped out by the coming New World Order.

As to the specific regions which will evolve, the prophet Ezekiel gives evidence of one of these regions when he speaks of the great northern confederacy that will invade Israel in the latter days; the prophet Daniel tells us of the King of the South, indicating a southern regional grouping of nations; and the apostle John tells us of the Kings of the East as well. Although not specifically identified as such, the Revived Roman Empire, another grouping of nations, easily fits the description of a great Western confederacy. All in all it is safe to say that the current movement toward regionalism should come as no surprise to the student of Bible prophecy.

Governing the World

It is worth restating the point once again that, according to the prophecies of the Bible, the New Europe and its charismatic leader will be the anchor of these global regions. But governing this new world order will be a big job. The United Nations, held by many people as the best hope for this task, has enjoyed a resurgence of respectability since the Kuwaiti crisis in early 1990. When Iraq invaded the tiny oil sheikdom, George Bush quickly united worldwide support to oppose the invasion. The way he did it made clear his vision of how the New World Order should be run. Every move he made, every sanction he called for, and every deadline he set were carefully coordinated through the United Nations. Indeed, "the Bush administration would like to make the United Nations a cornerstone of its plans to construct a New World Order."[10]

The degree to which Bush wanted to push this vision along was shown in the same crisis when he went to the United Nations Security Council instead of the United States Congress to obtain permission to begin a military assault on occupied Kuwait. As former American Ambassador to the United Nations Jeanne Kirkpatrick notes, one of the underlying goals in Bush's handling of the entire crisis was to show the world how a reinvigorated United Nations could serve as a global policeman in the New Order.[11]

This second coming of the United Nations has made evident the huge problems that have made this organization completely ineffectual in the first generation of its existence. Beyond the now-fading East-West division that split and stymied the organization, other structural problems still plague the global confederacy. None of these is more evident than the problem of having too many voices trying to guide the ship. The one-nation/one-vote principle (which, for example, gives Cuba an equal voice with the United States) is completely unworkable. All analysts agree that if the United Nations or any future organization is going to rule the world effectively, there will have to be a much smaller center of power. Paul Mazur, a leading internationalist, is blunt in his appraisal of the situation:

> . . . finally the large number of governmental bureaus that will have their orbits in the atmosphere of our planet cannot be allowed the freedom to compete and collide with one another. So, in order to control the diverse bureaucracies required, a politburo will develop, and over this group organization there is likely to arise the final and single arbitrator—the master of the order, the total dictator.[12]

The Ten Kings of Revelation

What makes this logical solution so incredible is that this is exactly what the Bible tells us will happen in the last days. According to the prophecies in the Bible, the Antichrist (along with a council of ten rulers) will rule over the whole earth:

> The ten horns which thou sawest are ten kings which have received no kingdom as yet, but receive power as kings one hour with the beast. These have one mind, and shall give their power and strength unto the beast (Revelation 17:12,13).

These "wise men" of earth, perhaps the leaders of ten global regions, perhaps ten of the world's most brilliant and respected thinkers, perhaps ten kings from royal bloodlines, will work with the Antichrist in an effort to seemingly bring peace, love, unity, and prosperity to planet Earth. However, they will eventually do much more than that. The Bible tells us that along with the beast and the False Prophet these kings will actually try to make war with the Lord Himself when He returns at the height of Armageddon.

Signs of the world's desire to have such a group of brilliant, noble men lead the way into a New World Order are definitely emerging. In recognition of the fact that the United Nations will have to be reformed to meet its new important role, Ramses Nassif, press spokesman for former U.N. Secretary General U Thant, sums up the latest thinking:

> Are the historic changes transforming the world making the United Nations irrelevant? To many of those who know it best, the answer is yes. . . . How then could the United Nations be reformed and modernized? I think a group or a commission of eminent persons is needed . . . Jimmy Carter . . . could make an able chairman for such a commission.[13]

Of equal interest have been the many other recent calls for the creation of councils of "Wise Persons" to lead the world through this great period of transition. Mikhail Gorbachev has called for the U.N. to set up a "Brain Trust" of the world's elite to "push global politics toward detente." He claims the Brain Trust should include "nobel laureates, diplomats and churchmen."[14] Likewise, the "United Nations Association of the U.S.A." has called for a "Global Watch Committee" of prestigious leaders to lead the international community. In reaction to Black Monday (the October 1987 stock market crash), Paul Streeten of Oxford University called for "a surrender of some national sovereignty and the transfer of sufficient power to the decision makers who could manage the system . . . a Council of Wise Persons."[15]

It was no surprise when 76 Nobel laureates gathered in Paris in January 1988 to discuss solutions to world problems. They have met several times since then, including a meeting in 1990 to discuss how religious intolerance threatens world peace. The participants at this particular gathering included Jimmy Carter, Vaclav Havel, Henry Kissinger, Francois Mitterand, Lech Walesa, and Elie Wiesel. The *International Herald Tribune* described this gathering as an effort to actually set up "a central steering committee, on the lines of the United Nations Security Council."

The problem is that these planners of the New World Order are not elected or answerable to anyone. It is ironic that on the way to this great new age of democracy and freedom of choice, democracy is the first victim! As Malachi Martin notes:

> In a truly one-world order, it would not be possible to regulate an election of high officials in the same manner as democratic egalitarianism requires. General referenda would also be impossible. So obvious has this difficulty been that warning scenarios have long since been prepared in the democratic capitalist camp itself. Scenarios that show in considerable detail just how and why, in the transition to a world order, the various processes of democracy would have to be

shouldered by select groups, themselves picked by other select groups.[16]

Of course, we are not saying that any of the participants in these emerging "Wise Persons" councils are necessarily going to be among the eventual ten kings who rule the world with the Antichrist. All we are doing is pointing out that the prophesied pattern is definitely beginning to emerge.

The Man-Made Millennium

As we already noted, German Chancellor Helmut Kohl sees a day when—

> The United States of Europe will form the core of a peaceful order . . . the age prophesied of old, when all shall dwell secure and none shall make them afraid.[17]

It is these millennial visions that best describe the goals of the would-be builders of the New World Order. Like the builders of the Tower of Babel before them, they believe that by coming together as one they can create the ultimate kingdom of peace without the presence of the Prince of Peace. While their visions of this peaceful and just New World Order are largely lifted from the millennial period described in the Bible, they purposely purge any reference to the fact that this can only happen after the return of Jesus Christ and will only succeed because He Himself will rule over the nations.

A perfect example of this manipulation is the United Nations' abduction of the millennial promise that the nations will beat their swords into plowshares. By accepting half-truths and the twisting of biblical promises to suit human ambitions, the world is being set up for a deception that staggers the imagination. The deception will be complete with the arrival of the false Messiah—the Antichrist—who will claim that the New World Order under his guidance is actually the fulfillment of the millennial prophecies. Unfortunately, like Adolph Hitler's stolen promise of a thousand-year Reich of Peace, it will be no more than a cruel hoax. The student of God's Word knows that the eventual outcome of this "fake millennium" will actually find people doing the exact opposite of the true millennial promise. The prophet Joel tells us that ultimately in this fake millennium people will beat their plowshares into swords and their pruninghooks into spears (Joel 3:10).

What few people realize is that this dream of a man-made millennium serves as the foundation which today unites Communists, capitalists, socialists, and religionists. For example, Western globalists speak of a worldwide community built on a foundation of freedom and plenty for all. Communists see a similar vision. According to Malachi Martin:

> The one poetic touch in Lenin's otherwise abrasive mind, in fact, concerned that almost dreamlike "Workers Paradise" he foresaw at the end of the proletarian rainbow. To find a parallel, you would have to go back to the early Hebrew prophets and their forecast of the Messianic Age . . . men and women, workers all, living in a stateless society under conditions of endless plenty, absolute justice and perpetual peace among nations. . . . [18]

Likewise, New Age leaders and New-Age-minded religious leaders hold up the same goal: an earthly kingdom built by and for man. There is no longer any question of whether there will be a New World Order, but only of when all the necessary pieces of this puzzle can be pulled together. No careful observer today believes that this moment is far away. Today the momentum has hit such a stride that Martin's 700-page report on development of this New World Order concludes that it is "something that is imminent . . . a system that will be introduced and installed in our midst by the end of the final decade of the second millennium." [19]

Will the Real New World Order
Please Stand Up?

On the surface this New World Order will be a brilliant solution to the planetary crises threatening the world. However, the belief that submerging national and cultural differences in some form of global unity can lead to an age of peace is a serious misdiagnosis of the problem. Mankind as a whole cannot know peace until people as individuals know the Prince of Peace. The Bible is very clear on this point. Although there will be "peace among men" during the millennium, Jesus warned that until that time when all people will live under the rule of Christ the goal will not have been peace but war for the souls and hearts of men. Any false, temporal, global peace before that time will only mask the true problem: sin in the hearts of men. The book of James clearly explains the root of the problem:

> From whence come wars and fightings among you?
> Come they not of your lusts that war in your members?
> Ye lust and have not; ye kill and desire to have (James 4:1,2).

The New World Order will not be able to change the hearts of people, and in fact will only feed their greedy, lustful desires by promising them peace, prosperity, and the right to live as they please. Under the leadership of the Antichrist this will work for a short time, but the sugar coating will not conceal the rotten core of this new order for very long.

After about 3½ years the facade will begin to crumble. The nations, perhaps beginning to recognize that they have been swindled, will begin to move together in a unity more representative of their spiritual state. They will begin a process of war leading to a global confrontation against Israel that will make the anti-Iraq coalition of 1990 pale in comparison. The unity built around this desire to destroy the people of God will only deepen as the whole world gathers together as one man to make war with the returning Lord Himself. This establishes the degree to which this New World Order, like the Tower of Babel before it, is the culmination of man's outright rebellion against the order ordained of God.

This time, however, far from simply confounding the desires of men, God will utterly destroy their efforts and establish the true thousand-year kingdom of God on this planet. Only then will the lion lie down with the lamb, only then will men beat their swords into plowshares, and only then will there be peace on earth and goodwill to all men.

The Quantum Leap and the Counterfeit Millennium

The laws of physics tell us that objects in motion tend to remain in motion and that objects at rest tend to remain at rest. This scientific law is true in political affairs as well. Things tend to remain as they are unless an unbalanced force, a shock to the system, causes them to change. This is one of the problems faced by the builders of the New World Order. Most agree that a gradual evolution to such a system would clearly fail under the never-ending international bickering, negotiating, and foot-dragging. Something more dramatic, worldwide, and instant is needed to propel the world headlong into the coming global age.

What could possibly trigger a change so dramatic that individuals would put differences to the side, nations would give up huge chunks of their sovereignty, and international coalitions would bow to the power of a handful of global leaders? Is there a conspiracy leading us in this direction? What role will lying signs and wonders play? How close are we to this New World Order? What will it be like? And how do we get from here to there? The Bible has answers to all these questions.

Section II

From Here
to There

Chapter 7

The Blueprint

One of the great debates among Christian observers of current events is whether there are powerful men and institutions quietly pulling strings behind the scenes to bring forth this New World Order. This question is very important because its answer will determine exactly how we are to understand the unfolding of world events. Are they just random occurrences, or are some of them carefully orchestrated incidents designed to lead us to the New World Order as simply as a cowboy leads his horse to water?

Some claim to see a tightly controlled conspiracy, and lay the guilt at the feet of the Jesuits, the Illuminati, the Bilderbergers, the Masons, the Nazis, the Jews, the international bankers, and countless other groups. Often the problem is that emotion and personal prejudices are put ahead of careful research. As a result of these frequently oversensationalized theories, many Christian researchers have discounted "conspiracy theories" completely. All too often we read that the only conspiracy is the supernatural one of Satan versus God. For example, one Christian book on the New Age movement states:

> It seems obvious that Christians spend far too much time on tracking down conspiracies and instigating witch hunts. . . . As far as the Bible is concerned there is only one real conspiracy—a spiritual one. . . . There

> is a worldwide conspiracy, but it is neither communist
> nor humanist. It is neither capitalist nor New Age. It is
> a spiritual conspiracy.[1]

There is no question that conspiracy theories have been sensationalized and oversimplified. However, bad research is not evidence that a secretive flesh-and-blood effort to move society toward world government does not exist. Indeed, it has been well-documented for years that one of the prime methods that the Soviets used to try to spread the Marxist revolution to all four corners of the globe was through the infiltration and contamination of Western institutions and organizations. By its very nature such an effort was based on secrecy.

Likewise, Marxist leaders and pro-Soviet Catholic Church leaders in Latin and South America worked for years to subtly permeate Catholic teachings with Communist ideals under the banner of Liberation Theology. Furthermore, powerful capitalist and internationalist organizations with world leaders in their membership, and with the stated aim of working toward a New World Order, also exist. These groups work in a quiet but calculated manner toward the establishment of a New World Order.

Words from the Corridors of Power

Rear Admiral Chester Ward, a member of The Council on Foreign Relations for 16 years, has given interesting testimony. He left that organization, which has included U.S. Presidents, Vice-Presidents, Secretaries of State, Secretaries of Defense, and CIA directors, as well as business, media, and economic giants, because of what he described as their desire "to bring about the surrender of the national sovereignty and the national independence of the United States."[2]

Longtime Senator and onetime presidential candidate Barry Goldwater is even more explicit. He released a book of his observations on this consolidation of power entitled *With No Apologies*. According to Goldwater, he never intended to release this book because he was "aware of the risks in speaking freely and candidly." However, this concern was overridden by the danger he believed the United States faced. He wrote, "We stand in danger of losing [our] freedom—not to a foreign tyrant, but to those well-meaning but misguided elitist utopians. . . ."[3]

Here is Barry Goldwater's warning to the United States. Keep in mind that this is a respected Senator and not some "conspiracy hound" speaking:

> Whereas the Council on Foreign Relations is distinctly national in membership, the Trilateral Commission is international. Representation is allocated equally to Western Europe, Japan, and the United States. It is intended to be the vehicle for the multinational consolidation of the commercial and banking interest by seizing control of the political government of the United States. Zbigniew Brzezinski and David Rockefeller screened and selected every individual who was invited to participate in shaping and administering the proposed New World Order. . . . The Trilateral Commission represents a skillful, coordinated effort to seize control and consolidate the four centers of power—political, monetary, intellectual, and ecclesiastical. What the Trilateralists truly intend is the creation of a worldwide economic power superior to the political governments of the nation-states involved. . . . As managers and creators of the system they will control the future.[4]

More recently, Senator Jesse Helms of North Carolina warned that a campaign of "systematic psychological warfare" is being waged against the American people:

> [The power of the Internationalists] resides in its control over our financial system and over a large portion of our industrial sector. The influence of

> Establishment Insiders over our foreign policy has
> become a fact of life in our time. This pervasive
> influence runs contrary to the real long-term national
> security of our nation. It is an influence which, if
> unchecked, could ultimately subvert our constitutional
> order. . . . In [this] globalist point of view, nation-
> states and national boundaries do not count for any-
> thing. . . .[5]

These examples should suffice to make the point. While it is
certain that some of the conspiracy theories have been simplistic
and misguided, it is equally irresponsible in the face of overwhelming evidence to conclude that there is no behind-the-scenes
manipulation of events. In fact, it is more likely that just the
opposite is true. While it is unlikely that the conspiracy is as
centrally controlled as some believe, the evidence does indicate
an unseen human hand helping to move the world toward the
global society of tomorrow. Indeed, common sense alone con-
firms FDR's conclusion that "in politics, nothing happens by
accident. If it happens, you can bet it was planned that way!"[6]

Can You Keep a Secret?

Whenever a group of people privately decide for other people
what is best for them, and then proceed to bring this about
inconspicuously, so that an uninformed society does not resist its
"best interest," the specter of conspiracy is raised. Whether the
intentions are good or bad, the outcome noble or selfish, the fact
that much of the effort to bring forth the New World Order has
been done covertly is cause for grave concern. Insider Carrol
Quigley, a Georgetown University professor who has no arguments with the drive toward the envisioned New World Order,
wrote in his 1300-page analysis of the internationalists:

> I know of the operations of this network because I
> have studied it for twenty years and was permitted for

two years, in the early 1960's, to examine its papers and secret records. I have no aversion to it or to most of its aims, and have for much of my life been close to it and to many of its instruments. . . . IN GENERAL MY CHIEF DIFFERENCE OF OPINION IS THAT IT WISHES TO REMAIN UNKNOWN, and I believe ITS ROLE IN HISTORY IS SIGNIFICANT ENOUGH TO BE KNOWN. . . . [Its aim is] nothing less than to create a world system of financial control in private hands able to dominate the political system of each country and the economy of the world as a whole.[7]

This aura of conspiracy is only compounded by the fact that the Council on Foreign Relations, for instance, composed of national political, business, and media leaders, has in its bylaws a prohibition against minutes being taken in any meetings and threatens any member with expulsion if they divulge the content of any of those meetings. UNESCO, an arm of the U.N., has long recognized and cried for an end to this secrecy:

If UNESCO is attacked on the grounds that it is helping to prepare the world's people for world government, then it is an error to burst forth with apologetic statements and denials. Let us face it: the job of UNESCO is to help create and promote the elements of world citizenship. When faced with such a "charge," let us by all means affirm it from the housetops.[8]

Tell-a-Vision

Another aspect of this secretive effort to bring forth a New Age of peace and prosperity that must be taken into account is the incredible power of the mass-media in today's world. Never in the history of mankind has it been possible to so subtly place ideas, values, and beliefs into the minds of virtually the entire world.

While we will discuss this matter at length in a later chapter, it is worth noting that there are those in media today who recognize the power they hold and have no qualms in using it to change the way the world thinks. Surely such a secretive mass-shaping of society could be described as conspiratorial.

Even the liberal *New York Times* labels the television networks' cooperative efforts to subtly shape and change public opinion on political, social, and environmental issues as an attempt to achieve "nothing less than a change in American social norms."[9] In confirming what the *Times* calls "a significant display of television's power to bring about social change,"[10] industry insider Jay Winstein warns that we have embarked on a road which leads to nothing short of "the application of Madison Avenue expertise to affect the population through mass-media."[11]

Hollywood attorney and environmental activist Bonnie Reiss is so convinced that the mass-media can covertly modify public perception that she has left her job in order to use her influence to have environmental themes woven into television, movies, and music. "I [feel] that there are a few thousand people who could affect a few million,"[12] she claims. Former NBC Chairman Grant Tinker fully supports the indoctrination efforts: "If we can start changing attitudes in this country we can start changing behavior."[13]

Even the Pope encourages the media in this "noble" effort. On World Communications Day he exhorted media leaders to transmit a "message of trust" to the world and reminded them that their "task seems to go beyond human possibilities: informing in order to form [public opinion]."[14] However, although the causes may often seem noble, the surreptitious implanting of ideas into the mass consciousness through the power of modern media is cause for serious concern. This is especially true when the media present a preprogrammed anti-American, pro-globalist perspective. For example, when Ted Turner was criticized for outright distortions in his much-publicized special "A Portrait of the Soviet Union," he responded, "When you paint a portrait, you can paint whatever you want; I didn't say it was a true picture."[15]

The Open Conspiracy

There is also another development well worth noting. Whether it has been the exposure of the media on international problems, the emergence of the New Age, or a combination of factors, "the conspiracy" has come out of the closet. Or, as H.G. Wells foresaw it a half-century ago, it has become the "open conspiracy."

We have watched this mind-shift unfolding over the last decade in our ministry at The Omega-Letter Publishing Group. We receive all kinds of letters. In the mid-eighties many of the letters of criticism said, "A New World Order? Are you crazy? It will never happen. We can't get together with the Communists. America is free and strong. We won't let it happen." However, in the last couple of years that tone has changed. Typically the critical letters now say "How can you oppose a New World Order? We can't survive without it. How can any one nation save the environment without everyone's cooperation? We're all in this boat together. It's time we got together!"

Suddenly it's not a covert conspiracy anymore; it's an almost inexplicable worldwide revolution in thinking. Or is it? Could it be that this "sudden" change in thinking is not just a spontaneous occurrence but the result of a tremendous propaganda campaign? Perhaps the conspiracy we've heard so much about, though loosely directed by an inner circle, is today being sold to the public by an outer circle of media leaders, political leaders, environmental activists, and New Age visionaries convinced that they are actually working to save the world.

Indeed, the evidence does seem to indicate that all of the "spontaneous" social movements which are directing mankind toward a global age are not as unrelated as they may initially appear to be.

Chapter 8

A Political Transformation

If there has been one overwhelming discovery in the last decade or so, it has been that the most powerful man or institution in the world is the one that shapes the minds and wills of mankind, not the one that has to put tanks on every street corner to protect his conquests. The collapse of the Soviet bloc is proof positive of this fact.

Another reality has also been perceived in this battle to fashion the collective will of mankind: In the news-saturated society of today, people do not take the time to study all the facts and make their own informed decisions. Instead, they increasingly rely on the perception of those who are presenting "the facts" to them. Thus an inherited perception has become for them the reality, no matter what the facts actually are. This leaves the front gate wide open to the manipulations of today's Pied Pipers who seek to lead us down the merry path of globalism.

A perfect example of this perception-over-fact mentality comes from U.S. Senator Timothy Wirth of Colorado:

> We've got to ride this global warming issue. Even if the theory is wrong, we will be doing the right thing in terms of economic and environmental policy. [1]

A recent study conducted by the Times Mirror Center for the

People and the Press entitled "The Age of Indifference" identifies the scope of the problem. It observes that today's under-thirty generation "knows less, cares less and reads less"[2] than any other generation in five decades and concludes that this makes them "easy targets of opportunity for those seeking to manipulate public opinion."[3]

Creating the Global Children of Tomorrow

Nowhere is this effort to shape perceptions more evident than in America's public school system. For years globalist themes have been quietly woven into children's studies while care has been taken to camouflage this effort. As one memorandum warned teachers:

> If we talk about the project as a global education project, it is likely to become a source of intense and long-term opposition from an extremely vocal minority. Temporary safe term is "multicultural/international curriculum development."[4]

Global education is not a class that children take. It is a theme, a point of view, that is being woven into all of their classes, from math and science to geography and history. Indeed, the National Education Association admits that they have begun to use the educational system "as a tool to bring about world peace" and to promote "the ideals of global community."[5]

A teacher's manual explains the goal:

> A global dimension should be given to all subjects and to many other school experiences. Children in the early grades should learn about the ideals of the United Nations.... Affective and active methods should be used which will involve pupils. Education should be profoundly changed.[6]

An internal report commissioned by the Department of Education itself concluded that global education had gone far beyond educating children and had actually attempted to enlist them in an anti-American, pro-globalist protest:

> When the heat is applied to the ostensibly bland globalist curriculum, it distills into a policy agenda of Utopian disarmament and national emasculation. The objective of those developing the globalist literature surveyed here is radical policy change. The curriculum's sponsors intend to achieve that objective by turning students into activists.[7]

However, this is only one of many areas in which the youth of today are being targeted with the one-world message. In virtually every area where youths spend their time and energies there can be found an easily discernible and concentrated effort to influence the way they view the world. To the builders of the New World Order the saying that "the young people of today are the leaders of tomorrow" is much more than just a nice phrase; it is the defining principle of a great number of their activities.

The Message in the Walkman

Unquestionably, if you want to reach the minds of people you have to reach them at the place where their hearts and love are. With the youth of the West that place is in their music. In the sixties it was Janis Joplin, Jimi Hendrix, and the Doors who were the leaders of the national youth culture. Their music and their words were the political and spiritual gospel to an entire generation of peace activists. In the 1990's the same principle is no less true. The words of singers Michael Jackson, Sting, or any number of others are usually given greater weight in the minds of this tuned-out generation than the words of the world leaders whom they often cannot even identify. It comes as no surprise, therefore, that music is at the very center of the efforts to propagandize the up-and-coming generation. As the *New York Times* observed:

The leftism linked with rock is most immediately visible in the periodic political benefits and tours undertaken by such leading rock performers as U2, Sting and Bruce Springsteen. Be it anti-nuclear protest or anti-apartheid or anti-political oppression or anti-poverty, likely as not your favorite rock stars are raising money for it or contributing their own money to it or writing songs about it.... Words may have political meaning, more or less explicit. But music operates on its own more powerful, more primordial agenda. People loved "Born in the USA" because of the catchy title/choral refrain, to be sure, but also because the music, huge and powerful and booming through a stadium sound system, galvanized them to a mass communal response. It is just that power to motivate the masses that has attracted totalitarian manipulators to popular music, not least Joseph Goebbels at the Nazi Nuremberg party rallies....[8]

Today, with the existence of a mass-media culture, complete with 24-hour-a-day music video channels, the idols of the youth have a platform to spread their message (or that of their puppeteers) which is staggering. More than ever this means that it "is going to be music that is politically expressive and activist," according to the publisher of the pop monthly *Spin*.[9] One of the most dramatic examples of this was the 1988 concert in London on behalf of imprisoned South African leader Nelson Mandela. Canada's *Toronto Star* newspaper affirmed its impact:

Pop music spectacle or worldwide political protest? From whatever side of pop culture's fuzzy philosophical lines, 750 million people watched or listened to ... the 10-hour Nelson Mandela FreedomFest Concert in London. No one can deny that the global village was drawn closer together to support a single political issue than any time in history.[10]

So fanatical were the statements made by performers at the concert that the BBC had to cut away from the concert several times during its coverage. Nonetheless, the concert achieved its goal. Organizers boasted even as the music marathon was just beginning that "on the strength of rock's popularity . . . the South African government was already chafing from the pressure musicians intend to generate internationally."[11]

The question that must be asked is, Who made these singers emissaries of the Secretary of State or the Foreign Office? As indefensible as apartheid is, and while no one would suggest that we should limit the freedom of speech and expression, there is little doubt that these singers have almost no understanding of the true issues involved and have been given an international voice based solely on their place on the music charts. Such power (which in this instance was the right to preach to 20 percent of the earth's population at one time) in the hands of *anyone* is potentially dangerous. But such power in the hands of a young, often naive, frequently stoned, and characteristically rebellious segment of the population is a prescription for disaster. Still more serious, given their popularity, is the certain fact that behind these symbolic voices are hands carefully choreographing their every protest.

Indeed, Harry Belafonte, one musician responsible for organizing the Live Aid concert and the corresponding "We Are the World" album in 1985 alluded to this very manipulation. He explained to *Billboard Magazine* that behind the stated goal of feeding Ethiopians lay a political objective as well:

> . . . it was Harry Chapin who provided much of the needed inspiration to bring artists together to join in the struggle. I think he saw the United Nations as ultimately the only institution that's going to serve as any kind of hope for global harmony. And he understood that the power of artists could do that. . . . Look at what Pushkin did to overthrow the Czar. It is no wonder that artists and the educators are always the

> first to be controlled or sought after by any system. . . .
> There are no boundaries on art; its universal power is
> absolutely awesome.[12]

Changing the Consciousness of the World

Live Aid in 1985 was an amalgamation of the biggest stars in the music world playing, by live satellite hookup, to a worldwide audience of 1½ billion people in 160 countries. However, it was much more than that. It was a watershed event which showed how major consciousness-raising extravaganzas could be combined with the latest telecommunications technology to create interconnected global events where participants in one country could see and hear those in other countries who were also participating in the same event. The sense of global unity created by such events is really mind-blowing. Indeed, Tony Verna, who produced the program, tells how inspired he became "during Live Aid when he saw Soviet youths waving to U.S. revelers in Philadelphia. 'That's when you feel the impact of Global TV!' "

Soon after that Pope John Paul II used this technology for his "World Prayer for Peace" global linkup in June 1987. Once again he could not only see and hear congregations from 16 different nations joining him in reciting the Rosary, but each of these congregations could also see and hear him, and each other, on giant television monitors.

Since the early days, when music stars used these global linkups to feed the poor and simultaneously push their latest left-wing political ideologies, the technology and the message have become much more pointed. By 1989 the procession had grown to include "Our Common Future," which featured a mixture of music stars and world political leaders extolling the virtues of environmental management. By 1991 the march of global programming added a global satellite telecast from Moscow, where the celebrities were no longer rock stars but political and spiritual leaders who had gathered together to preach the "gospel of this earth."

We Are the World

While it all seems so noble, without a doubt the common denominator in all of these events is *one-worldness*. Live Aid participant John Oates (of the music duo Hall and Oates) explains, "I've always believed in one-worldness. It's important to look beyond the small barriers of politics and nationality." Australian Prime Minister Robert Hawke, participating in "Our Common Future," applauded the consciousness-raising effort and rejoiced that "this extraordinary global event, which is drawing together hundreds of millions of people, reinforces the reality that increasingly we are all part of a global community." The Pope's global prayer for peace ended with a picture of the earth seen from space while the narrator closed the telecast with these words:

> So as we see our world in an actual live picture from space, we can appreciate the power of technology to bring people together and the power of prayer to bring about one-world at peace under God.

The picture of the earth as seen from space is a very powerful symbol of global unity. For this reason it has been at the core of all the global telecasts. As one visionary foresaw over 40 years ago, this is a symbol whose time has come:

> Once a photograph of the Earth, taken from outside, is available . . . a new idea as powerful as any in history will be let loose.[13]

Designed to complement this symbol on the Global Forum telecast were live images from a rain forest in Costa Rica, a split-screen sunset and sunrise, and a live picture from the Soviet space station. All of these images, perceptions, and symbols are carefully being worked together to draw our generation emotionally into the New World Order. Unfortunately, in a generation of hype over substance, impression over intellect, and feeling over fact, there is virtually no resistance to the manipulation.

Revelation 17 on TV

We should also take a moment to reflect on just how far this consciousness-raising progression has come. To the student of Bible prophecy the sight of political and religious leaders joining together on a global telecast in the name of a New World Order is a powerful sign of how close we may be to the return of the Lord. This is the exact coalition that the Bible tells us will rule the world right after the rapture of the believers in Jesus Christ has taken place! Yet according to the *Global Forum* newsletter:

> Every nation on earth now recognizes that our planet and all living things on it are in danger. All of us are responsible for these problems—and for the solutions. To change the harmful ways we deal with each other and with our environment, the Global Forum involves the two pillars of our communities—spiritual and parliamentary leaders—in a process of intensive dialogue. The two groups of leaders are central to the process of change because they are the opinionmakers and policymakers who work most closely with people at all levels, from the local to the global. Through dialogue and interaction, the Global Forum gives them the opportunity to influence not only each other— ethically, morally and practically—but to extend this influence to the communities they serve worldwide.[14]

This was the purpose to which the latest in this series of global consciousness-raising was dedicated. As previously noted, for the first time in history both the Intelsat and the Intersputnik satellite systems, with 129 member countries, granted free access to such a project, which reached over two billion viewers!

Global Television

However, these global spectaculars are only part of the picture. One of the things that has puzzled prophetic scholars over the years has been the question of how the whole world's thinking will be changed and unified in a very short period of time to accept the New World Order of the Antichrist. Even with the monumental changes of the past few years there is still some distance to go in picturing the single world government, the single world economy, and the single world religion which the Bible tells us will come to pass in the last days. In centuries gone by such major change would have taken decades to unfold. However, the prophetic Word of God seems to indicate that these events will happen very quickly at some moment of international crisis and turmoil.

One of the developments peculiar to this generation that makes sudden and widespread change possible is the emergence of instantaneous worldwide media coverage. The recent war in the Persian Gulf was a perfect example of this. We all watched live as Peter Arnett, John Holliman, and "Bernie" Shaw reported on the initial air raids into Baghdad. Instantaneously we would join Wolf Blitzer for the latest news from the Pentagon. Then it would be over to Charles Beirbauer at the White House. Next we would pray with the people of Israel as the SCUDS fell all around them, and then we would duck with a frightened Charles Jaco in Saudi Arabia. This is truly the time when the world was first really dazzled with the technological power that the media now possess to draw the whole world emotionally together at one time.

It is also this power that has made our rapid acceptance of Soviet overtures possible. The recent peace offensives, proclaiming the collapse of Communism, now assure night after night on the evening news that the Soviet Union is no longer our enemy but our troubled friend. Graphic footage, pronouncements, and concessions used with Madison Avenue precision have overwhelmed Americans into an acceptance of the Soviet promises. Without the convincing media hype such an occurrence would have taken many years or decades to unfold. And in turn those years would have forced the East Bloc to prove their sincerity. But with the power of today's media the change is so quick that the time of testing has been lost.

Senator Jesse Helms worries that this instant society we live in today threatens to make us more vulnerable than ever to propaganda and outright distortion as we rush to embrace seemingly good news:

> Who can deny that the American people and Congress have been subjected to an unprecedented campaign by the major American news media to portray Mr. Gorbachev as a benign reformer whose only desire is openness and restructuring in Soviet domestic affairs and normal relations with the United States? . . .
>
> Having heard the word "glasnost" so often on U.S. television and read so much about it in the U.S. press, I asked my staff to look up the word in a Russian-English dictionary. The media tell us that the word means "openness," which might lead us to believe that there is a relaxation of controls inside the Soviet Union and a new friendly attitude toward the West.
>
> The Library of Congress sent me a page from a Russian-English dictionary published in Moscow. The entry under "glas" gives the meaning of "voice." The entry under "glasnost" gives a meaning of "publicity." Several specialists on the Soviet Union, who are native Russians, have told us that the current meaning is a bit stronger than just "publicity." These specialists say that "glasnost" in current usage means "propaganda."
>
> This is a far cry from what the media would have us believe. But this distortion of the meaning of words, warfare in the field of semantics, is typical of the media diet that the American people are being fed. This distortion of the meaning of words is typical of

> the ethical standards of American journalists today.
> These journalists are not reporting the facts about the
> news. They are, rather, engaged in polemics and pro-
> paganda in a war against traditional American culture
> and values. . . .[15]

We live in one of the most dangerous times in the annals of human history. Monumental changes are unsettling the very foundations of the present world system. Combining this fact with the globalist propaganda being thrust upon an unsuspecting West through "global education," plus the pronouncements of idolized singers and actors, forces one to acknowledge the almost inescapable net that has been cast over the minds of men. *TV Guide*, speaking of the Cable News Network, noted that—

> . . . Ted Turner and a handful of other entrepreneurs
> are radically altering the world's television landscape.
> . . . The empire builders of the 1980's regard the whole
> planet as their domain. . . . They are a new breed of
> television tycoon, and together they are propelling
> television into the global age.[16]

This is a menacing amount of power in the hands of one who said, "When you are painting a picture you can paint whatever you want; I didn't say it was a true picture."

Chapter 9

The Pied Pipers

Years ago students of Bible prophecy who watched the world scene for signs of the prophesied New World Order had a much easier time of it. All they had to do was observe a few key organizations such as the United Nations, the Aspen Institute, the Council on Foreign Relations, or the Trilateral Commission and see what plans they were espousing to build a world community. Their lofty plans and goals were seen as a foreshadow of the prophetic events we knew would one day come to pass.

However, the emergence of the New Age movement and the thousands of different groups working toward this New World Order has made the task of discerning the true centers of global power much more difficult. This increasing difficulty has to do not only with the vastly increasing number of groups but also with the fact that many of the groups working toward this New World Order do not appear on the surface to be doing so at all.

World Government—Piece by Piece

One deceptive method being used by globalist organizations is called *piecemeal functionalism*. The concept has been pushed forward by many internationalist groups, including the Trilateral Commission. This powerful group of politicians, media leaders, business executives, and bankers has been one of the leading proponents of the New World Order over the last couple of decades. Zbigniew Brzezinski, one of the group's organizers explains it this way:

> In general, the prospects for achieving effective international cooperation can often be improved if the issues can be kept separate—what we now call piecemeal functionalism. . . . Coalitions of specialists can be built across national boundaries in specific functional areas, blunting the nationalism that otherwise might hinder agreement. . . .[1]

The concept of piecemeal functionalism was originally codified by the Aspen Institute's Harland Cleveland. He observed that trying to directly create a New World Order through large all-encompassing organizations such as the U.N. has not worked. By employing the concept of piecemeal functionalism these groups expect to achieve much broader success. By appearing to address separate issues piece by piece, treaty by treaty, law by law, issue by issue, and organization by organization, the New World Order is in fact being assembled virtually unnoticed. New Age leader Mark Satin sees the pattern clearly:

> The new politics is arising out of the . . . social movements of our time: the feminist, environmental, spiritual, human potential . . . and world order movements. . . . The contributions come together like the pieces of an intricate jigsaw puzzle.[2]

Several things can be learned from this. In the first place, the Trilateral Commission and countless other groups were looking to build a network of loosely related issues and groups all working in the same general direction. Today we see the New Age movement, animal rights groups, political protest groups, and environmental groups fulfilling that role. These organizations receive millions of dollars of funding from corporate sponsors, many of which have globalists at their helm.

However, it is also worth noting that the Trilateral Commission paper also points out that this indirect approach to world government will "blunt the nationalism that might otherwise hinder agreement." It cannot be made any clearer that there are those who have the power to move the world in the direction of a New World Order and want to do so by camouflaging what they are actually doing. While this may fall short of the definition of "conspiracy," it certainly does indicate careful manipulation. Indeed, Richard N. Gardner (professor of International Organization at Columbia University, Trilateral Commission member, Council on Foreign Relations member) argues against the old philosophy of attempting to achieve "instant world government." He claims that "an end run around national sovereignty, eroding it piece by piece, will accomplish far more than the old-fashioned frontal assault."[3]

A Managed Crisis?

Globalists have not been content to see their goals achieved in the normal course of time. Therefore they have utilized a method known as "management by crisis" to help move their agenda forward. Management by crisis is a technique as old as politics itself. However, its widespread use on an international scale is much more recent. The objective of a managed crisis is to have people accept something as a solution to a particular crisis that they never would have accepted if that "crisis" had not been brought to their attention.

Simply stated, a "managed crisis" has three stages. First, those who desire a change in a specific direction, and who have sufficient resources, present a crisis to the public. The crisis can be created or invented, or an existing crisis can be adopted. Second, the crisis is widely publicized. Finally, when there is sufficient public alarm the "managers" propose their academically hailed solution to the crisis.

Here's an example. A small coastal community strongly opposes the building of a large factory in their quiet community.

Suddenly new government regulations are announced severely limiting the number of fish the community's fishermen can catch. Fear of unemployment created by the regulatory crisis causes the community to drop their opposition to the factory. Thus, as the direct result of an unrelated crisis, the people are willing to accept a "solution" that they strongly opposed before the crisis.

Today we see many widely publicized crises: the environment, overpopulation, the arms race, the collapse of national financial systems, the Middle East. The common, academically hailed solution being proposed for all of these is the formation of a New World Order. If we can understand that some of these events can be used and amplified for the purpose of making us move in a certain direction, then we can often perceive the propaganda that is being directed our way.

The Economic Crisis

Take the world economic crisis, for example. The crisis today is compounded by the interdependence of national economies. This was evidenced when the New York stock market crashed on "Black Monday" in October 1987. The effects were immediately felt worldwide. Likewise, multinational corporations which span the globe have moved beyond the control of the individual nation-states in which they operate. Furthermore, national political stability is increasingly threatened by crushing debt. This used to be limited to the Third World, but no longer. The foundations of the Soviet Union and even the United States are being rocked. The financial effects are being felt even in the world's most prosperous nations, Japan and Germany. As one former Secretary of the Treasury put it:

> I've been in government service all of my life, and I have dealt with the monetary affairs of this country and the world for decades, but I have never seen the situation [Third World debt] so bad. It is virtually

impossible for these nations to repay the money; if they are squeezed any harder, it will create national and international upheaval and even revolution. In fact, we're already on the verge of that now. . . . It was greed, pure and simple, by the big banks and I have no idea what we are going to be able to do.[4]

A tremendous testimony to the power of crisis to change thinking is revealed by the fact that in a poll conducted a month after Black Monday, "getting the U.S. out of debt" was the number one priority of Americans.[5] The *New York Times* quoted the cry of the financial community, "Here's the problem—you fix it. If you have to cast aside your entire political philosophy, so much the better. All we want is a restoration of confidence."[6]

And what is the perceived cause of the global financial crisis? According to the *New York Times*, ". . . while the marketplace is global, political constituencies end at the borders of the nation-state. . . . Nationalistic concerns, analysts say, set the stage for the collapse October 19."[7] As economist and futurist Gerald Mische put it, "There are few issues that so clearly demonstrate the fiction of territorial sovereignty as this debt bomb crisis."[8]

And what is the solution to the crisis? We are told that international political authorities must be empowered to oversee what has already become a de facto New International Economic Order. Simply put, since the corporations and banks have already created a world economy, we had better create a world political body that can control and regulate it. Richard Cooper, writing in The Council on Foreign Relations' *Foreign Affairs* magazine, would like to press this concept a step further:

> I suggest a radical . . . scheme . . . the creation of a common currency for all of the industrial democracies, with a common monetary policy and a joint bank of issue to determine that policy. . . . But a single currency is possible only if there is . . . a single authority issuing the currency and directing the monetary

policy. How can independent nation-states accomplish that? THEY NEED TO TURN OVER THE DETER-MINATION OF MONETARY POLICY TO A SUPRA-NATIONAL BODY.[9]

Likewise, Paul Streeten, professor emeritus at Oxford University, in examining the fallout created by Black Monday, called for a "surrender of some national sovereignty and the transfer of sufficient power to the decision makers who would manage the system."[10] Far from being outside the mainstream, it is these very ideas that are fueling the creation of a central bank for all of Europe as the European Economic Community rushes toward economic unity by 1992.

The Environmental Crisis

Another example of a managed crisis is the environmental crisis. It is probably the most powerful, recent example of this piecemeal approach. The environmental movement was born in response to the Club of Rome's "Mankind at the Turning Point" report and has rapidly expanded due to a heavy media campaign in the past few years. It has now spawned thousands of specialized environmental groups and global events, such as Earth Day.

As a result of massive consciousness-raising efforts, a recent *National Geographic* poll has shown that while 18–24-year-old Americans ranked last in an international test to locate their country on a map—

> When it came to environmental issues, Americans are downright perspicacious. Most [84 percent] are aware that fluorocarbons and other chemicals may be destroying the earth's ozone layer; they know that wind patterns, not the ozone layer, spread fallout... and most know that acid rain is a particular problem to North America.[11]

Environmental threats have now been elevated on the world's problem agenda. The *Bulletin of Atomic Scientists* with its now-famous doomsday clock claims that environmental concerns have passed nuclear war as the greatest threat to planetary survival. Assistant Secretary of State Frederick M. Bernthal notes that environmentalism could easily be "the major threat of the 21st Century."[12] Columnist Patrick J. Buchanan even goes so far as to argue that "environmentalism is now well on its way to becoming the third great wave of the redemptive struggle in Western history."[13]

This heightened awareness has placed environmental issues squarely onto the political agenda. A *Times Mirror* survey found that 64 percent of Americans believe that "proposing laws to protect the environment"[14] is a top priority for the Bush administration. A Canadian survey found that a political party which makes environmental protection its top priority would immediately capture 20 percent of the vote regardless of any other policy positions.[15] According to the pollster, "This country is on the verge of a Green Revolution . . . [that could] lead to a society very much different from what it is today."[16] All over the world environmental consciousness is growing. The cry is simple: "Something must be done to save the environment."

You will recall that for the purposes of management by crisis it makes no difference whether a particular crisis is real or invented. The critical issue is *convincing the world that something must be done to resolve the crisis*, even if it involves drastic measures. Once persuaded, the door opens for the final phase: proposing the solution.

In the case of the environmental crisis, the solution is again a global managing body. Prime Minister Robert Hawke of Australia recently launched a "One World or None" campaign. He speaks of the environment as reinforcing "the reality that increasingly we are all part of a global community."[17] Canadian Environment Minister Tom McMillan argues that "the world's environmental problems are greater than the sum of those in each country" and that "they can no longer be dealt with on a purely nation-state basis."[18] What we need, according to French Prime Minister Michel Rocard, is "a world mechanism of authority with the capacity of decision and control."[19] Former U.S. Senator Mike Gravel of Alaska is calling for a referendum on "the delegation of our individual sovereignty to a world government with respect to our security, our human rights, our environmental safety, and our economic well-being."

The environmental and economic crises are not the only issues being used as the basis in calling for a New World Order. In fact, when one begins to watch the highly publicized crises of the world today and the solutions being proposed to solve them, it becomes evident that in each instance the proposed solution almost always leads toward a world government, a world court, world law, worldwide banks, and so on. This will become increasingly evident in the pages ahead.

The issues at the center of these crises seem unrelated, but globalist groups have noticed the power of each of these issues in the call for world government and are admittedly using them to move the world in the desired direction. This is proving out the Trilateral Commission's assertion that the movement toward a New World Order can be greatly facilitated if they "can keep these issues [to appear to be] separate . . . [and thus] blunt the nationalism that might otherwise hinder agreement."

The world system is in critical condition. The creation of a global management system does seem to make a lot of sense. These powerful men are not selling snake oil. Many have the noblest intentions. They are proposing a pseudomillennial kingdom peace. But like the tower of Babel, any "kingdom of peace" built without the Prince of Peace cannot ultimately stand.

The Moment of Change

At what point could all of these separate issues be pulled together to actually bring a New World Order into existence? One hypothesis can be found in the theory of societal Darwinism.

Ervin Laszlo is the former head of the United Nations Institute for Training and Research (UNITAR) and a leading proponent of this theory. He argues that "societal systems evolve just as humans have!"[20] Thus societies evolve when the present system (such as the present nation-state system) becomes outdated or obsolescent because of "new realities" or inventions. These new realities cannot be integrated into the present system, and therefore they work both to destabilize it and to serve as the basis for the new system. An example of this would be the societal evolution from the largely agricultural society to the industrial age with the invention of machinery. Laszlo explains it this way:

> In most general terms, systems evolve when they reach a sufficient level of complexity and when their normal functioning is disturbed. The ... disturbance ... is the evolutionary trigger. It must be of a specific kind and level. If it undershoots the critical level ... evolution fails to occur. But when just the right level of disturbance obtains, the system enters a phase of critical instability: it moves out of its normal routines and is propelled into basic transformations.[21]

Simply stated, when a crisis, discovery, or revolution of incredible proportion occurs, the existing society is pushed into a phase of critical instability and a new society evolves. What makes this theory so significant in today's world is the number of voices who proclaim that we have reached that moment of critical instability. Says Laszlo:

> ... There's evidence that shows that the [present] system cannot be indefinitely sustained, that in fact it is already on its last leg. ... As in nature, so in society, there is no true evolution without crisis ... profound and lasting change comes only when the system itself is critically destabilized by new conditions. ... Humanity is now approaching a point of critical instability. ...

This is the "checkpoint Charlie" which could mark humanity's passage into a new age—or into oblivion.[22]

Willis Harman, a former consultant to the National Goals Research Staff of the White House, agrees. His perception is that "we are in the early stages of a change much more far-reaching than the Industrial Revolution. It is a metamorphosis that will transform every institution, every profession, every aspect of modern society."[23]

Seizing the Moment

The moment of critical instability that will shake the very foundation of the present nation-state system will theoretically be brought on by some massive crisis or series of crises. It is at that moment of crisis that these analysts believe it will be possible to seize the opportunity and actually influence the evolution to a new society in the direction of their choice. As Laszlo put it, "In the coming period of transformation we shall, indeed, have a chance to be masters of our own destiny."[24] According to the Communications Era Task Force, by "our ability to see the historical turning point at which we stand we can more deliberately and consciously influence our direction."[25] Laszlo warns, however, that "conscious human beings, equipped with a basic knowledge of societal evolution, could exploit whatever degrees of freedom such evolution offers and influence the direction of evolution to their own advantage."[26]

Here is the crux of the matter. It is here that we begin to see the way that many globalists and New Agers see the evolution to the new society. It will be an evolution born in turmoil and rapid change. And it is the window of opportunity provided by such a moment of turmoil that New Age and globalist groups are waiting for. Dieter Heinrich, Executive Director of the World Federalists of Canada, explains it this way:

The fact that the world as-it-is is not yet ready for world government does not mean that World Federalists are too early with their ideas, or that we should wait while more people change their thinking.... Thinking can change very suddenly in the wake of crisis.... We must be ready when things start shaking loose. This is how evolution occurs, not in a smooth curve of progression, but in fits of crisis and change.[27]

What Crisis?

What possible crisis could unite the entire world? What common cause could unite mankind and cause him to leave the old order behind and bravely leap toward a new order? One of the possibilities discussed by New Agers and one-worlders is a near nuclear disaster.

Imagine, so the reasoning goes, that the world turns on the evening news one night and hears that the Soviet Union has launched a full-scale nuclear attack on the United States. Next it is announced that the U.S. has launched a counterstrike. Suddenly the whole world realizes that the events are completely out of their hands. It is only a matter of moments until most of the world is destroyed. The father sits with his son unable to protect him in any way. The mother, in desperation, wants everyone to go to the basement to prolong their certain fate an instant longer, hoping against hope that it is all a dream. Quickly a sense of common fate sweeps the world. The man in Moscow realizes that the man in Washington is in exactly the same boat. The thousands of miles that once separated their worlds has vanished. The whole world sits in a common hopeless despair.

Now imagine that somehow the crisis is averted. A world leader arises and addresses a world which gives him their full, united attention. He announces how the disaster has been averted and then explains how such a crisis can never be allowed to take place again. He urges the world audience to realize the oneness of the planet and how they will live or die together. He tirades against petty national, cultural, and religious differences and urges the world to come together as one in this great "spaceship earth."

Such a scenario is not completely unrealistic. In the face of such a disaster the world could well be ready to accept the compromises and sacrifices that such a "global village" would require. It almost reminds one of the process of a managed crisis that we discussed earlier.

The world has learned in the last 40 years that totalitarian regimes which impose an ideology by force have by and large been economically infeasible. As one researcher put it, "The granting of 'freedom' to Eastern Europe was no more than a corporate divestiture of deficit-ridden subsidiaries."[28] However, in the event of such a nuclear crisis, the New World Order, envisioned by those "well-meaning but misguided utopians," would not likely have to be imposed by force. The change of thinking caused by such a crisis would make the system seem not only desirable but also imperative for the salvation of mankind.

Furthermore, such a near-disaster could easily cause a worldwide economic collapse as well, only compounding the need for global systems of recovery. National political alliances would be in shatters and totally obsolete in the face of building a world system of governance. Add to this the common problems of environment and population, and the pull toward a global system would be virtually irresistible. It is this point in time to which the globalist and New Age visionaries point as the moment when their foresight and planning can come into effect. As World Federalist Dieter Heinrich says:

> Obviously we are not praying for a good crisis, but the likelihood of one in the absence of world federation is high. We must be ready in great numbers to push for the necessary changes when things start shaking loose. This is how evolution occurs . . .[29]

Likewise, The World Constitution and Parliament Association has already written a World Constitution and a number of "World

Legislative Bills" that are ready in case of a collapse of the present nation-state system. And while this gesture may be largely symbolic, it is representative of the world's rush to set up "alternative systems of control" in the event of a collapse of the present system.

Is It Enough?

Would such a near nuclear disaster be enough to push the world into the arms of the New World Order? Or is it possible that something more may be involved? Historian Lewis Mumford has noted that every major transformation of the past has rested upon "a new metaphysical . . . base . . . a new picture of the cosmos and the nature of man."[30]

In the light of Bible prophecy, such a religious element would seem to be at the forefront of transformation. Indeed, the Bible warns that the last days will be defined by religious deception (Matthew 24:4,5,23,24). Perhaps the New World Order, so carefully planned by "misguided utopians," actually has an unseen spiritual hand moving in the background with a parallel but distinct agenda in mind. Maybe this hand is just using the world's most brilliant men as little more than pawns. If such a possibility is considered, then all kinds of signs and lying wonders could accompany the moment of transformation.

Imagine, for example, instead of the confusion being caused by a near nuclear disaster, it is caused, at least in part, by the disappearance of millions of human beings from planet Earth!

Chapter 10

The Gospel of Antichrist

Most world leaders today proclaim that we have embarked on the road to lasting peace. Although they note the exception of the Persian Gulf crisis in early 1991, politicians, retreating Communist leaders, and supporters of the Reagan era buildup all purport to be responsible for the thaw in the Cold War. However, they are not the only ones vying for the world's appreciation and admiration.

> The Berlin Wall crumbled, democracy has invaded Eastern Europe and capitalism can't be far behind. While America's conservatives and political strategists pat themselves on the back, we all know where the real credit goes. Harmonic Convergence. Surely you remember. Harmonic Convergence was a cosmic communion two years ago in which thousands of New Agers gathered at sites they believe to be sacred to pray, chant and meditate in one mighty metaphysical effort to propel the planet into a new era of peace. . . . "It definitely worked. . . . It's not a joke. Things are tumbling really quickly now," a new age disciple explained.[1]

Likewise, another article explains that the revolution in world events, while caused by a cosmic gathering, is not the result of Harmonic Convergence—but the World Peace Day.

> Picks, chisels and jackhammers reduce the Berlin Wall to rubble. Governments topple. . . . Dictators fall. . . . Cosmic coincidence? Historical inevitability? Or is it something deeper, set in motion 3 years ago when the collective consciousness of an estimated 500 million people around the world simultaneously focused for an hour on a single thought—peace.[2]

Not to be left out, Transcendental Meditation's founder, Maharishi Mahesh Yogi, who now offers his secrets to national governments, claims that the rush to peace is proof positive that he holds the keys to the New Age. Charles Alexander, a professor at Maharishi International University, is convinced that his mentor is right. He says, "As a scientist, I think it's very important that the cause of these events be known. I'm really confident that we are the cause of what's going on. . . ."[3]

Such far-out claims initially bring a slight smile to our faces. That smile disappears, however, when we think of the millions of people that are involved. Far from being confined safely to the lunatic fringe, the idea that we can create our own future through esoteric mind-over-matter techniques is literally sweeping the world. One recent poll found that fully two-thirds of Americans believe in some or all of the central occultic teachings of the New Age movement.[4] Indeed, an honest appraisal of the late-twentieth-century record reveals that while he is exploiting the greatest technologies and scientific discoveries in history, mankind is also turning in record numbers to the ancient mystery religions and occult techniques which once dominated the world.

Corporate executives take part in seminars to learn how to put "metaphysics, the occult and Hindu mysticism" to work in the world marketplace.[5] The Soviets and CIA race toward dominance in the new field of psychic warfare.[6] A U.S. Senator has introduced a bill that would establish a commission to study "everything from ESP to biofeedback."[7] Public educators lead public school children through hypnotic techniques so powerful that a cassette tape of the sessions warns adults not to listen to the tape while operating a motor vehicle. The U.S. Government spends millions of dollars a year trying to contact E.T.'s while leading laboratories are trying to regress scores of people into previous lives!

All of the evidence indicates that the world, and the West in particular, is undergoing a religious revival unparalleled in history. However, far from being a revival of biblical Christianity, it is actually a resurgence of ancient paganism.

The Lie That Binds

This revived form of paganism is exactly the glue that the Bible tells us will bind the prophesied New World Order together. The apostle John described this last-day religious power as "Mystery Babylon." This "mystery" religion, we are told, will center around Rome but will eventually be made up of all religions. The unity will be based on the teachings of Babel. Of course, the first key to understanding the end-times Mystery Babylon is to understand these ancient Babylonian practices. On this point the Bible is very clear. The heart of Babylonian religion is, and has always been, the same old spiritism. The prophet Isaiah reminded us of this almost 2700 years ago.

> Come down and sit in the dust, O virgin daughter of Babylon. . . . Stand now with thine enchantments and with the multitude of thy sorceries, wherein thou hast labored from thy youth, if so be thou shalt be able to profit, if so be thou mayest prevail. Thou art wearied in the multitude of thy counsels. Let now the astrologers, the stargazers, the monthly prognosticators stand up and save thee from these things that shall come upon thee (Isaiah 47:1,12,13).

Even the most durable skeptic has to admit that this 2700-year-old list reads like the schedule to the latest New Age or psychic fair. That is because Satan's lies never change. Through this revival of Babylon, the Word of God tells us, all those who are left behind after the rapture will be seduced into believing Satan's original lie.

What is this lie? It is the exact same falsehood that Satan told to Eve in the Garden of Eden. He simply convinced her that she could achieve enlightenment, tap into her divine nature, and become a god herself (Genesis 3:1-5). Actually, the history of this seductive promise goes back even further than that. It was this lie that caused Lucifer to be cast out of heaven in the first place. He thought he had the divine potential within himself to actually unseat God. Isaiah, through the inspiration of the Holy Spirit, recorded this initial uprising for us:

> How art thou fallen from heaven, O Lucifer, son of the morning! How art thou cut down to the ground which didst weaken the nations! For thou hast said in thine heart, I will ascend into heaven, I will exhalt my throne above the stars of God; I will sit also upon the mount of the congregation, in the sides of the north; I will ascend above the heights of the clouds; I will be like the most High (Isaiah 14:12-14).

Today this same seducing fabrication is literally sweeping the planet. Maitreya, who New Age leader Benjamin Creme claims in *The Reappearance of the Christ* to be the "new Christ," claims that "man is an emerging God. . . . My plan and my duty is to reveal to you a new way . . . which will permit the divine in man to shine forth." Maharishi Mahesh Yogi, the founder of Transcendental Meditation, counsels followers to "be still and know that you are god." Ernest Holmes, founder of the Church of Religious Science believes and teaches that "all men are spiritually evolving . . . until each will express his divinity." The Mormon Church's Brigham Young even went so far as to say:

The devil told the truth [about godhood]. . . . I do not blame mother Eve. I would not have had her miss eating the forbidden fruit for anything.[8]

However, this is only the tip of a giant spiritual iceberg. Scores of gurus from India today carry that identical message to the West. Homespun evangelists of the same gospel, such as Shirley MacLaine, also unceasingly preach the deity of man as the great hope of enlightenment. According to the actress and guru:

You are everything. Everything you want to know is inside of you. You are the Universe. . . . Maybe the tragedy of the human race was that we had forgotten that we were each divine. . . . You must never worship anyone or anything other than self. For you are God. To love self is to love God. . . . I know that I exist, therefore I am. I know that the God source exists, therefore it is. Since I am part of that force, then I AM that I AM.[9]

Today, in an incredible sign of the times, this very lie, the same one that led to Lucifer's uprising in heaven and Eve's fall in the Garden of Eden, is also the emerging common denominator in the evolving world religion. Everywhere we turn, confirmations of the tremendous inroads that this gospel of Antichrist is making are driving home the reality that there is another gospel contending for the hearts and souls of this last generation before the return of Christ.

An Opiate for the People

This New Age religion is a perfect fit with the New World Order. The belief that we are unfulfilled gods, who through discovering our own innate potentials can control our own destiny, is exactly the kind of "faith" and belief that many believe will be needed in shaping the new order. We should not forget that it was this very combination of aspirations that led to the building of the Tower of Babel those many years ago. In today's world, as in ancient Babylon, other corresponding New Age beliefs (for example, "We are all spiritually interconnected with each other and with Mother Earth herself") are very powerful forces in helping to unite people in the "gospel of this earth." That is why these religious teachings are being vigorously promoted by well-meaning globalists and New Agers. After all, the cause is nothing less than saving the planet.

A Guiding Image

The Pied Pipers of this new order are fully aware that in the upcoming transition to a new order a common belief and hope must unite the world. Without this hope, the unity necessary to make such a transformation possible won't exist. Dutch scholar Fred Polak explains the importance of such a vision:

> Any student of the rise and fall of cultures cannot fail to be impressed by the role played in this historical succession by the image of the future. The rise and fall of images precedes or accompanies the rise and fall of cultures. . . . Discovery of a suitable guiding image of the future is clearly our society's most crucial task.[10]

So what could serve as a suitable guiding image for this New Age? According to Willis Harman, a former consultant to the National Goals Research Staff of the White House, there is only one idea that could prove strong enough to capture the hearts and minds of mankind. He points to the startling discoveries in the areas of psychic powers, ESP, parapsychology, telekinesis, and telepathic communications as a perfect religious foundation for the new order:

> If such a paradigm, involving a basic shift in the accepted vision of reality, were to become the basis of

presently industrialized society, its institutionaliza-
tion would amount to one of the most thoroughgoing
transformations in the history of mankind. We might
apply to such a change the Greek word *metanoia*: a
fundamental shift in mind, as in a religious conversion.[11]

It is this explosion of Eastern mystical ideas that will make the
whole process work, according to Dieter Heinrich of the World
Association of World Federalists:

No one supposes that World Federation will be
accomplished through revolution. Nor can it be imposed. It must be wanted, which means that the need
for it must be widely appreciated and its purposes and
principles widely understood. This means that when it
does come, it will be in a world which is very different
from today's. . . . Most of the problems people have
with world federation at first arise from trying to
imagine it overlaid on the world as it is, instead of
seeing it in context, emerging in a world in which
consciousness is also changing.[12]

"The sense of oneness with mankind, the planet and the
universe that comes out of this Eastern view will actually begin
the process that will see this emerging spiritual view begin to
express itself on the political plane," says Zbigniew Brzezinski,
the organizer of David Rockefeller's Trilateral Commission.
"Ultimately, every human being, once he reaches the stage of
self-consciousness . . . wants his social organization to corre-
spond to that feeling. This is happening on a world scale," he
explains.

The obvious social organization corresponding to a feeling of
oneness with the world is a world government. Here we see
clearly that the religious and political aspects of this new order
are not developing in separate vacuums. The religious feeds the

political and thus it should come as no surprise that this "new" religion is literally being shoved down the throats of the would-be world citizens of tomorrow.

However, any political leader who thinks he can use and manipulate this religious force for his own purposes is in for a big surprise. The Word of God states clearly that in the prophesied New World Order the religious will dominate the political! The opiate that man is trying to use for his own political ends will take on a life of its own as the spiritual principalities and powers are set loose for their last-days role in deceiving the hearts and minds of men.

Just how intense is the effort of globalists to force-feed this New Age gospel to the world? Every indicator seems to show that, far from being confined to the guru-worshiping sects, the mind-science cults, and the New Age communities, this gospel is being introduced to unsuspecting millions of people at a dizzying rate and intensity. Nowhere is this more evident than in the cartoons, computer games, and videos that this generation is being raised on.

Goodbye, Yogi Bear

Recently my nephew, who is being raised in a fine Christian home, was asked by his Sunday school teacher what he would do if he were trapped in a lion's den like Daniel was. Without hesitation he explained to his teacher that he would simply put on his golden ring and call Hercules! Needless to say, his cartoon viewing has been sharply restricted. Quite simply, Saturday morning TV isn't what it used to be. The Flintstones, Bugs Bunny, and Porky Pig have all lost their place in prime time. Try asking a child who Daffy Duck is, and you'll probably get nothing more than a blank stare. Now ask that same child who the Teenage Mutant Ninja Turtles are, and this time you'll get a much different reaction. "Everybody knows the Turtles" might be the reply. But more than the names have changed; the entire nature of cartoons has changed as well. It's no longer cat against mouse or coyote against roadrunner. Now it's good against evil and light against darkness. If the roadrunner wanted to find his way back into prime time today, he would have to change his ways. Speed could no longer be the clever bird's major strength. The new roadrunner might now use his familiar "Beep, Beep" as a chant, allowing him to tap into the magical powers that flow through the universe. This is the gospel of the Saturday morning cartoons.

Perhaps the best example of how explicit the schooling being given to our children through their cartoons can be is found in the opening of the He-Man cartoon.

> Travel with us now through the dimensions of time to the most amazing planet in the heavens. This is Eternia, a land of . . . swamps where unseen demons lie in wait. Eternia's cities are centers of highly advanced science and technology. Eternia is a land of sorcery and magic. There are powerful forces at work throughout the land. But no place is as magical and mysterious as Castle Gray Skull.
>
> Within these walls are mystical secrets and powers beyond imagination. . . . I am Adam, prince of Eternia; defender of the secrets of Castle Gray Skull. Fabulous secret powers were revealed to me the day I held aloft my magic sword and said, "By the power of Gray Skull—I am the power." I became He-Man, the most powerful man in the universe.[13]

It is immediately striking that the hero in this epic, set in "Eternia," is named "Adam." The name "Eternia" has the obvious connotations of eternity. Likewise, Adam is the name of the biblical father of the human race. Adam fell as a result of the lie that the serpent perpetuated on Eve—namely, that we can achieve enlightenment and become as gods in our own right. That belief, and the rebellion it inspired, caused Adam and Eve to be ejected from the Garden of Eden. In the "gospel" of He-man, however, when Adam raises his magical sword and proclaims "I am the power," he finds the serpent's promises immediately come to pass as "fabulous secret powers" are revealed to him and he becomes "the most powerful man in the universe." In the gospel of He-Man the serpent's lie is vindicated and the children's hero is the one who imitates man's first act of rebellion against his Creator. But that is still not the extent of it. Other central tenets of the New Age lie are also prevalent in He-Man. The sorceress speaks to the other characters through telepathy. Orco, a wizard, levitates objects and uses incantations to cast magical spells. The evil Skeletor utilizes the power of the "third eye," long a core teaching of the occult.

Sadly, He-Man is far from the exception in present-day television fare.

The Teenage Mutant Ninja Turtles

The hottest cartoon characters on the market at the time of this writing are the Teenage Mutant Ninja Turtles. We recently rented one of their videos entitled "The Incredible Shrinking Turtles." Of course, since much of the protest that has surrounded these characters has been because of the violent nature of these "heroes in a halfshell," this is what we expected to find. However, by a long shot the "gospel" that this video presented was far more dangerous to the minds of children.

At the beginning of the movie, the Ninja Turtles are playing games in Central Park. Suddenly, Nown, an alien from Dimension X, falls from the sky into a lake. The turtles pull the drowning alien from the water, but too late. As Nown dies, he tells them of a crystal, called the Eye of Zarnoth, which broke into three pieces as he fell. He doesn't know where it landed. The alien, with his last breath, tells the turtles that they must find all three pieces before anyone else because "when the three pieces are joined, the possessor will have power undreamed of in your world."

We see here in the Eye of Zarnoth a not-so-subtle reference once again to the third eye of the occult. This is the eye which, according to mystics, is located in the forehead and can be opened through metaphysical techniques such as meditation and visualization. Once the eye is opened the enlightened seeker gains access to his divine nature and incredible spiritual powers. In the movie, the turtles race with the evil Shredder for the three pieces of "The Eye." When Shredder initially gains control of it he attaches it to the front of his helmet in a position right over his forehead, instantly giving him supernatural powers. However, Shredder loses the helmet and it is found by Blodget, a reporter who has just lost his job. Blodget takes the helmet home and puts it on his head as he sits on the sofa, wondering what to do about all his troubles.

"What am I going to do now?" Blodget asks his cat, Mortimer. In response, his cat quietly hands him a cassette tape entitled "How to Fix Your Messed Up Life." Skeptically Blodget decides to listen to the tape, which tells him:

> Yes, you too can achieve your dream of a better life
> through the power of positive wishing. Do you yearn
> to own a luxury limousine? It can be yours if you
> simply put your mind to it.[14]

Suddenly beams begin to emanate from the Eye of Zarnoth on the helmet which Blodget is wearing and he finds himself sitting in a beautiful limo. "It works!" he shouts, extolling the powers of his new mind powers. All of his efforts at making a better life had failed. Even "positive wishing" had failed. But all that ended when Blodget tapped into the power of the third eye!

Some would argue that this is just a cartoon. Kids, they would contend, can separate fiction from reality. The problem with this argument is that it fails to recognize that these ideas which are picked up in children's programming are then reinforced in many other areas, not the least of which are in their video games and their classrooms. It is even confirmed to them on Sunday morning television when they hear one of America's leading preachers spew forth the message of the power of positive thinking, for which the power of positive wishing is only a thinly veiled imitation. Clearly the seed has been implanted: Through the power of your mind you can create reality and have all that you desire, if, as the cartoons tell you, you can just manage to open your third eye.

For those who do not think there are people who are consciously pushing this message on viewers, the words of New Age visionary Shirley MacLaine should be considered. She tells of how ABC approached her and convinced her to do a miniseries detailing her spiritual journey.

> ABC television approached me to consider making a miniseries film of my book *Out on a Limb*. They spoke of metaphysical search being popular now and extra-terrestrials and UFOs as something the public was genuinely interested in. Brandon Stoddard [head of entertainment at ABC] was well aware of the growing spiritual hunger in the American culture and wanted to be the one who had the courage to okay the nourishment.... "All I ask," Brandon went on, "is that you make sure the audience understands cosmic justice and that we each are responsible for our own reality. That's what the viewers will want to respond to.... Now make up a budget. Twelve, fifteen million, whatever it is. Hopefully, we've got an Event here.... There are more people into this stuff than you think. And I want ABC to be first."[15]

The Classroom of the Nineties

Some may argue, incorrectly, that these themes have always been in the cartoons and movies. However, even if that were true, we are witnessing a new phenomenon today. As noted, once the seeds have been planted in the "fictional" world of television and video games, these ideas are then legitimized in other places, including the public school system. Indeed, it has now become clear that religion is not being thrown out of the public schools at all—only Christianity is! And, while Christianity is being unceremoniously booted out the front doors of these schools, every conceivable form of Eastern philosophy and tradition is quietly being slipped in the back doors.

The list of reasonable concerns in these areas today has grown well beyond the usage of games like Dungeons and Dragons and the Ouiji Board. Johanna Michaelsen details the scope of the current problems in her book *Like Lambs to the Slaughter.* She quotes one teacher as explaining:

> ...we do some pretty amazing things: psychic healing, shamanism, crystals, witchcraft...[and] meditation in class, either guided or open, and then they write about it.... We burn candles and hold a full moon ceremony once a month.... I must have a divine light around me because I've had no flack from anyone.... One time, though, I was conducting a spring equinox celebration for the kids; I mean I had the altar all set up—flowers, the candles were lit on the altar—and the principal walked in! Fortunately, he was a new principal and he was thrilled with what we were doing.... I was lucky...I have to walk a fine line on the religious issues. Some might say that I've crossed it.[16]

Distressingly, this is only the most obvious evidence of the problem. One of the greatest dangers in the educational system are techniques that are being disguised as simple concentration exercises, scientific skills for relaxing students, or exercises to boost their self-confidence. One example of a procedure to deal with stress is given by Larry Ciglen and Les Ann Ciglen, two teachers in the Ontario, Canada, public school system.

> ...physical relaxation is very important for calming and settling our bodies. Techniques of muscle

> relaxation, deep breathing and visualization are used to accomplish this relaxed state. . . . After assuming a comfortable position, the children practice breathing deeply and repeating, "I am relaxed." . . . Students learn how to isolate their muscles and through a process of tightening and releasing muscles individually and in a set sequence, relax their bodies. When imagery, seeing the muscles relax in their minds is added, the technique becomes even more effective.[17]

However, as harmless as this may sound, this is the exact technique employed by Eastern mystics to open their third eye! This works, they say, because it allows them to overcome the limitations of their natural mind by achieving an altered state of consciousness. *OMNI* magazine explains how the Tibetan yogis get to this state:

> Take a deep breath, let it out slowly, stretch your muscles, and relax. Now imagine that warm currents of mental energy are very slowly moving up from the soles of your feet toward your ankles. Feel the muscles in your feet gradually warming and relaxing as you imagine the currents flowing through them. . . .[18]

Clearly, these two techniques are virtually identical. Yet the yogis tell us that the purpose is to achieve altered states of consciousness while these educators say the goal is simply to help students become relaxed! Mary Bell, a graduate of the Berkeley Psychic Institute Teacher Training Program, is explicit in admitting that the goals are really the same. "Concentration skills," she writes, "have been around curriculum guidelines for a long time. Being 'one-pointed' can lead not only to creative genius but to communing with God."[19]

Unfortunately, many educators are well aware of the realities of what they are doing and are purposefully changing their semantics to disguise their intentions. Deborah Rozman, for example, tells teachers in her book *Meditating with Children* that "if you still have trouble . . . when bringing this program to your children, parents, family, school administrators or board of educators, use alternative terms like . . . awareness training, concentration, centering, awareness games, relaxation, holistic learning, creative imagery, etc. . . ."

This is religious teaching. The fact that the names have been changed to those sounding less religious should not confuse the issue, but sadly it does. As one New Ager boasted in an article entitled "Infiltrating the New Age into Society":

> One of the biggest advantages we have as New Agers is, once the occult, metaphysical and New Age terminology is removed, we have concepts and techniques that are very acceptable to the general public. So we can change the names and demonstrate the power. In so doing, we open the New Age door to millions who would not normally be receptive.[20]

Spirit Guides to the Future

At the core of many Eastern and New Age teachings is the belief that the development of the "higher self" can be greatly accelerated through contact with spirit guides. These guides are variously seen as souls between incarnations, manifestations of the great unconsciousness, or spirits from other dimensions. Gurus and mystics promise that once a seeker has contacted his own spirit guide, whoever or whatever it may be, he is on the fast lane toward enlightenment. Christians understand that the contacting of these entities has been at the core of the occult for millennia, and that these spirit guides are nothing other than demons playing with and deceiving the minds of men.

Unfortunately, the effort to contact such guides has now also entered the public schools. This process follows logically with the "relaxation" techniques that have already taught children how to achieve trancelike states. Once these altered states of consciousness have been attained, children are often led through so-called mental exercises. For instance, in the Success Imagery program, developed by Dr. Charles Stoebel, the child is instructed to picture himself or herself in a peaceful location. It can be by a lake or on a mountain, he is told, as long as it is a place where he is completely at peace. Then he is told:

> Now a figure is coming toward you. He is friendly and can be young or old. Speak to the wise person and welcome him into your safe place. Get to know your wise person. You can invite him back anytime.[21]

Likewise, according to Beverly Galyean, in Confluent Education the students are instructed to "look into the sun and as you do the face of a very wise person slowly appears... listen to this person speaking.... You may engage in a conversation."

Who are these wise persons? They are the exact spirit guides that permeate mysticism, and they were contacted in the exact same way that mystics have contacted their guides! However, as has become the norm, those who know the truth of the matter cover it up. Confluent Education originator Beverly Galyean is a perfect example of one who recognizes these "spirit guides" for what they are, yet who admits that "we don't call them that in the public schools. We call them imagery guides."[22]

Of course, as Christians we know that these spirit guides are actually demons leading people into a world of delusion. Yet contacting these guides has virtually become a universal pastime in our society at large. Could it be that the ideas which the children gain in the cartoons are then put to the test in the public schools until the students have become proficient in working in this realm? The evidence that this is exactly what is happening is overwhelming.

And the delusion continues well beyond the classroom. Whether it is the housewife taking a morning class at the YMCA, a corporate executive taking a management seminar, or a curious seeker signing up for a course in Silva Mind Control, they are being opened up to the exact same lies and the exact same spirit guides. It is not too difficult to picture a day ahead when all of these trusted spirit guides will point to the Antichrist and identify him as the true Christ! The stage is being set for a deception so powerful that if it were possible, even the very elect would be deceived.

The cause seems so noble. These visionaries of the New Age believe that they are introducing the world to the very ideas and beliefs that will unite the world in the days ahead. Indeed, these very beliefs, it is argued, will actually play a huge part in the quantum leap of consciousness that will propel the world into the New World Order. Tragically, they will also propel the world into the arms of Antichrist.

Chapter 11

Signs, Wonders, and the Rise of Antichrist

As we noted earlier, the question that faces the planners of this New World Order is how they will actually propel the world into such a system. One of the ideas that we have already discussed is the possibility that a crisis such as a near-nuclear confrontation would put so much fear into the people of the world that they would then be open to the move toward a completely new order. However, historian Lewis Mumford noted that all major transformations in history "have rested on a new ideological or metaphysical base . . . a new picture of the cosmos and the nature of man." Could it be that there will be a spiritual dimension to this transition? There certainly is a new view of the nature of man emerging.

Today through the New Age revival of "Mystery Babylon" people are becoming deceived into believing that they have godlike inate powers and abilities which they are just beginning to tap into. Such widespread acceptance of the paranormal could well pave the way for spiritual events that could trigger the birth of the New World Order and prepare the way for its charismatic leader. In the light of Bible prophecy it is important to remember that both of these things must happen. Far from just becoming convinced globalists, the citizens of the last-days world are also going to become committed worshipers of the Antichrist himself.

> And they worshiped the dragon which gave power unto the beast; and they worshiped the beast, saying, Who is like the beast? Who is able to make war with him?... And all that dwell upon the earth shall worship him, whose names are not written in the book of life of the Lamb (Revelation 13:4,8).

In the light of these passages it would seem that far more than a near-nuclear-holocaust will have to come upon this world if we are to explain why the Antichrist will be worshiped as God Himself. Of course a nuclear scare could be part of it, but there will simply have to be a spiritual dimension as well.

UFO Landing

One thing that could change the way the world thinks almost overnight would be a close encounter of some type. While UFO's have been the subject of much scorn over the last several decades, it now appears that the technology that made the space shuttle possible, combined with the popularity of movies like *Star Wars* and *E.T.*, have left many millions of people open to the possibility of an extraterrestrial ("E.T.") visiting planet Earth. Hal Lindsey in his book *The 1980's Countdown to Armageddon* explains just such a scenario:

> Authorities now admit that there have been confirmed sightings of unidentified flying objects.... Reports held in U.S. Air Force files reveal that whatever these flying objects are, they move and turn at speeds unmatched by human technology. It is my opinion that UFO's are real and that there will be a proven close encounter of the third kind soon. And I believe that the source of this phenomenon is some type of alien being of great intelligence and power. According to the Bible, a demon is a spiritual personality in a state of war with God. Prophecy tells us that demons

> will be allowed to use their powers of deception in a grand way during the last days of history. I believe these demons will stage a spacecraft landing on Earth. They will claim to be from an advanced culture in another galaxy. They may even claim to have planted human life on this planet and tell us they have returned to check on our progress. Many scientists—not to mention movies and television shows—are putting forth similar theories about the origin of life on Earth. If demons led by Satan, their chief, did pull off such a deception, then they could certainly lead the world into total error regarding God and His revelation.[1]

While this is only one example of the type of spiritual event that could transform the world, it does show how much more powerful this type of event would be in changing the world's thinking than a purely natural disaster.

One particular episode of the "New Twilight Zone" laid out a scenario in which, during a heated and completely stalled arms reduction session at the U.N., a UFO appeared and hovered over the United Nations complex. Then an alien being materialized before all the delegates. He explained that he had planted life on this planet and that he had come back to check up on their progress. After performing several signs and wonders to convince the nations of his incredible godlike powers, he gave them just 24 hours to solve their differences. And they did. The show concluded with this statement: "For those of you who doubt that world peace is possible, remember that it happened first in the twilight zone."

Almost as if he had seen that particular episode, Ronald Reagan shared the same idea when he met in Geneva with Mikhail Gorbachev in 1985. The U.S. President reflected on how a close encounter would cut through all the preliminaries and instantaneously unite the world.

> If suddenly there was a threat to this world from some other species from another planet, we'd forget

> all the little local differences that we have between our two countries, and we would find out once and for all that we really are all human beings on this earth together.[2]

However dramatic such an occurrence would be, there is an established link between UFO's and the occult. Unfortunately, such a link would be quickly forgotten in the excitement and reality of the moment. Jacques Vallee, an astrophysicist, computer scientist, and one of the world's most credible researchers in the area of UFO's, has noted this occult connection:

> A few investigators—notably Ray Palmer, John Keel and Salvatore Freixedo—have suggested both in public statements and in private conversations with me that there may be a link between UFO events and occult phenomena. At first view the very suggestion of such a link is disturbing to a scientist. However . . . the phenomena reported by [UFO] witnesses involve poltergeist effects, levitation, psychic control, healing and out-of-body experiences. . . .[3]

Vallee's research has lead him to the conclusion that UFO's are real but probably not physical; they are part of some evil scheme for the victimization of humans; and one of their major purposes is to manipulate human consciousness and to program mankind psychologically for some ultimate deception.[4] Author Whitley Strieber, writing in his bestselling book *Transformation*, also reveals that a great majority of the people who have purported to have contact with E.T.'s have also been involved in occult practices at some point in their lives. Speaking of his own experience, Strieber writes:

> Increasingly I felt as if I were entering a struggle that might be even more than life or death. It might be a struggle for my soul, my essence, or whatever part of

> me that might have reference to the eternal. . . . This
> led me back to something else I had noticed about the
> visitor experience. From the experiences of people . . .
> and from dozens of the letters that were pouring in, it
> was very clear that the soul was very much at issue.
> People experienced feeling as if their souls were being
> dragged from their bodies. . . . "We recycle souls,"
> they had said.[5]

This scenario of a UFO landing on planet Earth in a spaceship and claiming to have planted life on this planet (proving his highly evolved nature with signs and lying wonders) certainly would be capable of deceiving the entire world. And with the connection to the occult clearly established, it is not difficult to imagine the spectacular display that the seducing spirits behind the phenomena could put on. However, this is only one of many different possibilities.

The New Age Christ

One of the most dramatic claims of the way the coming transformation will occur is given by New Age leader Benjamin Creme. Creme believes that in the very near future the New Age Christ, "Maitreya," will reveal himself to the world. Creme, who claims to be the John the Baptist for Maitreya (who was supposed to appear as early as 1982), claims that when the world is sufficiently ready to receive the appearance of the Christ there will be a "Day of Declaration." On that day, according to Creme, Maitreya—

> will be invited to address all the world through world-
> wide television and radio hookups. At that time, he
> will mentally overshadow all of humanity . . . he will
> communicate with us telepathically . . . on our televi-
> sion screens. We will see this man, and we will silently
> hear his words drop into our minds, in our own

> language. We could turn off the sound on our own
> television sets and still hear him. ... Everybody, every-
> where, will hear it no matter what they are doing. In
> this way [by overshadowing] he will reveal his true
> nature, inspiring within all men and women the cer-
> tainty that this man is indeed the Christ. And si-
> multaneously throughout the world, hundreds of
> thousands of healings, cures, apparently miraculous
> cures will reinforce, if necessary, that this is the
> Christ that we are watching.[6]

Once again, this is something that only the Antichrist or very powerful demonic forces which had been allowed the right to go forth by God could truly accomplish. We must also realize that millions of people are already opening themselves up to their inner voices through such occultic practices as meditation, yoga, hypnosis, and mind-expanding drugs. In addition, school-children involved with programs such as Success Imagery, QR, and Confluent Education are not only being instructed on how to open themselves up to their inner voices but are also being told to do "whatever that voice tells them to do." It is entirely conceivable that the demons behind the voices are preparing these seduced individuals for the day when they will point to the Antichrist and identify him as "God"!

The World Healing Day

When one speaks of evolution, the first thought to come to mind is the debate about the origins of man. However, the evolution debate today has taken on new meaning. New Agers and other evolutionists now spend a great deal of their time talking about the next step of evolution. Mankind, they contend, is on the verge of the next step of evolution. However, this time the evolution they foresee will not be *physical* but *spiritual*. This school of thought was given a great boost by an article appearing in the *National Geographic* by Phillip Tobias. According to the physical anthropologist:

> From my lifetime of studying hominid fossils, I know we've hardly shown any anatomical changes in our bodies for 100,000 years. And I don't think we're suddenly going to start again showing anatomical change. I believe that our physical and anatomical evolution has become less and less significant, whilst our cultural, behavioral, linguistic and spiritual evolution has become more and more important.[7]

This spiritual evolution, we are told, will happen very rapidly in the days ahead. This idea of a "swift" evolution is known as punctuated equilibria. Interestingly, it is a relatively new theory put forward by evolutionists because of their complete inability to prove even one instance of the evolutionary process from the fossil record. This theory maintains that instead of animals evolving very slowly over millions of years, the transition from one species to another happens very suddenly. This, they say, is why they cannot exhibit proof of their "scientific" theory of evolution!

However, outside of the scientific arena, this idea that the next step in our evolution is spiritual, and that it will happen very quickly, has become the basis for several different mass-participation events in the past few years. These have included The World Healing Day, Harmonic Convergence, and countless think-in's. The World Healing Day, which began in 1986, is held every year on December 31 at noon, Greenwich mean time. Millions of participants (organizers claim in excess of 200 million) gather together in different countries with one common purpose: They believe they can trigger this next step of evolution by simultaneously thinking thoughts of peace and unity.

> For this one, you don't have to donate money, stand in line. . . . At the most, you may want to light a candle.

But, put simply, this is a thought process, one giant think-in. Brain power. Do it with friends; do it while you drive to work. Do it with the 249,999,999 other people who are expected to take part in this experiment in metaphysics. All you have to do to participate is to concentrate for one hour—on thoughts of peace and global harmony.[8]

Unfortunately, millions of people treat such outlandish beliefs with deadly seriousness. Former Colorado Governor Richard Lamm's wife is one of the enthusiastic supporters of these mind links. She explains that the entire gathering is based on something called "The 100th Monkey Theory":

The Japanese monkey, Macaca Fuscata, has been observed in the wild for a period of over 30 years.

In 1952, on the island of Koshima, scientists were providing monkeys with sweet potatoes dropped in the sand. The monkeys liked the taste of the raw sweet potatoes, but they found the dirt unpleasant.

An 18-month-old female named Imo found she could solve the problem by washing the potatoes in a nearby stream. She taught this trick to her mother. Her playmates also learned this new way and they taught their mothers, too. This cultural innovation was gradually picked up by various monkeys before the eyes of scientists. Between 1952 and 1958, all the young monkeys learned to wash the sandy sweet potatoes to make them more palatable. Only the adults who imitated their children learned this social improvement. Other adults kept eating the dirty sweet potatoes.

Then something startling took place. In the autumn of 1958, a certain number of Koshima monkeys were washing sweet potatoes—the exact number is not known.

Let us suppose when the sun rose one morning, there were 99 monkeys on Koshima who had learned to wash their sweet potatoes.

Then it happened!

By that evening, almost everyone in the tribe was washing sweet potatoes before eating them. The added energy of this hundredth monkey somehow created an ideological breakthrough!

But notice: A most surprising thing observed by these scientists was that the habit of washing sweet potatoes then jumped over the sea. Colonies of monkeys on other islands and the mainland troop monkeys in Takasakiyama began washing their sweet potatoes!

Thus, when a certain critical number achieves an awareness, this new awareness may be communicated from mind to mind. . . .

There is a point at which if only one more person tunes into a new awareness, a field is strengthened so this awareness is picked up by almost everyone! The "hundredth monkey" may be likened to the person on the edge of a new consciousness. The person who has not yet been convinced, the "just one more" who will make the difference, and cause the sudden shift in a conceptual or organizational paradigm.[9]

This story is, of course, pure fabrication. No such experiment ever truly took place. Nonetheless, it is this belief that a small but critical percentage of people meditating on thoughts of peace and justice and telepathically transferring this thought to all other people on the planet that is the basis of the World Healing Day each year. This belief was also central to the "Harmonic Convergence" in the summer of 1987. As bizarre as this may sound, don't forget that millions of people are being set up for the "strong delusion" spoken of in 2 Thessalonians 2:16-12.

The occult connection is once again found very easily. John Randolph Price, the originator of the World Healing Day, explains that this whole idea was given to him by his personal spirit guide, whom he contacted through meditation, yoga, and hypnosis. Additionally, it was revealed to Price that the coming "Christ" will rule over a New Age on earth, while the Antichrist is anyone who denies the deity of man! Of course, this is just the exact opposite of the biblical teaching, which tells us that an antichrist is anyone who denies the deity of Jesus Christ.

> Who is a liar but he that denieth that Jesus is the Christ? He is antichrist that denieth the Father and the Son. . . . These things have I written unto you concerning them that seduce you (1 John 2:22,26).

Changing the Mind of God

According to organizers of the annual "World Healing Day," this "100th Monkey Theory" is possible because of the "true" nature of the universe that is being revealed to them by their spirit guides. First of all, they believe and are teaching the standard Eastern belief that "God is all and all is God." In other words, God is simply the sum total of everything in the universe. As such, each individual is one small part, or a cell, in God.

However, just like in the human body, they say, each cell contains "the code" to remake the entire body. This is the principle that makes cloning a possibility. In the theory of cloning, we are told, by taking one cell from the human body and extracting the DNA code which contains every piece of information about that individual, we can actually make a perfect carbon copy of that person. Of course, this is just a theory. Outside of the science fiction movies it has never really happened.

However, the argument of New Agers is that if God is just the sum total of all of us, then, like the cells in the human body, we must have within us all the "DNA" code that makes up God Himself. Therefore all the secrets of the universe are within me. All that is God is within me. I just have to tap into and break the code to discover that I am God. Shirley MacLaine explains that is the message not only of the spirit guides but of most of the world's spiritual masters:

> ... when each person experiences the higher self,
> the conversations are almost identical. The lessons are
> all the same ... entities channeling through a variety
> of people in many countries in many different lan-
> guages were saying basically the same thing. Look
> into yourselves, explore yourselves, you are the uni-
> verse. ... The spirit masters had all said the same
> thing.[10]

The second part of this "revelation" is that since we are little
gods, then if we tap into our divine powers, whatever we visualize
or imagine or meditate on can come to pass. This is science-of-
mind teaching, or as it is better known, "mind over matter." It is
also this ability to tap into our divinity that purportedly makes us
able to utilize psychic powers, ESP, telepathic communication,
and so on.

Finally, New Agers would have us come to the understanding
that the mind and will of this force called God are simply the
culmination of all of our minds and wills. And since we are all
brain cells in this global brain, then whatever a majority of
individuals are visualizing or thinking will be reflected in the
"mind of God" and will then be manifested on the physical plane.

Therefore, if much of the world is thinking negative thoughts,
then God (the collective unconsciousness) will bring negative
events to pass. And if enough people in the world are thinking
positive thoughts, then God (the collective consciousness) will
bring forth positive events in the physical realm. The "World
Healing Day" and "Harmonic Convergence" were nothing more
than attempts to affect this balance.

The Quantum Leap

While it should seem clear that these ideas are bizarre and
without biblical foundation, we must realize that they form the
core of the Eastern religions, the cults, and the New Age movement which is being received with open arms by the spiritually

starving West. They are also at the very center of what spirit guides—contacted through yoga, meditation, TM, trance channeling, corporate management seminars, and even relaxation techniques used in the public schools—are telling the masses.

There is little doubt that the entire globe is being set up for some unthinkable delusion. Indeed, the organizers of the "World Instant of Cooperation" are convinced that one day soon, when enough people begin to simultaneously meditate and visualize a world of peace and prosperity, there will be a spiritual transformation that they say can only be described as a "Planetary Pentecost."

A Planetary Pentecost

New Age leader Barbara Marx Hubbard, an executive director of the World Future Society, a former member of the Presidential Committee on National Curriculum, and a Democratic Party nominee for the Vice-Presidency of the United States in 1984, claims that the World Healing Day could well trigger a "Planetary Pentecost" that would bring about—

> ... a mass transfiguration and empowerment of millions at once ... a second coming through lifting our consciousness, transforming ourselves as Christ transformed himself. ... Such events are now being prepared.[11]

Hubbard even goes so far as to claim that during this "Planetary Pentecost," participants will have the powers of Christ to "heal" and "resurrect" the dead. Likewise, John Randolph Price claims that through meditation he sees "images of a new heaven and a new earth." However, this is not the new heavens and the new earth that the Bible speaks of. "We can let the kingdom come," he claims:

> ... we can let the will of God be done in earth as it is in heaven ... which means that this world can be

transformed into a heaven—right now—in the 1980's and 90's. This is no fantasy. This is not science or religious fiction. This is the main event of our individual lives. . . . And through our collective efforts on December 31 . . . we can literally turn on the light of the world, dissolve the darkness, and begin the new Age of spirituality on planet earth.[12]

The transformation that will supposedly occur at this coming moment is called a quantum leap. It is, according to New Agers, the next step of evolution for humanity. According to Hubbard:

It will not come as the light that blinded St. Paul on the road to Damascus. . . . It will not come to the peoples of Earth one by one. It will come to the peoples of Earth together in one instant of time. This is the great instant of cooperation. Cooperation does not mean being nice to each other. It does not mean agreeing with each other. It does not mean peace, comfort or working together to solve a problem. It means cooperating with God. It means co-evolving with me. It means co-experiencing the same force at the same time and acting together in accord with the idea which you all have from within.[13]

Of course, we know that a certain number of people meditating is not going to do anything. It is certainly not going to affect the universal unconsciousness because such a consciousness simply does not exist. However, demons acting behind the scenes could coordinate these efforts with the moment when the Antichrist is revealed. Regardless of what dramatic event triggers the birth of the New World Order and the rise of the Antichrist, there is little doubt that demons will be given the power to make it look like the unified meditations of the world's critical mass brought this great event to pass. In fact, the theological base is already being laid to explain away the one event that will certainly have the largest transforming effect upon the world as the Antichrist rises to power.

Christians and Our Coming Quantum Leap

According to John Randolph Price and New Age groups who are preparing for this quantum leap, the only thing that could stop this evolution to heaven on earth would be if "there were massive and dedicated counter-forces to offset the benefits" of this worldwide collective, unified effort. The only group capable of doing this, according to Barbara Marx Hubbard, are those who are sticking to a worn-out, divisive theology, which believes that it has the "only" truth. Of course, this is a clear reference to Bible-believing Christianity.

Nevertheless, Hubbard and other New Agers are not concerned about opposition to this great revelation of human unity, divinity, and the ensuing quantum leap. The reason is simple: They have been told by their "spirit guides" that when the moment of transformation arrives all opposition will be eliminated. Almost predictably the way in which these spirit guides claim this will be done sounds exactly like the biblical description of the rapture.

New Age leader Peter Russell, author of *The Global Brain*, explains that, as with the others, so also it was revealed to him that each person is a cell in the global or universal brain, which is God. However, he claims that there are some "cancer cells" in this global brain who cause division, and therefore bring malfunctioning and illness to mankind. According to Russell, these brain cells (people) will have to be exported into a nonphysical realm! John Randolph Price asserts that his spirit guide showed him that the earth's inhabitants who do not join in this quantum leap will be "removed" from earth. However, they will be reincarnated once they have grown spiritually, he claims. Barbara Marx Hubbard, in her commentary on the book of Revelation, attributes these words to the "spirit guides" who, she maintains, coauthored the commentary with her:

Humanity will not be able to make the transition from Earth-only to universal life until the chaff has been separated from the wheat. The great reaper must reap before we can take the quantum-leap to the next phase of evolution. It is a free choice. Evolution is good but it is not nice. Only the good can evolve. Only the God-centered will survive to inherit the powers of the universal species.... This act is as horrible as killing a cancer cell. It must be done for the sake of the future of the whole. So be it; be prepared for the selection process which is now beginning.... We have no choice, dearly beloveds. It is a case of the destruction of the whole planet, or the elimination of the ego driven, godless one-fourth who, at this time of planetary birth, can, if allowed to live on to reproduce their defective disconnection, destroy forever the opportunity of homo sapiens to become homo universalis, heirs of God.... Fortunately you, dearly beloveds, are not responsible for this act. We are. We are in charge of God's selection process for planet Earth. He selects, we destroy. All those souls who are less energetic will not pass on in new bodies. They will either play out their education elsewhere, or choose extinction. They will not be allowed to reincarnate on planet Earth....[14]

New Age author Ruth Montgomery's spirit guides are even more to the point. She quotes them as telling her:

Those who survive the shift will be a different type of people.... The souls who helped to bring on the chaos of the present century will have passed into the spirit to rethink their attitudes.... Millions will survive and millions won't. Those that won't will go into the spirit state....[15]

The True Trigger of the Quantum Leap

There is no question that there will be a mass disappearance of people from this planet at the same time as the Antichrist rises to power. Actually a "quantum leap" is a pretty good description of the "jump" that we will be taking. It is the rapture of the believers in Jesus Christ. However, as we can see here, the foundation is being laid for a lie that will convince the world that it is the "bad people" who have been taken because they stood in the way of the global unity and spiritual development that was finally leading mankind into the next stage of evolution.

I agree with author Dave Hunt that the rapture of the church of Jesus Christ will be the instrumental event in triggering the mass change of consciousness and thinking on this planet. These other corresponding events may be allowed as a smokescreen of what really happened, but the rapture is the event that will change the consciousness of the world instantly.

It will do so for two reasons. In the first place, the very trauma of the disappearance of millions of people and the resulting chaos will literally transfix world attention. Imagine the coverage that CNN and "Nightline" will be trying to provide! Everywhere they will be looking for answers. They will know that no simple scientific answer will do. They will know that something completely unique in human history will have happened. What a perfect time for the rise of one who comes with all "power and signs and lying wonders"!

Related directly to this is a second aspect of the rapture that we must remember. With the disappearance of the body of Christ, the restraining power of the Holy Spirit which indwelt believers will also have disappeared. The bridle which held the spread of evil and deception in check will cease. The Antichrist, the false prophets, and the spirit of deception will have full sway over the earth.

> For the mystery of iniquity doth already work; only he who now restraineth will restrain until he be taken

out of the way. And then shall that wicked one be revealed . . . even him whose coming is after the working
of Satan with all power and signs and lying wonders,
and with all deceivableness of unrighteousness in them
that perish, because they received not the love of the
truth that they might be saved. And for this cause God
shall send them strong delusion, that they should
believe a lie (2 Thessalonians 2:7-11).

The Mortal Head Wound

One other incident that the Bible specifically mentions is that
the Antichrist will receive some type of head wound that will
initially appear to be deadly. We are told that his miraculous
recovery from this head wound will cause the world not only to
wonder and worship him but also to worship the dragon which
gives him his power.

I saw one of his heads as if it were wounded to death,
and his deadly wound was healed; and all the world
wondered after the beast. And they worshiped the
dragon which gave power unto the beast; and they
worshiped the beast, saying, Who is like the beast?
Who is able to make war with him? (Revelation 13:3,4).

Some students of Bible prophecy believe that since the Word of
God describes both the Antichrist and his kingdom as the beast,
we should understand this passage to be referring to the revival of
the Roman Empire from which he rises. After all, they argue, the
Roman Empire has been dead for years but today is rising once
again. I do not believe that this is what the apostle John is telling
us. Even with the enormous changes in this world over the past
few years—the collapse of Communism, the spread of democracy, and the birth of the United States of Europe—people are far
from being so dramatically affected. Instead, it would seem that
the Word of God is revealing that the Antichrist will be wounded

in such a way as would considered to be unquestionably fatal. It is his miraculous healing that will stun the world.

The key phrase of the last days is *spiritual deception*. When Jesus was asked what would be "the sign of His coming and of the end of the world," the first thing He said was:

> Take heed that no man deceive you. For many shall come in my name saying, I am Christ, and shall deceive many (Matthew 24:4,5; cf. Mark 13:5,6; Luke 21:8).

Referring to the power of this delusion, Jesus warned that "there shall arise false Christs and false prophets, and shall show great signs and wonders, insomuch that, if it were possible, they shall deceive the very elect" (Matthew 24:24; cf. Mark 13:22). There is undoubtedly going to be a strong delusion that will come upon the world. With the exception of the rapture and the head wound, none of the other events that we have discussed may come to pass. But each one does serve to foreshadow just how powerful the delusion accompanying the appearance of the Antichrist will be.

Chapter 12

A Deceptive Christ

Almighty God can make the impossible possible, can change all human hearts, through the queenship of Jesus' mother, Mary.

—Pope John Paul II when he
visited Czechoslovakia

Regardless of the way the Antichrist rises to power, and regardless of the exact nature of the signs and wonders that accompany his rise, we know that he will accomplish three main objectives. First, he will convince the Jews that he is their long-awaited Messiah. Secondly, he will convince the false church that is left behind after the rapture that he is the true Christ. Finally, he will convince everyone that this is actually the beginning of the millennial period spoken of in the Bible during which people live together in peace and harmony for a thousand years. He will accomplish this while at the same time quoting the Bible. He will play on people's lack of true biblical knowledge and on the spirit of deception that has fallen on the world to twist the Scriptures to suit his own ends.

He will convince Israel that he is the Messiah by bringing a false peace to Israel that will simulate the true peace that Jesus Christ will bring seven years later at the height of Armageddon.

He will bring together all the nations of the world to sign a peace pact guaranteeing the protection of the chosen people and allowing them to rebuild the temple. This peace pact that he inaugurates will be the hub of the global false peace that he brings to the whole world. He will proudly point to the Scriptures and proclaim to be fulfilling the prophecies of the Messiah.

At the same time he will convince a heavily deluded world that he is Christ, who has returned to set up his thousand-year kingdom on this earth. The disappearance of millions of people from off the face of the earth will leave the world ripe for such a supernatural explanation. Indeed the Bible seems to indicate that no one left behind after the rapture will believe that it was the rapture that just happened. The strong delusion that God looses upon the world at that moment will help to blind the world to that fact.

As we have already noted, the New Agers and the spirit guides who have been leading them will proclaim that this is a great moment of evolution for humankind and that it is the bad people who have been removed. The Antichrist and his False Prophet, who will also be somehow propelled to world prominence at the same time, will be ready for just that moment.

Once again, in the same way that he will deceive the Jews into believing that he is the Messiah, the Antichrist will convince the rest of the world that he is the Christ by turning to the Scriptures and stealing the biblical explanation of what will happen at the end of the seven-year tribulation period. This is when, at the return of the true Christ, the exact opposite of the rapture of believers takes place; this time the unbelievers are removed from the world so that the true kingdom of God can begin. The only participants allowed in the kingdom will be the believers who were caught up in the rapture seven years earlier and who have now returned with Christ, and also those who became believers on earth during the tribulation period.

> As therefore the tares are gathered and burned in
> the fire, so shall it be in the end of this world. The Son

of man shall send forth his angels, and they shall gather out of his kingdom all things that offend, and them which do iniquity, and shall cast them into a furnace of fire; there shall be wailing and gnashing of teeth. Then shall the righteous shine forth as the sun in the kingdom of their Father (Matthew 13:40-43).

This is the beginning of the true millennial reign, when Jesus will rule upon David's throne in Jerusalem. However, you will notice that just the opposite of what will happen at the *beginning* of the seven-year tribulation period takes place: Instead of the rapture of the "pure in heart" this will be a catching away of the "evil ones." Those who commit iniquity are taken out of the world so that the true kingdom of God can begin.

The counterfeit Christ, who comes before the true Christ and who claims to be inaugurating this millennial period, will point to these passages and claim that this is exactly what has happened. The evil ones, who stood in the way of this new evolution of mankind to higher spiritual powers and the kingdom of God, have been removed. Then he will point to the new miraculous powers that now flow freely in the world as further proof that the millennium has come:

For there shall arise false Christs and false prophets, and shall show great signs and wonders, insomuch that, if it were possible, they shall deceive the very elect. Behold, I have told you before (Matthew 24:24, 25).

Signs in the Sun

If the Antichrist is to be a perfect counterfeit of the real Christ, one of the prophecies he will probably try to duplicate are the signs in the skies that will foreshadow the coming of the true Christ at the end of the tribulation period.

> There shall be signs in the sun and in the moon and in the stars, and upon the earth distress of nations, with perplexity, the sea and the waves roaring. . . . And then shall they see the Son of man coming. . . (Luke 21:25,27).

There is little question that in the moments following the rapture, just as at the time of the second coming, there will be perplexity and distress in the nations. Any great sign in the skies at this time would be the final proof the world needed that the man with all power and signs, who claimed to be Christ, is indeed who he said he was.

Fatima, Portugal: October 13, 1917

One of the greatest signs in the skies that has ever been witnessed by man took place in Fatima, Portugal, on October 13, 1917. On that day an apparition that claimed to be the Virgin Mary appeared for the sixth consecutive month to three small children at a spot called Cova da Iria. By the time of this sixth appearance, word of the affair had spread so widely that over 75,000 people were gathered in the tiny hamlet.

Then it happened. One of the children cried out, "Look at the sun!" As the crowd looked up, the sun turned to a silvery color and began to spin at high speeds, throwing off colors that bathed the crowds below in every tint contained in a rainbow. The sun then began to roam around the skies, moving this way and that. Occasionally it would stop and once again begin spinning and shooting forth the colored lights before it would go back to roaming the heavens. Finally it stood still, pulsating and trembling in the sky.

Then without warning it plunged from its position in the sky, heading directly toward the people below. The sun grew bigger and bigger and the heat became intense as the fire came down from the heavens. People began to scream and panic, thinking that the end of the world had come. At the height of their panic the sun stopped its descent and began to climb back up to its conventional place in the sky. All returned to normal. The show was over.

The crowd then noticed, as a wind blew upon them but seemed to have no effect upon the trees, that they were completely dry. This was in spite of the fact that it had rained for days prior to the event and the whole night before. Even the ground was parched and cracked as if no rain had fallen in months.

There is no question that something happened on that October afternoon in 1917. Some 75,000 people who had come from all over the world witnessed it. People from up to 40 miles away who were not even with the crowd also saw it. Newsmen and secular reporters of every type were there too. Everyone agreed that something completely beyond the control of mankind had taken place. Most, of course, believed it to be a great miracle of the Virgin Mary. Clearly it was either that or an unusually powerful deception being worked on the hearts and minds of men.

Rome, Italy: May 13, 1981

Exactly 64 years to the day after the first appearance of Mary at Fatima, the head of the Roman Catholic Church, Pope John Paul II, bent down to pick up a little girl who had a picture of Mary pinned to her sweater. As he did so, the first two bullets from the Browning Automatic that Mehmet Ali Agca fired at his head sailed over him. The next two bullets found a place in the Pope's body.

While he was recovering, John Paul began to wonder if it was more than coincidence that the one he worshiped as the Virgin Mother and to whom he had dedicated his papacy had saved his life on the anniversary of the first appearance at Fatima. Quickly he had his answer. As he lay convalescing, John Paul believes he had a supernatural vision. That vision, he says, included an exact repeat of the "miracle" seen by the 75,000 people at Fatima 64 years earlier. Whatever else John Paul saw remains a secret, but he was so moved by the event that this man, who had come to the papacy as a dyed-in-the-wool globalist, changed his entire approach to bringing forth his envisioned New World Order:

> Gone, too, was the Pope's presumed time frame involving a leisurely and relatively peaceful evolution from the traditional system of sovereign and interacting nation-states to a veritable new world order. Instead, there was now no doubt in John Paul's mind that in Heaven's agenda, all would be thrown into the cauldron of human judgment gone awry; of human evil sanctioned by men as normal; of unparalleled natural catastrophes, and catastrophes caused by the panic. . . .[1]

This panic, this world gone out of control, will be, John Paul believes, the result of some event that will evoke "an utterly new state of consciousness in all of mankind."[2] This sounds exactly like the effect that the rapture could have on the world.

However, according to the vision that John Paul II had, it will be something quite different. Or, as we shall see, it could well be a combination of both. We know that John Paul speaks of an upcoming event that will resemble the occurrence that took place in Portugal those many years ago. We also know that the Pope believes that it will in some way be related to the Bible verse which tells of a "woman clothed with the sun, and giving birth to a Son who rules the nations with a scepter of iron."[3] Of course, this passage is found in the twelfth chapter of the book of Revelation.

> There appeared a great wonder in heaven: a woman clothed with the sun, and the moon under her feet, and upon her head a crown of twelve stars; and she being with child cried, travailing in birth, and pained to be delivered. . . . And she brought forth a man child, who was to rule all nations with a rod of iron; and her child was caught up unto God, and to his throne (Revelation 12:1,2,5).

There is little question as to the identity of the "Man Child" in this passage of Scripture. Revelation 19 makes it very clear that He is none other than Jesus Christ, the "King of kings and Lord of lords." There is also little question that the woman spoken of in this passage is Israel.

However, the current head of the Roman Church, which to this day has not recognized the existence of the State of Israel, seems to believe that this woman is not Israel at all but the "Queen of Heaven," Mary. He believes that there is going to be some type of repeat of Fatima. He believes that at some point in time the world will dedicate itself to Mary, and he will be propelled to a position of unimaginable power as the moral leader of the world, and then a New World Order will be born. Furthermore, it would seem from this verse which the Pope believes has direct bearing on this event that a "Man Child" who rules the world with a rod of iron will be thrust forward onto the world stage!

It would seem obvious that this Man Child will be either the true King of kings or else a clever impostor. The answer to that question can easily be found by determining the identity of this "Mary" who appeared at Fatima and who has now "appeared" to John Paul.

Is It Really Mary?

This vision of John Paul is extremely disturbing for a number of reasons. The greatest of these, of course, is the source of the vision. As previously noted, the position that the Catholic Church gives to Mary is not biblical. Indeed, Mary is often placed above Jesus Himself as the Savior of the world. The "Mary" that appeared at Fatima was equally unbiblical. This apparition appeared many times, and each time imparted a message to the children who saw her. In the first visit this spirit asked three small children if they were—

> ... willing to offer yourselves to God and bear all the sufferings he wills ... as an act of reparation for the

> sins for which he is offended and of supplication for the conversion of sinners.[4]

The idea that three small children could or needed to make reparation for the sins of the world is completely contradictory to the Word of God. The Bible is clear: That act of reparation has been completed, once and for all, solely by the work of Christ:

> ... by his own blood he entered in once into the holy place, having obtained redemption for us. ... So Christ was once offered to bear the sins of many. ... But this man [Christ], after he had offered one sacrifice for sins forever, sat down on the right hand of God. ... For by one offering he hath perfected forever them that are sanctified (Hebrews 9:12,28;10:12,14).

At a later date, after showing these terrified children a vision of a tormented hell, this "Mary" told them what they were to do:

> You have seen hell where the souls of the poor sinners go. To save them God wishes to establish in the world devotion to my immaculate heart. If what I say to you is done many souls will be saved and there will be peace. ...
> Pray the rosary in honor of our Lady of the Rosary every day in order to obtain peace for the world ... because only she can help you.[5]

There is so much here that is completely at odds with the Word of God that it is difficult to know where to begin. First of all, the idea that only Mary can help the world is so unbiblical that it seems unimaginable that it goes on unchallenged. Jesus is the light and hope of the world, not His earthly mother. Likewise, it is Jesus who will bring peace to this world. He, not Mary, is the Prince of Peace. And ultimately true peace can only come to the heart in which Jesus is allowed to reign.

Furthermore, to suggest that God desires to establish devotion to Mary's immaculate heart presupposes the belief that Mary even has an immaculate heart. This is completely unscriptural teaching originating within the Catholic Church. According to this dogma Mary was conceived sinless and lived a sinless life. Yet the Word of God makes it plain that "all have sinned, and come short of the glory of God" (Romans 3:23). The true Mary acknowledged her own sinful nature and exclaimed, "My spirit hath rejoiced in God my Savior" (Luke 1:47). Certainly if she had not sinned she would have had no need of a Savior. Again, the idea that God wants us to worship Mary in any way is completely absent from the Bible. Instead, Jesus told us:

> Thou shalt love the Lord thy God with all thy heart, and with all thy soul, and with all thy mind. This is the first and great commandment (Matthew 22:37,38; cf. Mark 12:30).

Obviously, we are confronted with a real problem here. This Mary of Fatima, and the Catholic teachings about her, are completely at odds with the Word of God. And the Lord warns us in no uncertain terms how serious a matter that is:

> But though we or an angel from heaven, preach any other gospel unto you than that which we have preached unto you, let him be accursed (Galatians 1:8).

There is no possible conclusion that we can come to except the one which tells us that this apparition which appeared in Fatima and to the present Pope must be a seducing spirit masquerading as Mary. If that is the case, the same spirit guides that are leading and directing the multitudes of New Agers are also deceiving the head of the world's largest religious organization.

The terrifying reality is that John Paul II, far from being only a nominal follower of this "Mary," believes that she spared his life for a divine purpose and that he now is marching under her direct orders. Therefore whether this repeat of Fatima ever occurs or not, this seducing spirit has gained an inside position to deceive this pontiff and his billion followers worldwide. And if this "sign in the sky" should reappear, it is not too difficult to see how this apparition could point to the convincing impostor and identify him as the "true" Christ.

Woman Who Brings Forth the Man Child

According to what we know of John Paul's vision, the sun and this apparition which calls itself Mary will play a central role, as at Fatima. However, when this sign in the sky appears we can deduce, by the Scripture verse the Pope cites, that it will supposedly announce the arrival of the "Man Child who is to rule the earth with a rod of iron." Once again, it would seem clear that seducing spirits could use this event to catapult forward their false Christ.

It is not inconceivable that this Mary could point to some man as "her son," and then the mesmerized citizens of the world would regard this Mary as the biblical "sign in the heavens" and "her son" as the true Christ. The Pope, who is devoted to this Mary that he awaits to appear, could quickly become the chief assistant to this Christ. Indeed, the papacy has always claimed to be the true representative of Christ on earth. Already that is how the Pope sees his upcoming role:

> John Paul knows only that his function will be as a servant; that his years of preparation as one of the world's leaders, a voice and a figure that have received international recognition, will culminate in the apostolic ministrations he must perform in a very different world from the world of the millennial endgame, and among nations that no longer rely on themselves to build on earth a City of Man.[6]

Interestingly, the Bible speaks of just such an apostle to a false Christ in the last days, whom the Bible identifies as the False Prophet. Even more interesting is the fact that one of the great signs that the False Prophet will be able to do in the last days is to make "fire come down on the earth"—exactly what began to happen at Fatima in 1917.

Of course, I am not identifying the present Pope as necessarily being the False Prophet. This scenario may not come to pass at all. It is just one clear example of the deception that is being set up for the "quantum leap" to the New World Order that lies ahead.

With that said, however, it should be noted that this scenario is compelling for a number of reasons. In the first place, it helps to explain how the false "Christian" church is pushed forward to a place of leadership over all the world's other faiths in the world religion that will quickly emerge. John Paul believes that this event will solidly establish him as the moral leader of all the world's religions.

Secondly, it gives a precise scenario for the rise of the False Prophet to world prominence. It also fits perfectly with the biblical explanation of the fact that the False Prophet will point to the Antichrist as the true Christ just like the Scriptures indicate he will do.

Thirdly, it provides an explanation for the fact that the religious whore will rule over the kings of the earth in the early days of the tribulation.

Finally, the vision paves the way for a seemingly "biblical" explanation for the rapture which convinces the world that the "bad seeds" have been removed. The world will believe that the millennium has begun and that they have been accounted worthy to enter. It is for this quantum leap that the present Pope now waits to catapult him to world power:

> Practically considered, the success of his papal participation in the endgame depends on an event whose timing and occasion he is powerless to determine, and the nature of which he cannot in any way influence or

fashion. Without that event, he will be impotent just at the height of the endgame. Backed up by that event, he cannot but emerge as the most powerful man alive in his time....

He is waiting... for an event that will fission human history, splitting the immediate past from the oncoming future. It will be an event on public view in the skies, in the oceans, and on the continental land masses of this planet. It will particularly involve our human sun, which every day lights up and shines upon the valleys, the mountains and the plains of this earth for our eyes. But on the day of this event, it will not appear merely as the master star of our so-called solar system. Rather, it will be seen as the circumambient glory of the Woman whom the apostle describes as "clothed with the sun" and giving birth to "a child who will rule over the nations with a scepter of iron." Fissioning it will be as an event, in John Paul's conviction of faith, for it will immediately nullify all the grand designs the nations are now forming and will introduce the Grand Design of man's Maker. John Paul's waiting and watching time will then be over. His ministry as the Servant of the Grand Design will then begin.... Like his Master, for this he was born and came into the world.[7]

Chapter 13

If They Hated Me...

In the emerging drive toward a New Age of peace and prosperity, it is becoming increasingly clear that all religious persuasions, philosophies, and lifestyles will be accepted as equals. Mikhail Gorbachev forewarns that "tolerance is the Alpha and Omega of the New World Order," and he is far from alone on this point. All are agreed that for the New World Order to work there will have to be an unparalleled unity and tolerance among the peoples of the world. This unity will be built around the common threats and fears that face mankind. The problem, of course, has to do with those who claim to possess the only way, the only truth, and the only life. As reported in *Time* magazine, April 18, 1988, Gene Roddenberry, the creator of "Star Trek," put it bluntly:

> If the future is not for the faint-hearted, it is even more certainly not for the cowardly.... Those who insist theirs is the only correct government or economic system deserve the same contempt as those who insist that they have the only true God.

Equally revealing of the spirit of the age is the fact that this statement was not made in an address to the American Civil Liberties Union or in a speech to some national atheist society, but in a three-page front-cover pullout in *Time* magazine.

Unfortunately, outside of the gospel of Jesus Christ, the New World Order may well be the very best hope that mankind possesses. Therefore those who oppose this move because of "petty" religious differences seem like huge millstones cast around the necks of a world struggling to stay afloat. They could almost seem guilty of committing treason against the New World Order. It reminds one of the Holy Roman Empire, where Christians were persecuted—not because they said Jesus was God, but because they said He was the only God! This was too divisive for a multicultural empire, and so they were charged with the crime of "hatred against the human race"! The same charge, as we shall see, may well be revived today, along with the empire that spawned it.

You Shall Be Hated

There is no doubt that one of the common unifying factors in the New World Order will be a common hatred for believers in Jesus Christ. His claims and promises will be simply too narrow for an empire claiming to be built upon the principles of "unity in diversity." Once again, this is exactly what the Bible has told us will happen in the last days. Speaking of the Antichrist, the apostle John says:

> There was given unto him a mouth speaking great things and blasphemies. . . . And he opened his mouth in blasphemy against God, to blaspheme his name and his tabernacle, and them that dwell in heaven. And it was given unto him to make war with the saints and to overcome them (Revelation 13:5-7).

About 700 years before that statement the prophet Daniel foresaw much the same thing:

> And he [the Antichrist] shall speak great words against the Most High, and shall wear out the saints of

the Most High, and think to change times and laws; and they shall be given into his hand until a time and times and the dividing of time (Daniel 7:25).

Of course, these Scriptures speak of the time during the tribulation period after the rapture of the church. The saints spoken of will be the ones who come to know the Lord after the rapture. However, just as we can already see the shadows of the coming New World Order, we can also see the beginnings of this coming united hatred against God and His people. The spirit that will run rampant throughout the tribulation period is beginning to show its ugly head already today.

Before we move on, the point should also be made that this does not mean there will be no persecution against the church before the rapture. All of the apostles suffered persecution, as did the prophets before them. The same is true of many believers in foreign lands today. As Jesus made perfectly clear, the world's hatred of true believers would be a virtual trademark of the faith:

Then shall they deliver you up to be afflicted, and shall kill you; and ye shall be hated of all nations for my name's sake (Matthew 24:9).

Blessed are ye when men shall hate you, and when they shall separate you from their company, and shall reproach you, and cast out your name as evil, for the Son of man's sake. Rejoice in that day, and leap for joy; for behold, your reward is great in heaven; for in like manner did their fathers unto the prophets (Luke 6:22,23).

The hatred exhibited in the tribulation period will only be the apex of the spirit which has waged war against the children of God for centuries. However, for the first time in history it will actually become one of the central factors uniting the whole human race. The mark of the Beast, spoken of in the book of Revelation, will be largely symbolic of this common hatred. I have often wondered, for example, how the Antichrist will get the whole world to accept the number 666. Everyone has heard of this number and recognizes its evil connotations. If the Antichrist has any brains at all, wouldn't he at least change the number to 665 or 667? However, the more I've considered it, the more I realize that it is the very stigma attached to this number that may make it acceptable.

Imagine the Antichrist rising after the rapture of the church. As we have seen, he will probably convince the world that it is the "bad people" who have gone. The world will worship this hero who speaks great swelling words against the outdated "Christian" God. He will tell the world that it is time to put superstition and silly divisive dogma behind them. As a symbol of the new enlightenment he may well suggest that the number 666 be used as the hub of his new system just to show how far the New Age has progressed beyond such silly superstitions. Even more than that, he may well proclaim that by this act of defiance against an outdated myth he is actually helping people to exorcise themselves of any remaining demons of the old age. Already the foundations for such a clear act of rebellion are being laid.

New Age or Bust!

As we've already noted, in the eyes of the man on the street, the world is finally pulling together as one to confront the crises which face it. There is only one group, however, who will not join the coalition. They are the ones who will not quit preaching that Jesus is the only way of salvation. Not only that, but these Bible-believers also call other religions "false gospels" and cults! They label as sin many activities that people take part in, and for some reason they seem more interested in the next world than in saving this one. These ideas fly in the face of the religious and moral tolerance, as well as the compromise, that will be central to the New World Order—and the friction is beginning to show. Nowhere is this friction more evident than in the emerging environmental movement, which has become a foundation stone in the "gospel of this earth."

Christian Beliefs Harm the Environment?

In 1989 *Time* magazine broke with its habit of naming a person of the year and instead opted for the "Planet of the Year." It was truly a milestone in the successful effort to bring environmental consciousness to the forefront of human activity. However, along with the message of environmental preservation came a direct attack upon the gospel of Christ. In that special report *Time* warned:

> The Judeo-Christian tradition introduced a radically different concept [than the Mother Earth concept of pagan societies]. The earth was the creation of a monotheistic God, who, after shaping it, ordered its inhabitants, in the words of Genesis [to subdue the earth and have dominion over it]. . . . The idea of dominion could be interpreted as an invitation to use nature as a convenience. Thus, the spread of Christianity, which is generally considered to have paved the way for the development of technology, may at the same time have carried the seeds of the wanton exploitation of nature that often accompanied technological progress.[1]

This lead by *Time* magazine was quickly picked up by other media leaders. The Southam News organization, which owns and operates newspapers throughout Canada, recently published a special 24-page insert which was included with all their newspapers. Called "Planet in Peril," this special was also distributed as a study aid in many public schools. One of the articles in that insert, entitled "Philosophy of Destruction," declared:

> More to the point, what would a Creator think of the contention that religions set up to serve Him have soiled the planet in His name?
> That's what some theologians and philosophers contend: That blame for the ravaging of earth can be

> squarely placed on the Judeo-Christian religious be-
> lief that nature exists to serve humans and support
> civilization.
>
> "At the moment, the most dangerous thing we
> possess as human beings is the exploitive idea of
> nature—and it is engendered by many religions," says
> Digby McLaren, president of the Royal Society, an
> association of Canada's most distinguished scientists.
> Put simply, he says, many religious beliefs are extremely
> dangerous to human survival. God's admonition to
> Abraham in Genesis to be fruitful and multiply—using
> the earth and its plants and animals—was the begin-
> ning of exploitation and dominance by humans over
> creation and is the basis of Christianity, Judaism and
> Islam, says McLaren. . . .
>
> But increasingly, there is a new religious vision of
> the human place in nature, a new perspective of shar-
> ing and connectedness, of recognizing that survival
> depends upon living in harmony with the rich web of
> other life forms on the planet.[2]

These direct attacks upon the Christian faith, which are
openly portrayed as dangerous to human survival, are seen in
stark contrast to the earth-loving religious beliefs so prevalent in
the Eastern religions and the New Age.

However, the environmental movement is not the only forum
being used for seemingly appealing arguments against the Christian faith.

World Peace and Unity of Belief

The ideas of Mortimer J. Adler, one of the leading thinkers of
our time, are representative of another compelling argument
being raised against the "divisiveness" of the gospel. He writes:

> World peace is impossible without world govern-
> ment. World government is impossible to establish and

prosper without world community. And world community requires a certain degree of cultural unity, a condition that certainly does not exist at present.[3]

Simply stated, Adler's entire philosophy contends that we will not be able to attain world peace until we forge a worldwide cultural unity based on nondogmatic principles. However, Adler quickly discloses the obstacle that stands in the way of the attainment of such a Utopian goal:

> We have no problem at all if religion does not claim to involve knowledge and it is not concerned with what is true and what is false. If, however, it claims to involve knowledge . . . [and it claims that] it alone has its source in divine revelation, accepted by an act of faith that is in itself divinely caused [and if] . . . religion claims to be supernatural knowledge—knowledge that man has only as a gift from God . . . then we are confronted with a special problem. . . .[4]

Here is a brilliant man, certainly one of the greatest minds of this century, arguing that any religious content in the New World Order will have to be hollow, shallow, and without content. The religion that he calls for will not claim to involve any knowledge and certainly will not presume to determine what is true and what is false. Furthermore, his direct reference to any religions which are "accepted by an act of faith" is a clear indication that Adler is referring to Christianity. Thus world peace cannot be achieved until Christianity itself is eliminated. Like Gene Roddenberry, he concludes that the Christian message of salvation being available only through Jesus Christ is—

> . . . as deplorable as nationalism, for both are irremediably divisive of mankind and present obstacles to world community and, therefore, to world government and world peace. A great epoch in the history of

> mankind lies ahead of us. It will not begin until there is
> universal acknowledgment of the unity of truth ... for
> only then will all men be able to live together peace-
> fully in a world community under world government.
> Only then will world civilization and world history
> begin.[5]

Far from being the rantings of a devoted God-hater, these are
the conclusions of a man who trains up-and-coming world leaders
at the Aspen Institute and who helped edit the *Encyclopaedia
Britannica*. Yet with the future of the entire human race at stake,
these arguments seem completely logical to the minds of men
who have no way of knowing that one soul is worth more than the
entire world. For this reason, efforts to minimize the role of
Christianity in the world, and to even outlaw it, have taken on
very real dimensions. A perfect example of this is the Genocide
Convention.

The Genocide Convention

Using Hitler's atrocities as a backdrop, globalist groups have
long sought after the worldwide implementation of the Genocide
Convention since its approval by the United Nations General
Assembly on December 9, 1948. Of course, the term "genocide"
implies the idea of war crimes and mass murder, so it seems that a
Genocide Convention would be a logical vehicle to put interna-
tional madmen like Saddam Hussein or Adolf Hitler on trial.
Article II of the Treaty states in part:

> Genocide, whether committed in a time of peace or
> war, is a crime under international law which the
> Contracting Parties undertake to prevent and pun-
> ish.... [It includes] any of the following acts com-
> mitted ... with the intent to destroy, in whole or in
> part, a national, ethnical, racial, or religious group
> [by] ... causing serious bodily or mental harm to a
> member of the group....[6]

However, for four decades U.S. Senate conservatives refused to ratify the Convention, warning of its potential infringement on American sovereignty. One of the legitimate concerns that underlay the American resistance was the belief that emotional fears of another holocaust were being exploited to cloak an effort to make the World Court the "Supreme Court of the World" in all matters related to this convention. That concern was compounded by the fact that under the terms of this treaty it would not just be *nations and their leaders* who would be answerable to the World Court. Instead, the treaty would place *every citizen* under the direct jurisdiction of the World Court as well. It was no wonder that American legislators balked at this power-grabbing pact. This would represent an unheard-of transfer of sovereignty. It was also why they were amazed to see Ronald Reagan sign the treaty in 1988.

The greatest danger of the Genocide Convention is the definition of genocide that it presents. The language within the treaty makes it completely possible to define an act of genocide as one person causing "mental harm" to a person of a different religious persuasion, since that person is "a member" of the other group. Countless experts have concluded that this is well within the wording of the treaty. Furthermore, they agree that "mental harm" could mean little more than offending their religious sensibilities. Thus a Christian missionary from America who witnessed to a Muslim in Malaysia could be charged with genocide because he hurt the Muslim's feelings![7] That missionary could then be tried by the World Court without the protection of the U.S. Bill of Rights.

And this is not restricted to the foreign mission field. A citizen of the United States who hurts the feelings of any identifiable group could be charged with committing genocide against that group—not just in Malaysia but in Cincinnati or Denver as well. But it doesn't end there. Article IV of the treaty provides that "private individuals" who are accused of any of the acts outlined above, including such vaguely defined areas as "conspiracy" or "complicity" to commit genocide, can also be prosecuted as criminals under international law. Thus church groups, missionary organizations, and Bible publishers could easily be dragged into the fray as well.

When we recall that Christianity is being seen as the stick in the spokes of the New World Order, it is not difficult to see where such laws could take us in the days ahead. Christian proselytization will undoubtedly be looked upon by those opposed to the faith as an "intent to destroy a culture" or as "causing mental anguish" to another identifiable group. In the New World Order, where all religious beliefs are considered to be equal expressions of the same truth, and where unity is the rule of the day, such divisive activities will simply not be tolerated.

Of course, we would like to think that this will never happen here. We would like to believe that Constitutional guarantees would override such a transfer of power. Unfortunately, the contrary legal opinions are compelling. They indicate that on numerous occasions the U.S. Supreme Court has held that treaty law overrides domestic law. As former Secretary of State John Foster Dulles noted:

> Under our Constitution, treaties become the supreme law of the land. They are indeed more supreme than ordinary laws, for Congressional laws are invalid if they do not conform to the Constitution, whereas treaty laws can override the Constitution. Treaties . . . can cut right across the rights given the people by the Constitutional Bill of Rights.

Without our even realizing it, the Genocide Treaty may well already be the supreme law of the land. All that lags behind now is the public acceptance of such stern measures to ensure the tranquility of the New World Order. Paving the way for such international measures of the future are national measures being adopted to deal with "hate crimes" today.

Hate Crimes and the New World Order

Like the word "genocide," the phrase "hate crime" is loaded with all kinds of implied meaning. Hate crimes bring to mind thoughts of gas chambers, Nazi swastikas, skinheads, and countless other things which are truly abhorrent to the civilized world. However, mounting evidence indicates, almost beyond a shadow of a doubt, that the true target of hate laws in the days ahead will be those people who hold up a moral and spiritual standard to the world. Already a number of countries, such as Canada, Sweden, West Germany, Britain, Israel, and the United States have enacted hate-crimes legislation. And in many of these countries, the hate-crimes laws are already being pointed menacingly at Christians.

In Canada, for example, the nation was protected for years by adequate libel and slander laws. Furthermore, the nation's Criminal Code, under Section 281(2) (2), ensured that "anyone communicating statements willfully promoting hatred against any identifiable group" would be charged and prosecuted.

However, a few years ago Canadian lawmakers decided to bring two test cases to public attention, demonstrating that Canada was in need of stronger hate-crime laws. These two test cases involved James Keegstra and Ernst Zundel. Keegstra, a high school teacher in the province of Alberta, was teaching his students that there is a drive toward a world government, world economy, and world religion. On this point he was right. However, Mr. Keegstra claimed that this was all part of some Jewish conspiracy. On this point he was wrong. The drive toward a New World Order consists of people of all national and religious backgrounds. Nonetheless, as a result of his claims he was charged and prosecuted under Canadian Criminal Code for "willfully promoting hatred" against the people of Hebrew descent.

Another case which took place around the same time was that involving Ernst Zundel. Mr. Zundel was charged and convicted under Section 177 of the Criminal Code for "willfully spreading news that he knows is false." In his book *Did Six Million Really Die?* Zundel questioned the number of deaths which occurred during the World War II holocaust.

The point is not that these men were correct in their opinions. They certainly were not. The point is that they were sharing these views with no more than a handful of people, and that the current laws in effect were more than adequate to deal with these charges. But by the time the media had finished its blow-by-blow coverage, a whole nation was made fully aware of these trials. Through what certainly appears to have been a carefully contrived blitz, Canadians were suddenly demanding stronger hate-crimes laws to deal with such hate-mongers. And they got what they asked for. Canada Customs began a crackdown on newly defined hate literature being imported into the country. Under a new ruling (Memorandum D9-1-1) the following goods were now deemed as hate literature:

1) Goods that blame an identifiable group for serious economic or social problems.

2) Goods alleging that an identifiable group is manipulating media, trade or finance, government or world politics to the detriment of society as a whole.

This was a quantum leap beyond libel and slander protection. It was also a quantum leap beyond protecting visible minorities from persecution. Suddenly any claims that any group, whether political or financial, is manipulating events is considered to be hate literature. The future implications of these laws, now that the precedents have been set, is that any publication or book claiming that there is a secretive push for a New World Order could be outlawed.

Confirming the seriousness of the change was the fact that former Ontario Liberal Member of Parliament David Smith was forced to resign from his post at about the same time because, while he found the views of Keegstra to be "repugnant," he did agree that he may have been right about the role played by the Trilateral Commission and The Council on Foreign Relations in a drive toward a New World Order. The critical point in all of this is that Smith never said a word about Keegstra's beliefs about a "Jewish Conspiracy," and in fact he said that those views were repugnant. He only said that Keegstra may have been right about the Trilateral Commission and the Council on Foreign Relations—two organizations of international bankers, financiers, and politicians who openly admit that they are promoting a world government.

Even U.S. Senator and onetime Presidential contender Barry Goldwater proclaimed that these groups do indeed fit the description of someone "manipulating media, trade or finance, government or world politics to the detriment of society as a whole." Here is what Goldwater said:

> Whereas the Council on Foreign Relations is distinctly national in membership, the Trilateral Commission is international. It is intended to be the vehicle for multinational consolidation of the commercial and banking interest by seizing control of the political government of the United States. . . . The Trilateral Commission represents a skillful, coordinated effort to seize control and consolidate the four centers of power—political, monetary, intellectual and ecclesiastical. . . . As managers and creators of the system they will control the future.[8]

Clearly, no one can question the fact that Goldwater blamed an identifiable group for the defined manipulations. Will books by respected political leaders such as Barry Goldwater, Jesse Helms, and others who question the drive toward this New World Order be banned from Canada? Although it may yet be a way down the road, there is no question that the legal precedent has been put in place. However, that is only the beginning. The cause of such hatred, we now often hear in Canada, is rooted firmly in the Bible. *Toronto Star* religious writer Tom Harper reflects a growing conviction in this northern country:

The Bible is a wonderful book. But in the hands of the naive or the willfully ignorant it has led to incalculable evil in the past and continues to do so today. . . .

The sad truth is that ultra-orthodox Christianity with its absolutist views of Jesus—i.e.: its claim that Jesus Christ is God—very easily slips over into a theology of hostility against all who disagree.

Thus, it holds all who fail to believe as it believes, be they Hindu, Moslem, Buddhist, Agnostic or whatever, are eternally damned.[9]

Likewise, an editorial in another Canadian paper called for "amendments to the Bible on the basis of its unconstitutional content." It advised:

Ridding ourselves of bigotry through education is redundant unless we first dispense with the cause of bigotry, mainly the so-called Holy Bible. . . . We need only to be reminded of the Hitler era, in which the butchers of six million all wore crosses and had Bibles in their pockets, to realize the dangerous connection between the Bible and lunacy. Our government is left with no choice but to tackle the inevitable task set before it, thus assuring peace and tranquility for all Canadians and perhaps the world.[10]

Lest it be thought that such ideas were restricted to the media, the following comments of Canada's first openly homosexual Member of Parliament are also indicative. Svend Robinson stood in the Canadian Parliament and began his campaign to have the Bible banned from the nation. Indeed, as we shall see, homosexual rights groups, desperate to throw off the shackles of sin, are at the forefront of hate legislation worldwide.

There are other forms of violence to which gay people are subjected. The violence of certain extreme elements of the evangelical community like the Jimmy Swaggarts of the TV world incites people to violence under the guise of Christian philosophy. When people say things like Jimmy Swaggart did in his publication, "The Evangelist," we know that there are problems. After quoting from the Old Testament, he said "In Old Testament days the practicing homosexual was stoned to death." He went on to quote from Romans and then said, "God is saying here that not only is the homosexual worthy of death, but [perhaps] also those who approve of homosexuality."

That kind of hate literature has no place in Canada today.[11]

Of course, a reading of Swaggart's article showed that the evangelist in no way endorsed the present-day killing of homosexuals. He was merely stating that homosexuality was sin and was punishable by death in Old Testament times. Today eternal death still awaits the unrepentant sinner of any type, including the homosexual. However, in light of the fact that Mr. Robinson so vehemently opposes what the Word of God says, it is clear that Jimmy Swaggart is not the ultimate target of pro-homosexual legislators—the Bible is!

The Hate-Crimes Statistics Act

The United States has also set the wheels in motion to banish *hate* and *prejudice* from American soil. Holding up the Aryan Nations, the Klan, and the Skinheads as examples of what society should outlaw, the media began paving the way for public acceptance of hate-crimes legislation several years ago. The outcome was the April 23, 1990, signing into law of the "Hate Crimes Statistics Act" by U.S. President George Bush.

Despite the fact that the law will require the FBI to track and record *all* acts of hate against *all* minorities, by inviting only *homosexual* groups to witness the signing of the bill, President

Bush showed that *they* were the group that the act was specifically designed to protect. Not one member of any other minority group was invited to the signing. By this action George Bush has earned the notorious distinction of becoming the first U.S. President ever to officially sanction homosexuals with an official White House invitation. Among the homosexual groups invited to the White House were representatives from the Human Rights Campaign Fund and the National Gay and Lesbian Task Force (NGLTF). According to *Christian World Report*, July 1990, Robert Bray of the NGLTF said homosexuals were "stunned" that they had been invited to the White House. "We think," said Bray, "the president sent a very clear message to bigots and bashers that he will not tolerate violence against gays and Lesbians."

Once again, it does not take a great stretch of the imagination to discern that Christians who preach that homosexuality is a sin will be the target of such complaints. Indeed, what few Americans know is that under the hate-literature laws of Sweden, an evangelical pastor was given a four-week sentence in jail for violating Sweden's "Anti-Hate" statute, a law which protects homosexuals and other minorities from "verbal violence." The pastor had simply preached from the Bible the account of God's judgment on Sodom and Gomorrah. He had told his congregation, which included homosexuals, that God is still angry at sexual perversion and will judge those who practice it.

Could evangelicals at home soon face the same possibility of a jail sentence for preaching God's Word? Indeed, the pattern clearly shows that the Hate Crimes Statistics Act will definitely be used to silence evangelicals who are opposed to the homosexual lifestyle in the days ahead. As we have said, despite the fact that the Act was ostensibly written to combat crimes based on "race, religion, ethnicity, or sexual orientation," homosexuals were the only group to witness its signing. This is of great significance in light of the fact that one year prior to the implementation of the Act, two government reports identified homosexuals as the victims of undue repression and mental anguish. And who were the victimizers identified in these reports? You guessed it—fundamentalist Christians.

Part of the report released by the Health and Human Services (HHS) federal task force on the issue of youth suicide blames society, Catholics, Southern Baptists, and evangelicals for the high suicide rate among homosexual teenagers. Although distribution and further printings have been halted, the report has been quoted from extensively since being distributed on Capitol Hill. The report, which was created by San Francisco therapist Paul Gibson, charges that Southern Baptist, Catholic, and other "fundamentalist" or "traditional" churches place undue pressure on homosexual teenagers to renounce their sexuality as immoral. According to the report's author:

> Gay youths may feel wicked and condemned to hell and attempt suicide in despair of ever obtaining redemption.[12]

The report also blames "fundamentalism" for the high suicide rate among homosexual, Lesbian, and transsexual youth. This, the report concludes, is because of their "negative self-image" which is engendered by the traditional religions.

The second report which is of significance was released in 1989 by the National Research Council (NRC), entitled "AIDS, Sexual Behavior and Intravenous Drug Use." This book-length report identified the Christian perspective of homosexuality as a "deep-rooted social pathology" and further blamed Christians for "stigmatizing" homosexuals and thus contributing to the spread of AIDS! The NRC report threatened that a more "enlightened" view of homosexuality should be preached in the nation's churches, or "those churches should face denial of tax exemptions."

Clearly, alternative religions will not be the only thing everyone is required to tolerate and condone in the New World Order. Alternative lifestyles and different "sexual orientations" will have to be admitted as normal and healthy as well. The only sin in the New World Order will be calling sin sin!

Helping to Enlighten the Masses

Of course, the public is not always aware of the contents of government reports. In its efforts to make the public more aware of the persecution which the homosexual community experiences from the hands of fundamentalist Christians, the media is doing its part. A notable example of this was the episode of "48 Hours" which was broadcast on CBS on June 14, 1990. The program, hosted by Dan Rather, devoted a major segment of its airtime to examining the problem of Christian churches who try to convert homosexuals and Lesbians from their "sinful" lifestyle. The segment began with a personal look at the homosexuals so that the viewer could empathize with their likableness and "normalcy." Then clips were shown of Christians brandishing their Bibles and praying over the homosexuals, exhorting them to repent. Those homosexuals who never turned their backs on the homosexual lifestyle tell how their involvement with the fundamentalists terrorized them, leading them to a brink of despair and causing them to hate themselves and even to consider suicide.

Now if these comments and the comments of the two aforementioned government-sponsored reports do not constitute hate literature, nothing does. However, as is becoming increasingly clear, the only group who seems to be exempt from the protection of hate-crimes legislation and human-rights regulations are Bible-believing Christians. In Pat Buchanan's article entitled "It's Hollywood vs. Christians," he noted how certain blasphemous scenes in *The Last Temptation of Christ* were without foundation in the Bible. He then wondered if the President of the Motion Picture Association, Jack Valenti, who defended the film, would defend a film depicting Martin Luther King as a relentless womanizer, or one portraying Anne Frank as an "oversexed teenager fantasizing at Auschwitz or romancing some SS guards." He answers for him:

> Of course not. We live in an age where the ridicule of Blacks is forbidden, where anti-Semitism is punishable by political death, but where Christian-bashing is

> a popular indoor sport and films mocking Jesus Christ are considered avant-garde. . . . With *The Last Temptation of Christ* Hollywood is assaulting the Christian community in a way it would never dare assault the Black community, the Jewish community or the gay community. And the reason Universal Pictures and Mr. [Martin] Scorsese are doing this is because they know they can get away with it.[13]

In the famous Lichter-Rothman survey in 1980, the researchers documented the slant of today's media. The survey showed that only 5 percent of television's elite felt that homosexuality was wrong, and 93 percent seldom or never attended worship services of any kind. This leftward slant of the mass media, which is far more liberal than the American public, is very dangerous because of the media's power to influence public opinion. Television or movie stars have access to the minds of the nation that is unparalleled in human history. This makes Hollywood's anti-Christian bias one of the most powerful influences in the nation.

Corbin Bernsen, one of the stars of TV's "LA Law" series, is a perfect example of the antireligious bigotry which has come not only to dominate Hollywood and the networks but is now even considered as "ultra-chic" in liberal media circles.

Bernsen recently told the *Washington Post* of his goals:

> Religion is real dangerous. We have to depopularize organized religion and fight for more spirituality. Religion has become an outdated mode, an outdated answer to our problems. Religion is the only reason women don't have control over their own bodies.[14]

Naturally, the philosophy of the entertainment industry's creators is portrayed in their creations. As a result, Christians are shown to be charlatans, idiots, hypocrites, and intolerant bigots. Preachers are often portrayed as adulterous, and are even shown from time to time to run houses of ill repute. Examples of the ways in which Christians are portrayed in a bad light could in themselves constitute a book. Every day anti-Christian slurs and jokes are woven in and out of program after program. One representative example occurred on NBC's weekly program "Heat of the Night." In this particular episode, a preacher from "The Church of the Chosen Few" was fighting with the police to have a bordello shut down because it was a disgrace to the community. Of course, the bordello operator was portrayed as a real nice lady who was just trying to earn a living. Later the preacher was shown peeping through the window, watching what was happening inside.

That same evening a prostitute was murdered, and because he had been seen in the area, the preacher was brought up on murder charges. During the investigation, neighbors of the church groups said the congregation was rude because they made a lot of noise in their services, which often carried on late into the evening. It turned out that it was a crazed congregational member who actually did the killing.

In early 1990 the American Family Association compiled a list that showed how Christians were depicted in prime-time TV shows which aired in 1989. The survey found 29 examples of blatant anti-Christian stereotyping, with just one single positive portrayal. Recent statistics confirm the troubling effect of these portrayals. Indeed, it seems that the secular media succeeded in linking dangerous "cult" types with fundamental Christians in the minds of the American public. A 1989 Gallup Poll suggests that religious cults take the lead in persons that the American public would not like to have as a neighbor. Fundamentalists followed close behind. Of about 1000 adults who were surveyed, 62 percent said they would not want cult members as neighbors, and 30 percent said they wouldn't want religious fundamentalists as neighbors.

The National Endowment for the Arts

The outright war against Christ and Christians has also seeped into the arts. An uproar arose in the Christian community when it learned of a so-called art piece by Andres Serrano. What Mr. Serrano calls art is a vivid photograph of Christ hanging on the cross, submerged in a jar of the "artist's" bodily fluids. In an indication of how far official policy is moving, the display was part of a tax-supported exhibition which received funding from the National Endowment for the Arts. And, the "artist" was awarded a $15,000 prize.[15]

Mr. Serrano has apparently started a new trend of so-called art. David Wojnarowicz created a collage which he calls "Tongues of Flame." The collage portrays Christ as a drug addict in the process of injecting drugs into his arm via a syringe. Once again, the NEA supported Wojnarowicz's work through a tax-supported grant. In yet another obscene portrayal involving body fluids, John Fleck was awarded $5,000 in tax funds by the NEA. Furthermore, the NEA gave a $20,000 grant to the Artpark in Lewiston, New York for a performance which was to take place September 1, 1990. The Artpark, however, cancelled the performance which was created by a group called "Survival Research Laboratories" (SRL). The SRL play is entitled "Bible Burn!" Promotional posters instruct people to steal Bibles for burning:

> Bibles can always be obtained for free from hotels, churches . . . and your parents' houses. Be advised that in certain instances theft is a moral obligation. . . .
>
> SRL will create large sexually-explicit props covered with a generous layer of requisitional Bibles. After employing these props in a wide variety of unholy rituals, SRL machines will burn them to ashes.[16]

After Artpark President David P. Midland cancelled the event, SRL arts director Mark Pauline complained he had caved in to pressure from "right-wing zealots."

The Separation of Church and State

Another source of the open warfare on Bible-believing Christianity is coming under the guise of attempts to enforce the

Constitutional call for the separation of church and state. However, according to U.S. Senator Bill Armstrong, what we are now witnessing is the "twisting of freedom of religion into isolation from religion."[17] Truly, the Senator argues, rooting out all spiritual influence from American public affairs "is becoming fashionable policy" in Washington:

> The scope of this mind-boggling trend isn't confined to churches and religious institutions. A judicial, legislative and administrative net has been cast far and wide to rope in all spiritual influence and authority. Government is trying to purge religion from community groups, humanitarian organizations and colleges as well.

The examples of the degree to which this purge of Christianity is taking place are as dramatic as they are frightening. The duplicity and hypocrisy that underly this warfare are revealed in two news reports that appeared during roughly the same time period:

> NORTH VERNON, Ohio—A witches' supper for children will be held at North Vernon Elementary from 6 to 8 tonight. The supper is sponsored by Psi Iota Xi Philanthropic Sorority, with proceeds going to Jennings County charities. Cost is $1.50, which includes a hot dog dinner, games, fortune telling, a talk with a witch, a coloring contest and costume parade. . . . The evening is designed for pre-school to third grade children.[18]

> Concerned Women for America have filed suit in Terre Haute, Ind. seeking an injunction to compel a local school district to rent its facilities to a Christian concert promoter, and to make it suspend enforcement of a policy prohibiting use of school facilities by individuals or groups engaged in "religious instruction."[19]

The public schools are not the only place where the battle to exclude Christianity is taking place. In 1989 the California Fair Employment and Housing Commission ruled against Evelyn Smith, a widow who refused on biblical grounds to rent her apartment to an unmarried couple. The case began when the couple, posing as husband and wife, placed a deposit on one of Mrs. Smith's duplexes. When it was revealed that the couple was not married, Mrs. Smith returned their deposit, saying she could not condone fornication because the Bible condemns it. The California Commission, however, ruled that Mrs. Smith was guilty of illegal discrimination based on marital status and fined her 954 dollars. They also forced her to place a sign on her rental properties, confessing her offense and pledging never to do it again! This is absolutely ridiculous, almost bringing to mind the days of the stock and pillary. Today, however, the criminal who is publicly humiliated is not one who committed a heinous crime, but one who upheld the simple principles of morality. The duplicity is once again all too evident. In writing about the case, syndicated columnist Patrick Buchanan noted:

> Legally, Grandmother Smith's case is compelling. First, the couple deceived her; second, she is only practicing a moral code that California itself has formally endorsed: All 19 state colleges forbid the campus cohabitation of unwed couples.[20]

In a society which claims to be promoting "mutual respect," it appears through dozens of cases like Mrs. Smith's that the United States is actually on the verge of criminalizing Christianity. Towns which have a cross on their water towers are having to remove them, parks which have a Christmas nativity scene can no longer display them, and a Christian ministry which found they actually had a witch working for them was fined for firing her.

A lady in Hallandale, Florida, believes she may end up in court defending her right to leave her "God Bless This Home" sign on her front door. The head of the condominium association is arguing that she "is not supposed to put anything strange on her door."[21] Have we come so far that a "God Bless This Home" sign is strange?

In Colorado, the Freedom from Religion Foundation is suing the state because of a monument of the Ten Commandments that appears on the Capitol grounds.[22] In other states the same organization pleads for a "warning label" to be put on any Bibles that are placed in state-owned hotels.[23] And recently the Salvation Army was denied a grant because a painting of Jesus hangs on their wall.[24]

All over the nation, Christianity is coming under attack. Bible classes and Bible clubs have become the target for groups like the American Civil Liberties Union and the Anti-Defamation League. Christian books have been banned from school libraries across the nation. Fifth-grade teacher Ken Roberts was forced by principal Kathleen Madigan to remove *The Story of Jesus* and *The Bible in Pictures* from his 200-volume classroom library. A federal court of appeals banned the Christian books. However, the court allowed books on native American religion and Buddhism to remain in the library. The court accepted ADL and ACLU arguments that the books on Native American religion and Buddhism do not constitute "religious tracts" like the Christian books. As syndicated Washington columnist John Lofton recently penned:

> The war against God in this country, specifically against Jesus Christ, is getting uglier, much uglier, and much more explicit. And make no mistake about it, please. This war is against Christ.[25]

Set Up for Holocaust

As we have documented earlier in this book, globalists who envision a New World Order believe that there must be a central unifying belief to bring all the peoples of the world together. One of the unifying factors often mentioned is that of an emerging acceptance of Eastern mysticism and paranormal experiences.

As we can see, however, another common denominator is beginning to emerge throughout the world: a common hatred and ridicule for the body of Christ. At its root this attack is not primarily because of Christianity's divisive claim that other religions cannot lead to salvation, or its determination to call sin by its rightful name, or its conviction that the salvation of individual souls is of greater importance than some loosely defined age of tolerance and understanding. This attack is coming primarily because the spirit that dwells in the unsaved is at war with the spirit of the person who is born again. All of these other issues are merely symptoms of man's rebellion against God and His plan. As Jesus promised to the true believer:

> If the world hate you, ye know that it hated me before it hated you. If ye were of the world, the world would love its own; but because ye are not of the world, but I have chosen you out of the world, therefore the world hateth you (John 15:18,19).

The Holocaust Museum

Everyone who has ever visited the Holocaust Museum in Jerusalem leaves there a different person from the one who walked in. That is because this museum focuses on the greatest atrocity in human history. Everyone asks the same question: How could it possibly have happened? As we visited this shrine to human cruelty I was particularly mesmerized by the faded newspaper clippings and the crude sketches which ridiculed Jews in pre-World-War-II Germany. I remembered long conversations with author Tal Brooke about how this museum held deadly clues for the future of our own generation. I read every clipping, I looked at every cartoon, and I reflected on how central this media portrayal of the Jews was to their soon-coming persecution. Most devastating was the realization that this anti-Semitic propaganda paled in comparison to the anti-Christian blitz that surrounds us today. In those days the only weapons were newspapers and posters, but today cable television, movie theaters, and home VCR's spread a far more sophisticated message of hate than was ever dreamed possible in Germany. One recent study noted the parallels:

> The attacks... on the leaders and organizations of orthodox Christianity parallel the Brown Shirts, pointed attacks upon the Jewish community in Germany during the '30's. Left unchecked, the momentum created by that hatred, presented as love of country, resulted in the death of millions of Jews, Christians, and others....[26]

By combining the deadly stream of propaganda that we see today with a message that is presented as "love of the world," we can quickly see how it could all happen again. Christians, the world is being told through every possible outlet, are the only hindrance standing in the way of global peace.

> Religious fundamentalists are convinced that we are living in the end times and that this era will end in a nuclear holocaust. The fundamentalists believe those who are born again will be removed by God to meet Jesus in the air through what they call the rapture before the great tribulation that will destroy the earth. ...There is a force in history that unites Humanity, but the fundamentalists do not share this vision.[27]

Recently Robert Runcie, the former Archbishop of Canterbury, hosted an ecumenical event where he gathered political and religious leaders from every spectrum and belief system to a forum on "global survival." The event included Buddhists, Shamans from South American rain forests, Muslims, and many others. The worldwide head of the Anglican Church then proceeded to tell those gathered that a new ecumenical movement, which recognized "the same spirit at the center of all faiths," was needed to help further the goal of world peace. The only persons who need be excluded, he continued, were those fatalists who believe that the crises the world faces are signs of the return of Christ.

> . . . nor can we accept the despair of those who interpret the various crises we face today in the political, economic and ecological areas of life as harbingers of the end of the world. The fatalism inherent in such a philosophy has no part in authentic religious awareness.[28]

Here in a nutshell we have the philosophical underpinnings of the New World Order. Two religious hindrances to the New World Order are spelled out. They are those who believe that there is only one true God and those who believe that the current events in the world are actually fulfillments of Bible prophecy and therefore foreshadow the return of Christ and the end of the world.

Section III

On the Prophetic Agenda

Chapter 14

The Sleeping Bear

In the last days, the prophets told us, Israel will be regathered into her homeland. We have already seen how that has come to pass. They also foresaw that a Revived Roman Empire would arise from a foundation in Western Europe. We have also seen how *that* has come about. However, they also saw that in this same time period another power would arise in the North and eventually invade the land of Israel. There is no question that the Soviet Union is the fulfillment of that prophecy. We know that for a number of reasons. The first of these is the fact that the Soviet Union is located to the uttermost north of Israel. This is precisely where the prophets told us this last-days invader would come from:

> Thou shalt come from thy place out of the north parts, thou and many people with thee.... And I will... cause thee to come up from the north parts, and will bring thee upon the mountains of Israel (Ezekiel 38:15; 39:2).

The full meaning of the Hebrew word here translated "north" is "uttermost north." Unquestionably, all of Russia is to the uttermost north of Israel. This geographical description alone clearly points to the fact that Russia is the fulfillment of this last-days power from the north. But students of the history of cultures and nations also point out that the names used by Ezekiel in speaking of this northern power refer specifically not only to Russia but to Moscow, her capital, as well.

The Soviets Will Invade Israel

The next thing of which we are certain is that at some point before the second coming of Jesus at the end of the tribulation period, the Soviet Union will invade the land of Israel. The prophet Ezekiel spells this out in convincing detail:

> Thus saith the Lord God: Behold, I am against thee, O Gog, the chief prince of Meshech and Tubal; and I will turn thee back, and put hooks into thy jaws, and I will bring thee forth, and all thine army, horses, and horsemen, all of them clothed with all sorts of armor, even a great company with bucklers and shields, all of them handling swords. . . . Be thou prepared, and prepare for thyself, thou and all thy company that are assembled unto thee, and be thou a guard unto them. After many days thou shalt be visited: In the latter years thou shalt come into the land that is brought back from the sword, and is gathered out of many people, against the mountains of Israel, which have always been waste; but it is brought forth out of the nations, and all of them shall dwell safely. Thou shalt ascend and come like a storm; thou shalt be like a cloud to cover the land, thou and all thy bands, and many people with thee. . . .
>
> Therefore, son of man, prophesy and say unto Gog, Thus saith the Lord God: In that day when my people of Israel dwelleth safely, shalt thou not know it? And thou shalt come from thy place out of the north parts, thou and many people with thee, all of them riding upon horses, a great company and a mighty army; and

> thou shalt come up against my people of Israel, as a cloud to cover the land; it shall be in the latter days, and I will bring thee against my land, that the heathen may know me when I shall be sanctified in thee, O Gog, before their eyes (Ezekiel 38:3,4,7-9,14-16).

One of the great debates among students of Bible prophecy is centered around the question of when this invasion will take place. Some believe it will happen before the rapture, since the Bible tells us that after God miraculously destroys the Russian army on the mountains of Israel, the Israelis will burn the Soviet weapons for seven years (Ezekiel 39:9). These students contend that the weapon-burning must be completed before the second coming, which occurs seven years after the rapture, and therefore the invasion must be at some point before the rapture.

The problem with this view is that the prophet Ezekiel tells us that when the Russian armies are destroyed, the whole world, and Israel in particular, will recognize that it is the God of Abraham, Isaac, and Jacob that has intervened:

> So will I make my holy name known in the midst of my people Israel; and I will not let them pollute my holy name any more; and the heathen shall know that I am the Lord, the Holy One in Israel (Ezekiel 39:7).

It seems inconceivable that the whole world would recognize the true God before the rapture and then immediately be deceived into accepting the Antichrist who arises thereafter. In fact, God states very clearly that after this event "the house of Israel shall know that I am the Lord their God from that day forward" (Ezekiel 39:22). This means that this invasion must take place after the Jews have been deceived by the false Messiah, the Antichrist. Secondly, there is no reason to believe that the seven-year period of weapon-burning cannot go on into the millennium after the establishment of Christ's kingdom of peace. Isaiah 9:4,5 makes it clear that there will indeed be "burning" weapons which will be the "fuel of fire" during this time.

To look at another possibilty in the timing of this invasion, we need to begin by looking at the current status in the Soviet Union.

The Soviets Declare Peace

"The evil empire." That was a phrase that accurately reflected the reality of the Soviet experience for over 70 years. It was also a fact that divided East from West for a generation. But now, we are told, that is all over. Mikhail Gorbachev is remaking the Soviet Union, and amazingly, he is remaking it in our image. Democracy, human rights, and the freedom of religion, he claims, will be the basis of the "new" Soviet Union. Herein lies the problem. The dramatic changes seem more like a religious conversion than political reform. It's just a little too radical, a little too sudden, and a little too perfect. Is it possible that what we are witnessing is not an end to Communism but a change in tactics?

> Wearing well-cut suits, Gorbachev preaches a message of reasonableness that is calculated to appeal to Western ears. His policy of glasnost, or openness, could almost have been invented on Madison Avenue.[1]

However, mere suspicions are not all that we have to go on in seeking to discern the motives of this new type of Soviet leader. Mikhail Gorbachev himself has been very clear in what his objectives are:

> In October 1917 we parted with the old world, rejecting it once and for all. We are moving toward a new world, the world of communism. We shall never turn off that road![2]

> I am a Leninist, devoted to achieving the goals of Leninism and the worldwide Leninist association of all workers under the banner of Marxism.[3]

Choosing to embrace, and present to the people, a hopeful vision of the changes in the Soviet Union, the Western media seldom presents these types of comments from the lips of "Gorby." The strategy that he openly claims to be utilizing is cut from the front page to make room for the pictures of this hero shaking hands with the masses on a downtown street corner.

Gorbachev explains this stategy for those who wish to hear. "We are carrying forth a Marxism-Leninism freed from the layers of dogmatism, staleness and shortsighted considerations," he says, "we are returning to its roots and creatively developing it in order to move ahead."[4] How this change in tactics will be played out is described by Gorbachev in his book *Perestroika*:

> It would be appropriate to recall how Lenin fought for the Brest Peace Treaty in the troubled year 1918. The Civil War was raging, and at that moment came a most serious threat from Germany. So Lenin suggested signing a peace treaty with Germany.
>
> The terms of peace Germany peremptorily laid down for us were, in Lenin's words, "disgraceful, dirty." They meant Germany annexed a huge tract of territory with a population of fifty-six million. . . . Yet Lenin insisted on that peace treaty. Even some members of the Central Committee objected . . . workers too . . . demanding that the German invaders be rebuffed. Lenin kept calling for peace because he was guided by vital, not immediate, interests of the working class as a whole, of the Revolution, and of the future of Socialism . . . he was looking far ahead . . . he did not put what was transitory above what was essential. . . . Later, it was easy to say confidently and unambiguously that Lenin was right. . . . The Revolution was saved.[5]

Seen in this light, Soviet maneuvers to make huge concessions to the West, and at the same time receive great financial assistance, portray an entirely different picture of the current Soviet motives than the one that is being fed to the American Public.

Particular heed should be paid to a speech made by Dimitri Manaillsky at the Lenin School of Political Warfare in 1931:

> War between Capitalism and Communism is inevitable... in order to win we will need the element of surprise, but the Bourgeoisie will have to be put to sleep, so we shall begin by launching the most spectacular peace movement on record. There will be electrifying overtures and unheard of concessions... stupid and decadent [Capitalist countries], they will rejoice to cooperate in their own destruction.[6]

Of course, the best way to judge a former opponent is by disregarding his words and carefully studying his actions. Despite "all the hope and optimism," U.S. Defense Secretary Dick Cheney reminds the West that "the United States faces a more formidable offensive strategic arsenal than when Gorbachev came to power."[7] The figures usually tell the story. According to Washington's estimates, Soviet military spending, far from dropping, is still growing at a steady rate of about 3 percent per year. As the *New York Times* reports, "Although there have been indications of a slowdown in certain categories of weapons, the modernization of the four military services proceeds under perestroika at the same tempo as in the "era of stagnation."[8]

The Common European House

Does this mean that the Soviet Union plans a surprise attack on the United States? That doesn't seem likely. Instead, the type of thinking now coming out of Moscow seems to indicate that they believe they can win the world without their military. Their plan is not to *fight* the New World Order but to *join* it. Then all they will have to do is await the "irresistible dialectic of material forces"[9] which will lead the whole world into their waiting arms. This is why Mikhail Gorbachev speaks so passionately about a "Common European House," which would include the Soviets in the heart of the New World Order. As his admission ticket to this "common house" he is promising both democratic reform and religious freedom. Although the Soviets will probably lie outside of the New Europe, there is no doubt that they will be a central part of the New World Order. In the meantime, to achieve their never-renounced goal:

> Everything must be done in the name of man's dignity and human rights, and in the name of his autonomy and freedom from outside constraint. . . .
> Do that . . . and in essence you will have Marxized the West. The final step—the Marxization of the politics of life itself—will then follow. All classes will be one class. All minds will be proletarian minds. The earthly paradise will be achieved.[10]

One Sad Surprise After Another for the Materialists

However, along the way to this great secular world order, something unexpected is going to happen to the Soviets. Along with the rest of the world, the leaders of secularism are going to fall under the spell of the Antichrist. These staunch Marxist-Leninists, who ridicule anything above and beyond mankind, will fall down before this great false Christ and worship him as God! The book of Revelation is very specific in its statements that *all* of the world will worship the Antichrist, that *all* of the world will come under his political rule, and that *all* of the world will be controlled by his global economic system. Those who have for years persecuted and attacked the gospel of Jesus Christ will embrace the impostor with open arms.

This fits well with the Scriptures which tell us that when the Soviet Union does invade Israel no one will be expecting it. It will be a great surprise because all will have thought that the Soviet Union was just another member of the peace-loving community of nations, living happily under the rule of "Christ" Himself!

Rising Anti-Semitism

The question that arises is this: Why in the world would Russia invade the tiny country of Israel? There are many reasons, but none is so central as the vicious anti-Semitism that exists within the confines of Russia. With the lifting of the iron fist of Communism and some limited ability to speak freely, one of the first topics of conversation now flowing throughout the Soviet Union is how the Jews have been responsible for much of the repression that has been suffered. According to the former Moscow Bureau Chief for the *New York Times*:

> Right-wing Russian nationalists are obsessed, as their writings and conversations testify, with what they see as the excessive influence of Jews in Soviet society. Despite their denials, anti-Semitism lurks barely beneath the surface of the Russian Right.[11]

A recent poll conducted by two University of Houston political scientists found that this is exactly the case. They found that while 18 percent of the Russian population is fully anti-Semitic, close to 65 percent of the people accepted the reality of anti-Semitic stereotypes.[12] The conclusion that is being reached by many is that the citizens of this superpower, which now seems to be in a state of decay, are looking for someone to blame. Soviet Film Director Andrei Smirnov expresses this reality:

> I agree with Solzhenitsyn that without repentance, we cannot change ourselves or our society. We must feel responsibility for our history. Who was it who made Stalin's terror? It was we—our fathers—and we must now pay for our fathers. But this is repulsive to most people. They want to blame others. They accuse Jews or someone else. They do not want to accept responsibility.[13]

The fear here is that right-wing groups in the Soviet Union, looking for a way to unite a crumbling empire, may well leap on this lurking anti-Semitism and use it as a unifying factor to pull the people together in some new patriotism in the name of the "Motherland." Clearly, the furor that could be raised by such a propaganda campaign could find its ultimate fulfillment in the reuniting of the world's most powerful military machines for an attack on the "nest" of Semites in Israel.

Food Shortages

When Saddam Hussein invaded Kuwait in the summer of 1990 there was little doubt in anyone's mind that this invasion was little more than an international hijacking. His economy was in ruins from the eight-year war with Iran, oil prices were low, and he wanted to have greater control over the market price of crude. Once he was in Kuwait, he also literally took the country apart piece by piece and carried it back to Baghdad. The prophet Ezekiel tells us that when the Soviet Union invades Israel in the last days many will be taken completely by surprise. Just like they asked Iraq in 1990, they will ask the Soviet Union in that day:

> Art thou come to take a spoil? Hast thou gathered thy company to take a prey? To carry away silver and gold, to take away cattle and goods, to take a great spoil? (Ezekiel 38:13).

Certainly, if Iraq's economic shambles were a part of the invasion of Kuwait, there is little doubt that the Soviet Union's economic crisis is at least as bad. Today the Soviet shelves are empty and discontent is at an all-time high. As one article claims, the final indignity occurred when supplies of bread ran out:

> "Now the one thing we could always depend upon has suddenly disappeared," said Marina Simyonova, storming out of a bakery near the Ukraine Hotel.

> "This fills your soul with tension, with anger. Is this
> what all our great reforms are about? If this is per-
> estroika, I've had about enough."
>
> "This is getting so humilitating that I wouldn't be
> surprised to see rebellions and food riots one day
> soon," said Galina Sokol as she left the store with one
> green onion.[14]

The tensions are growing every day. The system is breaking
down. In fact, the Soviet Union actually produced bumper crops
in 1990. It was the lack of fuel, machinery, and parts that made it
impossible to harvest the grains that literally rotted in the fields.
The frustrated farmers have now gone so far as to threaten that
"unless the city people help in the vegetable fields, they will not
get a single gram of food."[15] In the face of all these problems, the
Soviet Union has only one strong card in its hand—one of the
most powerful military machines in human history. If reforms
fail and the people are starving, it is not hard to imagine a hard-
line government taking military action to get what they need
elsewhere.

Swindled by the Antichrist

We cannot be dogmatic about how or when this invasion will
come about. I personally believe that it will happen at about the
midpoint of the tribulation period. One possible scenario could
run like this.

The Soviets, beginning to sense that this "messiah" is not
really who he says he is, become angry that as good Marxist-
Leninists they were taken in by this fraud and his religious
sidekick. They will set out to show the world that this New World
Order doesn't need any of these silly religious trappings. They
will "devise an evil thought" and launch a great invasion on the
heart of the New World Order—the regathered children of Israel.
The attack will come as a complete surprise. Israel will see too
late that they have placed their faith in one who is not truly the

Messiah. But, alas, they have no weapons to defend themselves. As the Soviets and their hordes reach the mountains of Israel, they meet an unexpected defender of the children of Abraham, Isaac, and Jacob.

> It shall come to pass at the same time when Gog shall come up against the land of Israel, saith the Lord God, that my fury shall come up in my face. For in my jealousy and in the fire of my wrath have I spoken, Surely in that day there shall be a great shaking in the land of Israel.... And I will call for a sword against him throughout all my mountains, saith the Lord God; every man's sword shall be against his brother.... And I will turn thee back, and leave but the sixth part of thee.... Thou shalt fall upon the mountains of Israel (Ezekiel 38:18,19,21; 39:2,4).

As we have already seen, the prophet Ezekiel makes it clear that when God Himself destroys the Soviet armies on the mountains of Israel, the whole world, Jew and Gentile alike, will recognize that the God of Israel has done this.

Enraged at the worship of Israel toward the true God, the Antichrist rushes into the rebuilt temple and proclaims that *he* is God. The children of Israel completely reject him, and so he sets about to destroy them. However, somehow the "earth help[s]" the children of Israel and she is protected from the Antichrist's wrath. We know that the Antichrist goes into the temple to declare himself as God at the midpoint of the seven-year tribulation period (Daniel 9:27). Combining this with the fact that the Scriptures tell us that Israel will be protected from the Antichrist for exactly 3½ years (Revelation 12:6) gives us a good indication that this will all happen at the midpoint of the tribulation period.

The sham of the false millennium will quickly come to an end. Now God's judgment begins to fall on the world. The Antichrist shifts his energies from religious deception to military might, and he and his kings destroy the "whore." In a world gone insane from plagues, judgment, and chaos, men will become more and more rebellious:

> And the rest of the men which were not killed by these plagues repented not of the works of their hands, that they should not worship devils, and idols of gold and silver and brass and stone and of wood, which neither can see nor hear nor walk; neither repented they of their murders, nor of their sorceries, nor of their fornication, nor of their thefts. . . .
>
> And men were scorched with great heat, and blasphemed the name of God, which hath power over these plagues; and they repented not to give him glory. . . . And [they] blasphemed the God of heaven because of their pains and their sores, and repented not of their deeds (Revelation 9:20,21; 16:9,11).

Finally they will join together in a great unity to complete the job that the Soviets failed to accomplish. However, this time, instead of meeting God the Father, they will meet God the Son!

Chapter 15

Testing the Mark of the Beast

The mark of the Beast. It is probably the best-known prophecy in all of the Bible. Virtually everyone, at one time or another, has heard of this prophecy which tells that in the last days no one will be able to buy or sell anything unless they get the "devil's mark." This widely held perception is very accurate. In the book of Revelation the apostle John tells us that under the reign of the Antichrist "no man might buy or sell except he that [has] the mark, or the name of the beast, or the number of his name" (Revelation 13:17). This mark, John tells us, will be universal. The false prophet will cause "all, both small and great, rich and poor, free and bond, to receive a mark in their right hand or in their foreheads" (Revelation 13:16).

This well-known prophecy is important for a number of reasons. First, it is a very clear prediction. There is very little room for interpretation. Either it happens or it does not; there are no gray areas. Therefore, as we see trends and technologies leading us toward its fulfillment, we have one of the most powerful proofs possible for the accuracy of the prophetic Word of God.

Unfortunately, it seems that this has proven to be a double-edged sword. In their anxiety to convince skeptics that this prophecy may soon come to pass, many people have sensationalized the issue with unproven and undocumented stories. One perfect example was the report in the early 80's that the U.S.

Government had issued checks which contained the restriction that they could not be cashed unless the recipient had a mark in his right hand or in his forehead! Yet of all the people that purportedly received these checks, not one of them ever thought to keep the check or even make a photocopy of it. Nonetheless, this unlikely and undocumented story was quickly picked up by Christian publications all over the country.

Then there was the giant computer called "The Beast" in Brussels which purportedly was keeping track of everyone in the world. The fact that no hard evidence of its existence ever appeared did not stop the rumormongers. In another instance it was reported that an entire town in Sweden had received the "mark of the Beast" as a test for the worldwide implementation of the system. An additional rumor had it that workers in high-security government projects in California were having micro-chips implanted under their skin for security purposes. In all of these instances, proof was never given or asked for.

The point is that with this clear, well-known prophecy we had better be very careful not to cry wolf too many times. This would take credibility away from the events that are paving the way for the fulfillment of this prophecy in the very near future. Instead, what we need is a very discerning look at the facts that we do have. As you will see, they are sensational enough on their own!

This prophecy is also extremely important because it is one of those prophecies that undoubtedly proves to us that we are the first generation qualified to be the last generation before the return of Christ. Such worldwide control of buying and selling would hardly have been possible before the age of computers, satellites, and cashless shopping. Today the technology neces-sary to bring this prophecy to pass exists. Moreover, the political and economic will to bring it to pass exists as well.

What Is the Mark of the Beast?

Although the mark of the Beast will be used to regulate a person's ability to buy or sell in the New World Order, it is far from confined to the economic realm. As Revelation 14:9-11 tells us:

> If any man worship the beast and his image, and receive his mark in his forehead or in his hand, the same shall drink of the wine of the wrath of God, which is poured out without mixture.... And the smoke of their torment ascendeth up for ever and ever; and they have no rest day or night, who worship the beast and his image, and whosoever receiveth the mark of his name.

Certainly God would not pour out such serious judgment upon anyone for purely economic reasons. Instead, as is evident from this Scripture, those who will accept the mark will also be making a spiritual decision coupled with the worship of the Beast and his image. Indeed, as we have seen, the mark of the Beast will almost undoubtedly become the actual symbol of allegiance to the Antichrist.

John's statement that the mark will be received in the hand or in the forehead gives a good clue as to the actual attributes of this mark. It could well be that what this prophet was referring to almost 2000 years ago was what is known today as the computer microchip. In fact, the microchips currently being used in "smart cards" could easily fulfill the definition of "the mark" which will be issued under the Antichrist regime. These chips can contain the complete financial, medical, and personal histories of the owner of the card. They can grant or deny access to bank accounts from automated teller machines, and that's only a small percentage of their capabilities. As far as the prophecy of the mark of the Beast is concerned, the only remaining requirement would be for the chip to be taken out of the card and actually be implanted into human flesh. That idea is not unthinkable. Already pet shelters across North America have been injecting rice-grain-sized microchips into the ears of cats and dogs to help owners easily identify and keep track of their lost pets.

The Cashless Society

The determination of just how close we could be to the fulfillment of this stunning prophecy must begin with a look at the current moves toward the cashless society. The following article extract from *USA Today* sums up what is sure to be the most substantial change in the way the world does business in the nineties.

> Imagine a "cashless society" where you can get groceries or gas, dine on fast food and make a phone call—all without a dime in your pocket. Robert Barone, president of Diebold, Inc., an automated teller machine (ATM) manufacturer, forecasts such a future:
>
> "You will soon be able to do anything that you do today with cash with a plastic debit or credit card.
>
> "There will be a proliferation of point-of-sale authorization terminals that allow a store to go to your bank, determine if you have the money in your account, and charge your account electronically.
>
> "You could do your grocery shopping with such a card. . . . One benefit to the consumer is he won't have to carry much cash around."[1]

Many observers felt that this cashless society would emerge in the 1980's. A study of why it did not finds that although the technology existed, the problem lay in public acceptance. A generation of people who had not been raised on computers and newer technologies simply refused to use them. One lady told me she was scared she would punch the wrong buttons on the Automated Teller Machine and start a nuclear war! Another man simply said, "I've dealt with a human teller all my life and I'm just not comfortable dealing with a machine."

Interestingly, for the younger generation, just the opposite is true: Many of those under 30 have seldom been in a bank branch;

they do all their banking with a machine! As this computerized generation grows up, the trend toward electronic banking will continue to develop. However, bankcard organizations are not just leaving it to chance.

> ...the Pearl River, N.Y., [program] is bringing automated payment systems to elementary and high school cafeterias. The system allows pupils to use magnetic cards instead of cash to pay for their meals. They insert the card into a reader, which is linked to a personal computer that holds account information. The computer deducts the charge from the child's account, which is prepaid by parents on a weekly or monthly basis. The cards are designed to withstand such punishment as spilled milk. . . . So far, some 35 public school districts across the county have given the system the go-ahead. . . .[2]

In another training program in Denver, children are being issued Kiddie MasterCards with a limit of only one hundred dollars.[3] As a result, children from ages 12 and upward are becoming completely comfortable with the cashless system of the future. The delays that hindered the implementation of the cashless society in the eighties will not be allowed to repeat themselves.

A Bonanza for the Banks

The primary reason for the push toward the cashless society is because of the huge savings that financial institutions will be able to obtain. For instance, imagine that you go into a grocery store and pay for your order with a credit card. The number of transactions that have to take place to complete the payment are surprising. First the store has to send a record of the purchase to the credit card company. Next, usually within a few days, the credit card company sends payment to the store. At the end of the month, the credit card company sends you your bill. Then, to pay the bill, you send them a check. They have to take that check and send it to your bank, or to a clearinghouse, to have the funds taken out of your account. Finally, the money that you spent at the store has to be credited to the account of the credit card company. In all, over six different transactions had to take place to pay for your bag of bean sprouts.

Compare that to the purchase of the future. In this instance, when you buy your groceries you give the clerk your credit card look-alike called a debit card. The clerk runs the card through a scanner, which is electronically linked to your bank. Instantaneously the money is removed from your account and put directly into the store's. That's it.

No wonder the banks and financial institutions are pushing so hard for the adoption of such a system! The savings will be absolutely astronomical. Some estimates put the savings of an electronic system over the processing of a check at over 700 percent, and even this figure may be conservative. Moreover, as one bank manager explained it to me, in an electronic system banks could tap into another huge area of savings. When a bank goes into a town they now have two choices. They can shop for a piece of land, build a large building on it, furnish it, hire and train staff, and pay property taxes, utilities, and wages—or they can slap an automated teller machine on a telephone pole or in a subway stop. The choice is painfully obvious. Thus the financial community is pushing for such a system with unrestrained enthusiasm.

Terry Galanoy, the former director of Communications for VISA International, is blunt in his assessment of the situation:

> Protesting too loudly about it isn't going to help either, because the disturbance you kick up is going to end up in one of your files. And on that come-and-get-it day when we're totally and completely dependent upon our card—OR WHATEVER SURVIVAL DEVICE MIGHT REPLACE IT—You might be left all alone without one.[4]

The Logical Reasons to Give Up Cash

Of course, when bankers and other proponents of the cashless society are selling the electronic age to the public, the reasons they give are not based on their own profitability. As in all good marketing campaigns, the benefits to the community and the individual are emphasized. Whether or not they are true benefits has little to do with the issue so long as they are *perceived* by the public to be advantageous. In the instance of the cashless society, there seem to be some good reasons being given in addition to the expected hype. The draw to a world cashless system is becoming virtually irresistible.

Destroying the Drug Trade

By its very nature the drug trade is based on cash—a suitcase-full at a time. Law-enforcement officials say that if cash were done away with, the drug trade could be dealt a serious blow. In a cashless system where all transactions leave a clear paper trail, transactions involving huge sums of money could easily be monitored. A letter to the editor in *Time* magazine is representative:

> Your report on drug smugglers converting drug-tinged money into clean assets shows that our Government's oversupply of U.S. currency is a prime cause of the growth of the cocaine trade. You explain that 80% of all the bills printed by the Treasury can't be located because so many of them are concealed by the dealers. As an assistant prosecutor at the county level, I am disheartened by the inaction on denying the drug kings their medium of exchange, currency. One way to catch them would be a surprise big-cash recall. Let's demonetize the drug trade.[5]

Kiss Crime Goodbye

However, by eliminating cash, not only the drug trade but the entire black market could be eliminated almost overnight, according to many observers. One particularly clear description of both the problem and the solution was given by a career foreign-services officer:

> William G. Ridgeway isn't so immodest as to suppose his plan would save the world. All he claims for it is that it would bust up organized crime, put an end to the deadly traffic in illegal drugs, reduce espionage and terrorism, drastically curtail corruption and tax evasion and begin a return to civility.
>
> Ridgeway's plan (dubbed Bold \$troke) would eliminate cash in favor of computerized, theft-proof "smart cards."
>
> Cash . . . is the criminal's vital accomplice, "the very mother's milk of the spy, the terrorist, the thief; the drug pusher, the drug user, the tax evader and the embezzler." Because it leaves no paper trail, it is "the interface between the legal and illegal world."
>
> Cash, in short, is the root of a heck of a lot of the world's evil, and Ridgeway would outlaw it in phases: large bills first, then successively smaller ones and, finally, coins.
>
> In its place: "smart cards." You've probably read about these electronic marvels, the technology for which already exists. On a foldable card the size of a dollar bill would be imprinted an astonishing amount of information: your bank balances, credit limits, medical records, passport, driver's license, photographs, welfare eligibility and other data including— this is key—your thumbprint.
>
> The thumbprint, which would have to be verified electronically with each transaction, would make the card worthless to a thief.
>
> Every single transaction would create its own record which could then be used for criminal investigations— just as checks, bank accounts and credit-card records are used now.

"The benefits of replacing cash (his plan would not affect credit cards or checks) would be incalculable," says Ridgeway. "No cash to smuggle. The sale of illegal drugs would stop, since no one would want a record of the transaction. The spread of AIDS would be curtailed, as drug use fades away. The cost of government would go down, as would the cost of private business. Tax evasion-payment in cash to avoid sales tax . . . [or failure] to report cash income would cease. The national debt could be reduced. Stolen items could not be sold without a trace. Personal security would be assured. Little old ladies could walk in the park again."

Ridgeway brushes aside the most obvious objections to his proposal: the Big Brother nature of a scheme in which every transaction is recorded. . . .

As for the intrusiveness of Big Brother—the threat to liberty—Ridgeway believes that our real concerns should run in the other direction. "Ever-rising lawlessness," he contends, "will cause the public to demand more and more repressive measures, a sure recipe for the demise of our democratic way of life . . . I know (from years in the Far East as a foreign service officer) what drugs, corruption and crime can do to a society. The same pattern of decline has started here, and the outcome is quite predictable."[6]

Ridgeway's assessment is extremely realistic. One recent report estimates that if tax-evaders alone could be thwarted it would put at least an additional hundred billion dollars a year into U.S. Government coffers.

The System Is Being Built

Crime and security concerns have indeed prepared the world to accept the necessity of increased security measures in addition to the elimination of cash. As *U.S. News and World Report* notes:

> In an era when virtually all Americans are asked to show I.D.'s ranging from driver's licenses to credit cards, the process of insuring that a person is who he or she claims to be is a big business and a matter of growing concern. No longer is the simple password, the I.D. badge or the magnetic encoded card sufficient, say security experts. Those traditional devices can be falsified, stolen, or discovered accidentally.[7]

With the proliferation of debit cards, particularly the automated teller machine cards, most Americans are now familiar with PIN's—Personal Identification Numbers. These are the numbers that the cardholder is supposed to memorize and then punch into the terminal wherever he makes a transaction. This is how the developers of the system have tried to make sure that the person using the card is actually the owner of the card. The thinking was that if someone stole a card it would be useless to him because he would not know the secret number. However, as a study by the Federal Reserve Bank of Atlanta has shown, this system is often inadequate:

> Current norms of security . . . in general have failed to provide much more than a rudimentary link between the individual and his access to funds in an account. . . . The magnetic strip card combination merely seeks to match a holder of the plastic card with the knowledge of a four to six digit code or PIN.
> A growing body of research indicated, ironically, that many cardholders—rather than memorize a PIN—carry a written copy of their PIN near their bank card. Others literally write their PIN directly on their plastic card.[8]

It is not just carelessness that plagues the system, however. The elderly, the mentally handicapped, and others may just not be able to remember such a number. Furthermore, it is not unthinkable that a robber could not only take someone's card but also force him into revealing his PIN number. Currently the damages from this security shortfall have been minimized by daily limits set on the amount of funds that someone can access from his account in any given 24-hour period. At my own bank the daily limit is 500 dollars. If someone stole my bank card, and if he somehow managed to find out my PIN number, he could only do minimal damage before the theft was reported. Actually, in my case he would probably get a message from the machine telling him to dream on!

If we move toward a cashless society, where bank branches cease to exist, these low limits would make it impossible to conduct normal business. Someone buying a house, a refrigerator, or a car would simply have to be able to access more than 500 dollars at a time. As a result, planners say that a new way is needed to make sure that the person using the card is its rightful owner. The report of the Atlanta Federal Reserve Bank noted that "some alternatives [are] being considered, such as signature dynamics and voice recognition [which] are based on nontransferable, biometric characteristics."

Biometric characteristics refer to physical qualities that are unique to the individual. Fingerprints are a perfect example of this. In addition to fingerprints, there are machines today that can verify a person's identity by the blood vessels in his eyes or hands, or by the tone and pitch of his voice. These machines may replace the old Personal Identification Number as a means of making sure that the person presenting the card is actually the owner of the card. Under this system a person who was about to make a transaction would present his card and then place his finger in an electronic fingerprint reader, or a hand scan machine, or a retinal reader. The machine would then compare the person's fingerprint, or other identifying characteristic, to the one digitally stored in the card. This would ensure that the person presenting the card was actually the owner of that card.

This transition is well underway. According to Benjamin Miller of *Personal Identification News*, "Biometrics will be a major part of our life by the year 2000." Likewise, the aforementioned *U.S. News and World Report* article concludes that many companies are betting that "consumers will be glad to give up their plastic cards and forget their passwords and personal I.D. numbers in favor of a system that reassures a unique physical characteristic."

The single problem with these systems is their extreme costliness. In one test system, being developed by a company called Identity System International, a smart card and a fingerprint reader are combined. The problem is that the fingerprint reader costs hundreds of times what the microchip in the card costs. You don't have to spend too much time thinking to realize that by simply taking the chip out of the card and implanting it in the person, you would get rid of the only expensive part of the system. In this way you could be assured that the holder of the microchip, which holds all the information anyway, would be the right person because the chip would be implanted inside his body. It would be rather difficult to steal someone's hand or forehead and present it at the checkout stand of the local supermarket. Today the technology for just such an implant exists. That technology, of course, is in the form of a microchip, much like the one presently used in smart cards.

Testing the Mark

Already, microchips are being implanted in animals for the purposes of foolproof identification. The following article from *Cat Fancy* magazine is descriptive:

> If you refuse to allow your cat to wear an identification collar because of the possibility the collar might get caught on something and hang the cat, you might be interested in this new method of Identification Devices Inc. It's an ultra thin microchip, which veterinarians will inject under the cat's skin. The microchip emits a numerical or letter combination code (about

4 billion are possible), which is assigned exclusively to that cat. . . . Its inventors believe that the widespread use of this technique of permanent identification could help save some of the thousands of animals euthanized each year by shelters that cannot trace the cat's owners.[9]

Of course, the microchip is not only suitable for cats; dogs are also being implanted. Likewise, horse breeders, cattle farmers, sheep farmers, and trout farm operators are also using the new technology. Identification Devices, the developers of this microchip, says the following in its promotional materials:

Suppose you were to make a list of the technical advances that are quickly reshaping the way we live: microminiaturization of electronic components, high-speed data processing systems, powerful new computer programming techniques, and extremely sophisticated telecommunications devices, as well as new methods of encapsulating delicate components so they function in unfavorable environments. Then consider how these innovations might be employed to solve the age-old problem of providing positive identification of people, animals and equipment. That's what the design specialists at Identification Devices did. . . . System I.D. transponders are encapsulated in an inert epoxy to protect the electronic circuitry during use. The specific epoxy chosen, of course, must be compatible with the intended application. Transponders implanted in animals, for example, have tissue-compatible coatings to prevent rejection by the body. The transponder is so small it is usually implanted in the animal with an ordinary syringe. And it is so durable it has a projected operating life after implantation of over 100 years.[10]

Identification Devices boasts the capacity to handle a network of 1 million terminals. This is definitely more than enough to coordinate the tracking of cats, horses, and fish. Furthermore, the company claims that "these innovations might be employed to solve the age-old problem of providing positive identification of people. . . ." There is simply no question that the technology necessary to bring forth the prophecy of the mark of the Beast is quickly falling into place. Like the cashless society, all that is really necessary is the acceptance of such an idea by the public. Today that acceptance seems to be at hand. It is coming for so many reasons that it is worth stopping to review a sampling of them.

Missing Children

In the decade of the eighties the enormity of the problem of missing children crept into our collective consciousness. Milk cartons and heart-wrenching television advertisements were a constant reminder that every day children were being abducted, abused, and often killed. Such a drastic problem has led to equally desperate proposals of ways to deal with the problem. One of them is the invention of Dr. Daniel Mann, a Florida-based plastic surgeon:

> A tiny homing device implanted behind the ear will help parents locate their missing children, says a plastic surgeon who developed the gadget using the same technology that led to cellular phones. The device, which emits electronic signals, could also help law enforcement officials find parolees and aid in the search for victims of Alzheimer's disease who have wandered off, said the developer, Dr. Daniel Mann. Private industry and government agencies have expressed interest in the mini-beeper, which measures less than an inch in size. Mann was awarded a patent last month for the device, which would work on an electronic energy system. The gadget emits a signal that could be monitored through a cellular system or

possibly by satellite. Reaction has been generally positive.[11]

Tom Bergsma, the developer of yet another implant for children, admits that "without a doubt, this device would be the ultimate invasion of privacy because they [the authorities] would be able to find you anytime they want." However, he argues, that this disadvantage must be weighed against the greater good. He says that "people are stealing our children and this device would make them responsible for their actions."[12]

Prison Overcrowding

Another highly publicized problem in today's world is the great strains being put on the criminal justice system by the growing numbers of people behind bars. Report after report shows the crisis proportions that such overcrowding has caused. The idea of letting less violent criminals serve the time at home seems very logical:

> In the Total Control Monitoring, Inc., system, the prisoner is required to wear an ankle bracelet which accompanies a cellular sending unit. If the prisoner wanders outside a designated radius, the sending unit emits a message to the monitoring device—operated by Brinks—who then in turn alert the correctional authorities. The sending unit can be tracked by the monitoring computer, and its whereabouts determined at any time, company officials indicated.[13]

Chronic Wanderers

As Dr. Mann noted, another problem in today's world are the elderly people or those with Alzheimer's disease who often lose track of their surroundings and just wander off. We recently visited a nursing home to see how they dealt with the problem and found that the residents are now fitted with a wrist or ankle bracelet that activates an alarm if they wander off. Indeed, according to a recent report:

> At the request of five federal agencies involved with the problems of the elderly, the Research Triangle Institute in North Carolina is studying the efficacy of attaching small transmitters to chronic wanderers.[14]

High-Security Areas

Today, with the power of technology, a great deal of damage can be done by someone with only brief access to certain areas. Whether it is information, financial records, military secrets, or nuclear facilities, security is the word of the day.

> Employees working on restricted projects would have a transponder embedded in a tamper-proof badge. The unique identification signal emitted by the device upon command permits access to secured areas. It is also used to automatically log each person's movements in and out of restricted areas. Should unauthorized entry be attempted, the system immediately alerts security personnel.[15]

Medical Emergencies

A recent newspaper article asked, "What happens if your child is rushed to the hospital and you're not there to consent to treatment?" The answer may be right at the kid's feet:

> CritiKid provides hospitals with a child's medical history—and parents with peace of mind. It's a chip of microfilm with information about allergies, heart problems, or other existing conditions, along with a signed parent's consent form. It is laminated and

attached to the lace or strap of the child's shoe. Hospital personnel remove the chip, read it with a microscope, magnifying lens or microfiche reader. More than 100 hospitals nationwide have adopted CritiKid, and more are expected to join. . . . [16]

Gun Control

With the rise in crime, a growing concern has been in the area of gun control. According to a report in *USA Today*, "A personal smart card that every citizen would carry is just one controversial idea the Justice Department has to keep guns out of felons' hands."[17] The microchip, embedded in the card, would carry such data as criminal records. Gun dealers would check for information that would disqualify potential buyers. The Justice Department also suggested that gun shops install high-tech fingerprint scanners to immediately verify the identity of all gun buyers.

Prison Escapes

Fingermatrix Inc., another high-tech security company, recently announced that it had received a $108,000 contract to install a fingerprint-based identification system for people visiting inmates at the U.S. Penitentiary in Leavenworth, Kansas:

> "We have people here that have a history of violence and escape," Leavenworth spokesman Dan McCauley said. "At any one time you have to figure that somebody is trying to plan some way to get out of this place, so your visiting becomes a security issue." Visitors to the prison will insert a finger into a small scanner. A record of the fingerprint will then be stored on a computerized database along with the prints of other prison visitors.
>
> "When you come out you'll put your finger in the system again and it will say 'Yep, that was you who

went in and now you've checked out,'" said Scott G. Schiller, director of investor relations for Fingermatrix. "What they're trying to protect here is that the wrong person doesn't leave."[18]

The New World Order

In the thirteenth chapter of the book of Revelation we are told that this "mark of the Beast" system will be installed to help manage the New World Order. We know from prophecy that this new order will consist of a global society that will grow out of the Western democracies in general and Western Europe in particular. That is why a recent conference held in Barcelona, Spain, was so significant. The conference was held under the theme "Borderless Borders" and was designed to address the problems of a "United States of Europe." According to the promotional materials:

> Card technology applications are being affected radically by the dramatic changes in a Western Europe in the process of uniting with an emerging, new Eastern Europe. . . .
>
> Issues which must be addressed include:
>
> Identification: What information is necessary? Who are the keepers of the database? Will international passports be issued by individual nations or a central bureau, for example, in the European Community (EC)?
>
> Security: How much identification is necessary to ensure a nation's security?
>
> Telecommunications: . . . Who will make the decisions—government, business or a worldwide entity?
>
> Banking/POS: Why should integrated Circuit/smart cards or debit cards replace cash? How much will

identification and social services requirements drive these card applications?[19]

There is little doubt here that the exact type of system spoken of in the Bible is now being openly discussed by world leaders. And the connection of this economic system to the New World Order is unmistakable. International Card Technology Institute President Arlen Lessin explains:

> This is a very important conference—and not just because of the issues to be raised. The purpose of this conference is to formally and informally create a dialogue among the people who must make decisions about how we are going to live in an open world.
>
> We are not yet a global community. But that is clearly the direction in which we are heading. Borders will tend to blur and disappear on levels of economic, technological, political, military and even social activities. How can the integrity and security of a nation be maintained if people are free to cross from one nation to another? Of course, there must be some constraints, some means of knowing who is wishing to cross, some means of monitoring and/or identifying people from various nations.[20]

What About the Outcry?

Not too long ago the Gannett News Service carried a story about this coming electronic society. Although the report indicated that the technology was ready, it also noted that people were a long way from accepting it:

> Gannett News Service—Here's a simple trick: Wave your hand over the computer code scanner at the grocery store checkout counter, and your bill is deducted from your checking account. The technology to

accomplish [this] feat already is here . . . said Tim
Willard, executive officer of the World Future Society,
a Washington organization that claims 27,000 members worldwide. But the will may not be.

"Just suggest something like an implant in humans,
and the social outcry is tremendous," Willard said.
"While people over the years may have grown accus-
tomed to artificial body parts, there is definitely a
strong aversion to things being implanted. It's the 'Big
Brother is watching' concept: People would be afraid
that all their thoughts and movements were being
monitored."[21]

Indeed, one would think that the possibility of such an intrusion, similar to the personal database of George Orwell's book
1984, would cause public outrage. But it seems that over the years
the public has been slowly weaned from their concern for privacy
to total passiveness toward computerized personal profiles. A
perfect example of this is the transformation of the Social Insur-
ance Number (SIN) in Canada. The original intent of the SIN
card, issued to Canadians 18 years old and over, was to ensure
that Canadians were not defrauding the government by accepting
undeserved unemployment benefits. However, as time wore on,
Canadian citizens were asked by retailers, financial institutions,
and credit card companies to give their SIN as identification.
Even though Canadians were not required by law to divulge this
number, eventually they were more than willing to use their SIN
card as a legitimate form of ID. The end result is that now the
government has access to a personal profile on every Canadian
citizen.

They know where we work and they know where we have
worked in the past. They know what fitness club we belong to.
They know what credit cards we have. And, since it is now
required by law for financial institutions in Canada to collect
their clients' SIN, the government now knows what bank accounts
we have, whether we have retirement funds, and whether we have

a safety deposit box or not. But this has not seemed to bother Canadians at all, since no cry has been voiced. We just don't seem to mind that the government knows a great deal about us. Dr. Ann Cavoukian, the Assistant Commissioner for the Information and Privacy Commissioner of Ontario, actually admitted at a recent symposium, "The SIN has indeed become the de facto national ID of Canadians."

It is no different in the United States. The government's intrusion into our private affairs may be even more pervasive. The Social Security Number (SSN) is now used by government agencies, financial institutions, and many other companies for identification purposes. Most states require the number before issuing driver's licenses.

The government's official collection agency, the Internal Revenue Service, now requires the number to be issued to *all* children over two years old, and soon will be required of newborn babies as well. Hilariously, the IRS wants the two-year-olds to sign the card to make it official! Humor aside, it is clear that this number is unlawfully being used for identification purposes, even though it was originally required *only* for those accepting employment for the first time. The *New York Times* notes how far we've come in just a few short years:

> Not long ago, Americans were still famous for detesting regimentation. In 1980, the idea of identifying aliens with Social Security numbers ignited outraged comparisons to concentration camp tattoos. Robert Ellis Smith of the Privacy Journal worried about "a European mentality of submitting to inspectors who tell you that your papers are in order." In 1982, The *Times'* William Safire called the idea "this generation's longest step toward totalitarianism." ...Americans once fiercely prized privacy, dignity and nuanced identity. Now, obediently, they punch in their PIN's and worship, cheerfully, at the touchscreen altar of convenience.[22]

In this generation, that altar of convenience is worldwide. Fiber optics, satellites, and computer databases have the potential to control the world in a way that boggles the imagination. Already national identification cards are being used in eight of the nations that make up the European Economic Community. Official government policies to wipe out cash and checks are being followed in places like Denmark, Australia, Israel, Singapore, and Thailand. High-speed international communications systems have developed to the point where it is now claimed that "the world's money follows the sun around the globe." There is little doubt that the technology to make possible the vision that the apostle John saw almost 2000 years ago now exists. Two recent reports show just how quickly things are moving:

> Sen. Albert Gore, D-Tenn., recently drew up a $1.75 billion plan to set up high-speed, high-capacity networks to link U.S. supercomputers—"the information superhighways of tomorrow," says Gore.
>
> Most supercomputer networks now run 2,000 times more slowly than the one he wants to see transmitting 3 gigabits, or 3 billion pieces of data, per second by 1996. By comparison, an average home computer printer spits out 200 characters per second.
>
> "The nation which most completely assimilates high-performance computing . . . will very likely emerge as the dominant intellectual, economic and technological force in the next century," Gore says.[23]

> IBM, MCI Communications Corp. and officials at a group of Michigan universities have quietly begun discussions with the federal government about creating a non-profit company that would operate a high-speed computer network that could one day reach every American home. The network would function as the nations [and the world's] interstate highway system, carrying not just computer data but television

images, telephone conversations and other forms of communication.24

Just One More Sign

When I speak about various prophecies in the Word of God, people often say to me, "It's just a coincidence." If there were just one or two vague predictions, I could understand that logic. But that is simply not the case. The Word of God has given us a very clear and detailed picture of exactly what the world will be like in the days just before the return of Christ. The prophecy of the "mark of the Beast" is only one of these. As we said at the beginning of this book, the evidence is clear. A simple analysis of the facts makes the conclusion almost inescapable: We live at the most expectant moment of history. As citizens of the 1990's we have front-row seats to those very events that will culminate with the return of Jesus Christ. In the last three chapters of this book we list several dozen prophecies to summarize the evidence for you and to remind you that—

> We have not followed cunningly devised fables when we made known to you the power and coming of our Lord Jesus Christ, but were eyewitnesses of his majesty. . . . We have also a more sure word of prophecy, whereunto ye do well to take heed, as unto a light that shineth in a dark place, until the day dawn and the day star arise in your hearts; knowing this first, that no prophecy of the Scripture is of any private interpretation. For the prophecy came not in old time by the will of man, but holy men of God spoke as they were moved by the Holy Ghost (2 Peter 1:16,19-21).

My greatest fear is that there will be some people who know all about prophecy and who know that the rapture is near, and yet will be left standing on this planet after the rapture. That is why mere knowledge and facts are simply not enough.

Chapter 16

God Is So Good

I remember when I first started studying Bible prophecy well over a dozen years ago. I was immediately captivated by the subject. Having been a student of economics, the idea of a coming new world order was not a far stretch at all. Every indicator seemed to prove that exactly what the prophets had said was true. I studied everything I could find on the subjects of prophecy and current world trends. I was convinced that everything was coming to pass and that it would happen in my lifetime.

You would think that this was the greatest revelation that any man could have. You would think it would change his entire life on the spot. But it didn't. Despite everything I knew, I still wasn't truly born again. I knew all the facts, but I didn't know the One "whom to know is life eternal." The knowledge in my head simply couldn't change my heart. I would sit and talk for hours to my friends about prophecy with a Bible on my lap, a beer in one hand, and a marijuana reefer in the other!

I kept thinking that one day all the information in my head would click, and then I would pull myself together and start living right. Unfortunately, just the opposite happened. I began on a downward spiral that brought me to the bottom of the world. How I thank God to this day that when I finally got to the bottom, I found a friend who sticks closer than a brother. As the songwriter says, "He brought me out of the miry clay, He set my feet on the rock to stay, Hallelujah!"

The Reality of Life

I never forget this sad reality when I preach or write about prophecy. Right now I am thinking about those who have read this book desperately hoping that the facts will "freak them out" enough so that they will start living right. I'm thinking of those who, having seen all the documentation, are saying, "That's it—I know it's true. I'm going to clean up my life." I have to tell you right now that if this is as far as you take it, it won't help you one bit. Such resolutions will not, in and of themselves, change you. A few days down the road, the dramatic proofs that you've seen will fade into the background as the very real concerns of this world and the equally powerful temptations of sin come calling. Mere facts will not help then. Neither will religious beliefs, good intentions, or even clean living.

My knowledge couldn't save me. My good works were not enough. Christ wanted to come and live in my heart. He wanted me to cut through all the excuses and self-will and give my life and love to Him. That's the heart of the gospel. Jesus loved me and died for me so that I could be free of all the entanglements in my life and have friendship with God Himself. He wanted me to be born all over again.

Saying Yes to Christ

I remember crying uncontrollably as a preacher that I had never met preached the gospel a few nights later. I sensed something beyond myself drawing me, and I knew that night that God loved me. I cried all night because I just didn't know what to do.

On Saturday, two days later, I still felt a presence around me. I had to walk to a mall, and as I strolled into the parking lot I decided, as I had for years, that it was time to get high. Without any hesitation I turned to walk back to my drug dealer's house, and I forgot all about the things I wanted to do at the mall. As I pivoted a voice spoke to me: "I can break the chain if you want me to." Without thinking I cried out, "Yes! I want you to!" Immediately the bondage was gone. I could feel it. I felt so clean that I literally began to jump around in the parking lot. I didn't even know the verse existed, but I instantly knew the reality of the fact that "if the Son shall make you free, ye shall be free indeed" (John 8:36).

As I lay in bed that night it hit me: I knew at that moment that I would never be the same again. I opened a Bible to a couple of verses that I suddenly remembered from somewhere:

> As many as are led by the Spirit of God, they are the sons of God. For ye have not received the spirit of bondage again to fear, but ye have received the Spirit of adoption, whereby we cry, Abba, Father. The Spirit itself beareth witness with our spirit, that we are the children of God (Romans 8:14-16).

The Goodness of God

The next morning I went back to church. My hair was still past my shoulders and my eyes were still bloodshot. But when we sang I sang the loudest of all.

> God is so good,
> God is so good,
> God is so good,
> He is so good to ME!

This is what God wants. He doesn't want some religious vow or some New Year's resolution; He wants to live in your heart—to be your Lord, Savior, and best friend. He will break every chain that binds you, if that's what you really want. My problem had not been with the drugs; it had been with my *will*. I didn't really want to give up my own way of doing things. When I finally did, I stepped into the power promised to every believer:

> It is the spirit that quickeneth; the flesh profiteth nothing. The words that I speak unto you are spirit and are life (John 6:63).

> [It is] not by might, nor by power, but by my spirit, saith the Lord of hosts (Zechariah 4:6).

If you've never entered into a personal relationship with Jesus Christ, now is the time. The Bible says, "Today is the day of salvation." If you don't do that, then you've missed the whole purpose of this book and the only important thing in the whole world. Jesus said, "One soul [your soul] is worth more than the whole world." This is why Jesus Christ came into the world. He knew that we could not make it by our own power. He knew that all had sinned and come short of the glory of God, and that only He, by dying in our place, could bridge that gap.

On the Right Track

The truth of the matter is simply this: You can't do it. You cannot pull yourself up by your bootstraps. You can't live for God without God living in you. But if you will quit trying to reach God on your own terms and by your own merit, and accept the fact that it is only Jesus' merit that makes you acceptable to God, then you are on the right track.

> Then said they unto him, What shall we do, that we might work the works of God? Jesus answered and said unto them, This is the work of God, that ye believe on him whom he hath sent (John 6:28,29).

It's just that simple. But it's not a lighthearted vow. I myself had spoken the words many times before. In reality, though, I didn't really believe. I had to come to a place where I truly got honest with God and opened my heart and life to Him. Will you do that? God will do the rest because He's the One who has brought you to this point of decision.

> No man can come unto me except the Father which hath sent me draw him . . . and him that cometh to me I will in no wise cast out (John 6:44,37).

> For it is God which worketh in you both to will and to do of his good pleasure (Philippians 2:13).

When you let Christ come into your life, you'll know a peace and joy "that passeth all understanding." Suddenly the focus of prophecy will no longer be on the signs but on what they foreshadow. It will no longer primarily be a consideration of *when He is coming* but of *the One who is coming*. As the songwriter has said, "The things of this world will grow strangely dim in the light of His glory and grace."

Remember the Blessed Hope

As I am writing these words, the thought of believers is also on my heart. Some have lost sight of the blessed hope of the soon return of his Lord. Maybe your church doesn't preach prophecy anymore. Maybe they think it's an interesting little sideline of no real relevance for today. I want to remind you that the prophetic hope of Jesus' return should be an important, central part of our daily walk:

> They themselves show of us what manner of entering in we had unto you, and how ye turned to God from idols to serve the living and the true God, and to wait for his Son from heaven, whom he raised from the dead, even Jesus, which delivered us from the wrath to come (1 Thessalonians 1:9,10).

Bible prophecy should remind the believer of his first love. It should stir him to look beyond the entrapments and struggles of this life and set his eyes on the glorious hope that awaits every child of God. Nothing is more important than keeping and holding onto that first love for the Savior. Unfortunately, it is so easy to forget the simplicity of the gospel message.

Peter and the Fish

The story of the apostle Peter is a perfect example of this. The Gospel of Luke explains how Peter first met Jesus. Peter was sitting washing his fishing nets when Jesus came by and asked him if He could use his boat to preach from. When He finished speaking, Jesus wanted to repay Peter for his generosity. He told the fisherman to launch out and let down his nets. Of course, Peter immediately told the Lord how they had fished all night and caught nothing. However, when he did as Jesus said, he pulled in so many fish that his nets began to break and he had to call his friends to bring another boat to help. By the time they were done, both ships were completely filled with fish. Then something amazing happened:

> When Simon Peter saw it, he fell down at Jesus' knees, saying, Depart from me, for I am a sinful man, O Lord. For he was astonished, and all that were with him, at the draught of the fishes which they had taken; and so was also James and John, the sons of Zebedee, which were partners with Simon. And Jesus said unto Simon, Fear not; from henceforth thou shalt catch men. And when they had brought their ships to land, they forsook all and followed him (Luke 5:8-11).

Instead of basking in the blessing that he received, Peter wanted more. What a glorious start to following Jesus! Peter forsook all that he had. He left the abundance of fish behind, which until that moment had been his livelihood, his supply, and his life. He forsook it all to follow Jesus. He left the blessing to follow the One who had blessed him. Peter had a heart after God. Too many Christians today miss the experience with God that Peter had because all they want is the blessing. Once they have their boatload of fish, they are satisfied.

Something Greater

For the next three years Peter followed Jesus. He saw miracles, he saw healings, and he saw the deliverances. He walked with Jesus on the water, he heard the teachings of the Lord day after day, and he was even given the revelation from God the Father that Jesus is "the Christ, the Son of the living God." But Jesus wanted him to have something greater:

> Simon, Simon, behold, Satan hath desired to have you, that he may sift you as wheat. But I have prayed for thee, that thy faith fail not; and when thou art converted, strengthen thy brethren. And he said unto him, Lord, I am ready to go with thee both to prison and to death. And he said, I tell thee, Peter, the cock shall not crow this day before thou shalt thrice deny that thou knowest me (Luke 22:31-34).

Peter thought he was ready. He honestly thought he was committed. He thought he was ready to die for the faith. But Jesus recognized that "the spirit is willing, but the flesh is weak." And we all know what happened.

> He began to curse and swear, saying, I know not this man of whom ye speak. And the second time the cock crew. And Peter called to mind the word that Jesus said unto him. . . . And when he thought thereon, he wept (Mark 14:71,72).

Imagine how devastated Peter felt! Imagine his agony after the crucifixion. He had failed the Lord in His most important hour. He had denied the One whom he had recognized as "the Christ, the Son of the living God." Many of us reflect on similar times when we have failed the Lord. The devastation can destroy our faith because "having begun in the Spirit" we have now tried to live "a good life" by our own strength.

God Is Not Finished

In spite of Peter's failure, God's message to him was clear: "I loved you when you were yet a sinner, and I love you still. I have not given up on you. If you still have that desire to follow me, I will make a way for you." Do you remember what happened? An angel told the women who had come to the tomb of Jesus:

> Be not afraid: Ye seek Jesus of Nazareth, who was crucified; he is risen, he is not here: Behold the place where they laid him. But go your way, tell his disciples AND PETER that he goeth before you (Mark 16:6,7).

The Lord did not forget Peter. He did not forsake him. Instead, He got the word to Peter that He was risen and that everything was okay. Maybe you feel you have failed so badly that the Lord has forsaken you, but it's just not true. Jesus wants you to know that "He is risen" and that "He goeth before you." It is *He* who is calling you back, for He is not finished with you yet!

Chapter 17

Geopolitical Signs

I remember the disappointment in 1988 of the many people who had placed their hope in the calculations contained in the book *88 Reasons Why Jesus Will Return in 1988*. When Jesus did not return on the given dates, all hope seemed to be lost. "I guess we just shouldn't get our hopes up," was the disheartened sigh. I thought at that time, "If these Christians only knew how many good, scriptural reasons we had for believing that these are the last days, they would not be so dissappointed when another date-setter missed the call."

It was then that I decided to make a simple list of some of the primary prophecies and the current events that are fulfilling them to remind us of how detailed a picture Jesus gave us of what the last days would be like. Not all the prophecies have reached their ultimate fulfillment yet, but where they haven't I give an indication of the trends which show that their fulfillment may be very close.

The Prophecy: Israel in Her Homeland

> I will take you from among the heathen, and gather you out of all countries, and will bring you into your own land (Ezekiel 36:24).

It shall come to pass in that day that the Lord shall set his hand again the second time to recover the remnant of his people which shall be left, from Assyria, and from Egypt, and from Pathros, and from Cush, and from Elam, and from Shinar, and from Hamath, and from the islands of the sea. And he shall set up an ensign for the nations, and shall assemble the outcasts of Israel, and gather together the dispersed of Judah from the four corners of the earth (Isaiah 11:11,12).

I will bring again the captivity of my people of Israel, and they shall build the waste cities, and inhabit them; and they shall plant vineyards and drink the wine thereof; they shall also make gardens and eat the fruit of them. And I will plant them upon their land, and they shall no more be pulled up out of their land which I have given them, saith the Lord thy God (Amos 9:14,15).

The Fulfillment

New York Times headline: ZIONISTS PROCLAIM NEW STATE OF ISRAEL; TRUMAN RECOGNIZES IT AND HOPES FOR PEACE; TEL AVIV IS BOMBED, EGYPT ORDERS INVASION.

TEL AVIV, Palestine—The Jewish State, the world's newest sovereignty, to be known as the state of Israel, came into being in Palestine at midnight upon termination of the British mandate. . . . [1]

This return of Israel to her homeland is the central fulfillment of Bible prophecy. It is around this return of the Jewish people to their homeland that all other prophecies relate.

It is not surprising that there has been tremendous opposition to this incredible prophetic development. Adolf Hitler and the

Third Reich tried to destroy the nation even before it was reborn in 1948. The PLO has vowed, Yasser Arafat's latest promises notwithstanding, to push Israel into the sea. Terrorism against the Jewish state is a daily occurrence. Attacked and outnumbered in 1956, 1967, and 1973, the land has remained in their control.

The Prophecy: Jerusalem Regained

> They shall fall by the edge of the sword, and shall be led away captive into all the nations; and Jerusalem shall be trodden down of the Gentiles until the times of the Gentiles shall be fulfilled (Luke 21:24).

The Fulfillment

> *New York Times* headline: ISRAELIS ROUT THE ARABS, APPROACH SUEZ, BREAK BLOCKADE, OCCUPY OLD JERUSALEM; AGREE TO U.N. CEASEFIRE; U.A.R. REJECTS IT.
>
> TEL AVIV, June 7—Israel proclaimed victory tonight in the Sinai Peninsula campaign against the United Arab Republic. On the eastern front, both the Old City of Jerusalem and Bethlehem were captured from the Jordanians. . . . After the fall of the Old City of Jerusalem, Defense Minister Moshe Dyan said there that the Israelis had reunited their capital and would never depart from it again.[2]

Recently when we were in Israel, our guide, who has fought in four wars defending Israel, told of the joy that spread throughout Israel on that day in 1967. He was on the Eygptian front in trenches with hundreds of other Israelis. They were, of course, tuned into their radios for the latest news updates. As five o'clock rolled around, they expected to hear the news begin with the top headlines as usual. However, the song "Jerusalem My Golden" began to play. The soldiers looked around at each other with a shrug of their shoulders. It didn't dawn on them what had happened until the announcer came on after the song and told the tiny nation that Jerusalem, which hadn't been in their hands since it was sacked by Titus and his armies in 70 A.D., was once again in their control. The soldiers began dancing and singing in their trenches in a celebration that had been on hold for almost 2000 years.

The Prophecy: Rebuilding of Solomon's Temple

Let no man deceive you by any means, for that day shall not come except there come a falling away first and that man of sin be revealed, the son of perdition, who opposeth and exalteth himself above all that is called God or that is worshiped, so that he as God sitteth in the temple of God, showing himself that he is God (2 Thessalonians 2:3,4).

He shall confirm the covenant with many for one week; and in the midst of the week he shall cause the sacrifice and the oblation to cease, and for the overspreading of abominations he shall make it desolate, even until the consummation, and that determined shall be poured upon the desolate (Daniel 9:27).

Behold, I will send my messenger, and he shall prepare the way before me; and the Lord, whom ye seek, shall suddenly come to his temple, even the messenger of the covenant, whom ye delight in; behold, he shall come, saith the Lord of hosts (Malachi 3:1).

The Fulfillment

It would seem from the prophetic Word of God that when the Antichrist arrives on the scene, the Jewish temple will be rebuilt.

It is into this temple that the Antichrist will go to proclaim that he is God. This is what Jesus called the "abomination of desolation." Also, since prophecy often has a double meaning, the passage in Malachi is often seen as being applicable to both the first and second coming of Christ. Thus the temple would have to be in place before Christ returns at Armageddon.

Today the call for just such a rebuilding is making the headlines. The riot on the Temple Mount in late 1990 ignited when Arabs claimed to have believed a rumor that a group called "The Temple Mount Faithful" were going to lay a cornerstone for the rebuilding of Solomon's Temple. The following articles from the Associated Press and the *Jerusalem Post* are indicative of how the groundwork for such a rebuilding is being laid. According to the Associated Press article:

> Hoping to rebuild the ancient Jewish Temple where Islamic shrines now stand, a group of Israeli rabbis are compiling computerized lists of potential priests, weaving seamless linen robes and reproducing a gem-studded breastplate described in Exodus.
>
> "All Jewish history as far as we're concerned is one big parenthesis until the temple is returned," said Rabbi Nahman Kahane of the Temple Institute. . . .
>
> The Temple Institute's 50 rabbis and artisans have made Temple vessels and produced a computerized blueprint of the shrine in preparation for rebuilding it on the site where it stood until A.D. 70, when the Romans destroyed it.
>
> More than $200,000 has been collected to finance the project, most of it from American Jews, according to institute director Rabbi Yisrael Ariel.[3]

The *Post* article updates these efforts:

> Led by a cohen in priestly robes, and equipped with special vessels for the Temple ritual, two rams' horns,

a clarinet and an accordion, members of the Faithful of the Temple Mount marched last week from the Western Wall to the Pool of Siloam to consecrate what they have designated as the cornerstone of the Third Temple.

Police had prevented the group from laying the "cornerstone" in the Western Wall Plaza, as they originally intended.

The one-metre-cube stone, which in accordance with the biblical precept was not hewn with an iron tool, was donated by Zion and Ezra Alafi, stone-cutters on Jerusalem's Hanevi'im Street. . . . During the procession, the three-ton stone lay on a flatbed truck which followed the group down the steep narrow road through Silwan village, past walls covered with graffiti in support of the intifada. Only a few local residents came out of their homes to watch scores of flag-waving marchers, almost out-numbered by police, newsmen and photographers.

At the spring, Yehoshua Cohen, a member of the priestly caste, wearing the woven linen priestly robes, drew water, as Gershon Salomon, leader of the FTM, led the group in reciting the sheheheyanu blessing, in which one gives thanks for having reached a special occasion. The robes and vessels were prepared by Yeshivat Habayit, which is dedicated to studying the practical aspects of restoring the Temple.

Another group, the Movement to Establish the Sanctuary, was represented by Yisrael Schneider, a Bratislav hassid, wearing the striped robes of the old Jerusalem Ashkenazi community.[4]

The Prophecy: A Great False Peace

Of the times and seasons, brethren, ye have no need that I write unto you. For ye yourselves know perfectly that the day of the Lord so cometh as a thief in the night. For when they shall say, Peace and safety, then sudden destruction cometh upon them, as travail upon a woman with child, and they shall not escape (1 Thessalonians 5:1-3).

Through his policy he shall cause craft to prosper in his hand; and he shall magnify himself in his heart, and by peace shall destroy many (Daniel 8:25).

The Fulfillment

In the midst of the most war-torn century in human history, world leaders today tell us that we are on the verge of an era of world peace unlike anything ever before experienced:

The United States of Europe will form the core of a peaceful order, the age prophesied of old, when all shall dwell secure and none shall make them afraid.[5]

A new partnership of nations has begun. . . . Out of these troubled times, our fifth objective—a new world order—can emerge: a new era, freer from the threat of terror, stronger in the pursuit of justice, and more secure in the quest for peace. An era in which the nations of the world, east and west, north and south, can prosper and live in harmony (President George Bush).[6]

In short, we in the Soviet leadership have come to the conclusion that there is a need for new political thinking. Furthermore, Soviet leaders are vigorously seeking to translate this new thinking into action, primarily in the field of disarmament. States belonging to different social systems can and must co-operate with one another in the name of peace. . . . We see a budding World Order in which peaceful co-existence and mutually beneficial cooperation based on goodwill will be universal norms (Mikhail Gorbachev in *Perestroika*).

The Prophecy: Cry for a World Leader

> All the world wondered after the beast . . . and they worshiped the beast, saying, Who is like the beast? Who is able to make war with him? (Revelation 13:3,4).

> There was given unto him a mouth speaking great things and blasphemies (Revelation 13:5).

> All that dwell upon the earth shall worship him, whose names are not written in the book of life of the Lamb (Revelation 13:8).

The Fulfillment

The Bible tells us that in the last days the world will be ready and desperate for a world leader. It is into this gap that the Antichrist will arise. Already the cries for such a world leader are beginning to echo around the globe:

> We exist in a leaderless world (Walter Cronkite).

> By forcing on mankind more and more lethal weapons, and at the same time making the world more and more interdependent economically, technology has brought mankind to such a degree of distress that we are ripe for the deifying of any new Caesar who might succeed in giving the world unity and peace (historian Arnold Toynbee).

> . . . a charismatic leader—scientific, political or religious—[will] be the world's only salvation from the social and economic upheavals that threaten to destroy civilization (Aurelio Peccei, founder of The Club of Rome).

...finally, the large number of governmental bureaus that will have their orbits in the atmosphere of our planet cannot be allowed the freedom to compete and collide with one another. So, in order to control the diverse bureaucracies required, a politburo will develop, and over this group organization there is likely to arise the final and single arbitrator, the master of the order, the total dictator (Paul Mazur).

We do not want another committee; we have too many already. What we want is a man of sufficient stature to hold the allegiance of all the people and to lift us out of the economic morass into which we are sinking. Send us such a man, and be he god or devil, we will receive him (Henry Spaack, former Secretary General of NATO).

The Prophecy: Revived Roman Empire

The fourth kingdom shall be strong as iron...and whereas thou sawest the feet and toes, part of potters' clay and part of iron, the kingdom shall be divided.... And in the days of these kings shall the God of heaven set up a kingdom which shall never be destroyed (Daniel 2:40,41,44).

The Fulfillment

In the great prophetic dream that Nebuchadnezzar had, God showed him the kingdoms that would rule over the earth. The last kingdom, Rome, was shown in two phases. The first phase, represented by the legs of iron, existed at the time of Christ's first coming. The second coming will find that empire revived. It is symbolized as being made of two substances, iron and clay. According to J. Dwight Pentecost:

> The final form of the Gentile power is marked by a federation of that which is weak and that which is strong, autocracy and democracy, the iron and the clay. . . .[7]

Since the decline and fall of the Roman Empire in 476 A.D., Charlemagne, Napolean, Hitler, and others have all tried to reunite Europe by force. But it never worked. Yet now, exactly as the Bible has prophesied, Europe and the rest of the Western world are coming together—not through the iron of force but through the clay of democracy. Who could have imagined, even just a few years ago, that democracy and not Communism would begin to sweep the globe?

The Prophecy: World Government Ruled by Antichrist

> Power was given him [the Antichrist] over all kindreds and tongues and nations (Revelation 13:7).

> The fourth beast shall be the fourth kingdom upon earth, which shall be diverse from all kingdoms, and shall devour the whole earth, and shall tread it down and break it in pieces (Daniel 7:23).

The Fulfillment

> We see a budding World Order in which peaceful co-existence and mutually beneficial cooperation based on goodwill will be universal norms (Mikhail Gorbachev in *Perestroika*).

> Just as the nation-state was a step in the evolution of the government at a time, we are now entering an era of new global interdependencies requiring global

systems of governance to manage the resulting conflicts... these growing tensions cannot be remedied by a single nation-state approach. They shall require the concerted effort of the whole world community.[8]

The Blueprint for a peaceful, loving and harmonious world has been drawn. Prayer, meditation, positive affirmations, spiritual families and global healing events such as Live Aid and the December 31st World Peace Event all contribute to this blueprint (Harmonic Convergence brochure).

The World Council of Churches... I guess it's similar to the United Nations of the church. I think that the future of the world is that we are becoming more of a village, that this is a global village. We are in one world, one community.... the church is going to have to aid the world in understanding that and the United States is going to have to come to grips with that (Rev. Franklyn Richardson).

... the establishment of an order based on justice and peace is vitally needed today as a moral imperative valid for all peoples and regimes... this is the only path possible (Pope John Paul II).

The Prophecy: Worldwide Economic System Ruled by Antichrist

He causeth all, both small and great, rich and poor, free and bond, to receive a mark in their right hand or in their foreheads, and that no man might buy or sell save he that had the mark, or the name of the beast, or the number of his name (Revelation 13:16,17).

The Fulfillment

> I suggest a radical . . . scheme . . . the creation of a common currency for all of the industrial democracies, with a common monetary policy and a joint bank of issue to determine that policy. How can independent states accomplish that? They need to turn over the determination of monetary policy to a supranational body . . . (Richard Cooper).[9]

In 1988 the respected *Economist* magazine, complete with a full-cover picture and feature article, announced the coming of a worldwide economy. The article, while noting that the international currency may be years away, did note that it "will be more convenient than today's national currencies, which will seem a quaint cause of much disruption to economic life in the late twentieth century."

The problem, according to the article, is that governments "are far from ready to subordinate their domestic objectives to the goal of international financial stability. Several more big exchange rate upsets, a few more stock market crashes and probably a slump or two will be needed before politicians are willing to face squarely up to that choice."

> I am very little concerned about the issue of foreign investment in the United States. On the contrary, integration of world economies is a desirable trend (Alan Greenspan, Chairman of the Federal Reserve Board).

> Here's the problem—you fix it. If you have to cast aside your entire political philosophy, so much the better. All we want is a restoration of confidence (*New York Times* reporting on the cry of investors on Black Monday).

The Prophecy: Redistribution of World's Wealth

> He [the Antichrist] shall enter peaceably even upon the fattest places of the province; and he shall do that which his fathers have not done, nor his fathers' fathers: He shall scatter among them the prey, and spoil, and riches; yea, and he shall forecast his devices against the strongholds, even for a time (Daniel 11:24).

The Fulfillment

Today one of the greatest problems that the world faces is the tremendous disparity in standards of living in the North and the South. It seems clear that the prophet Daniel saw this disparity over 2600 years ago. In the days ahead the Antichrist will spread the wealth of the world around. Once again, the calls for just such a move are emerging today:

> Now the choice he [Maitreya—supposedly the New Age "Christ"] will place before humanity is to do nothing, continue as we are and annihilate ourselves or accept the basic principle of sharing. That the food and the raw materials and the energy and the technological know-how of the world must be shared among all people, so we do not have the division, the dangerous divisions, which we have today between the north nations and the south nations, between east and west, and so create peace (Benjamin Creme).

> Fundamental change and improvement in policy is urgently needed... industrial nations must reverse the downward trend of their economic and technical assistance to poverty-stricken countries... (The Global 100 Group).

> We took this challenge very much to heart as we discussed how to teach about hunger and global development. We wanted to encourage the students to think

about poverty and hunger and we wanted them to explore their assumptions about the distribution of the world's wealth and resources . . . (*Global Perspectives in Education*, The Stanley Foundation).

The Prophecy: Rise to Power of Soviet Union

The word of the Lord came unto me, saying, Son of man, set thy face against Gog, the land of Magog, the chief prince of Meshech and Tubal. . . . And thou shalt come from thy place out of the north parts . . . it shall be in the latter days (Ezekiel 38:1,2,15,16).

The Fulfillment

In the last days, according to these Scriptures, a nation will arise that God refers to as Magog. The leader is referred to as Gog. As William Goetz explains in *Apocalypse Next*, we know several things about this nation:

A) It is located to the "uttermost north of Israel."

This is described as the north quarters [or north parts] in Ezekiel 38:6,15 and 39:2. The full meaning of the Hebrew word here translated "north" is "uttermost north." There can only be one nation which qualifies as being at the uttermost north of Israel. (By the way, all compass directions in the Bible are given in reference to the Holy Land). Get a globe. Run a line from Israel to the North Pole. You'll find that it passes through Moscow. Unquestionably, all of Russia is to the uttermost north of Israel.

This geographical description alone clearly points to the fact that Russia is the fulfillment of the prophecy of Gog and Magog. But there are two more items which help confirm this conclusion.

B) They follow the correct genealogy.

The names [given are] . . . Gog, Meshech and Tubal. (Many scholars point out that the word "Gog" should properly be translated "the prince of Rosh.") Students of languages and their meanings agree that these words refer to Russia, Moscow, and Tobolsk. Dr. Merrill Unger in *Beyond the Crystal Ball* and Hal Lindsey in *The Late Great Planet Earth*, quote famous nineteenth-century Hebrew lexicographer William Gesenius as their authority for saying, dogmatically and emphatically, that "Rosh" is to be equated with Russia.

"Meshech" and "Tubal" are identified as the Mushki and the Tubali of the Assyrian records, who over the centuries moved north into the Volga River basin and the present-day Moscow and Tobolsk.

C) They oppose God with a policy of official atheism.

Ezekiel's prophecy declares that God says, "Behold, I am against you, O Gog" (Ezekiel 38:3). A statement that God is against any people is unusual. He is revealed in the Bible as a God of love, mercy, and patience. It almost appears that this statement is out of character for God. The only obvious reason, then, for God's opposition to Russia has to be her atheism and her overt opposition to God.

The official Soviet position is that God does not exist. Following the teaching of Ludwig Feuerbach in his *Essence of Christianity*, Marx rejected the idea of a God and declared that religion was merely the opiate of the people. The Manifesto plainly states that "Communism abolished eternal truths, it abolishes all religion and all morality." Despite Gorbachev's current claims that Russia is a Christian country it appears that God, at least, is not fooled. This ploy, which is designed to pave the way for Soviet participation in the New Europe and ultimately the New World Order, will ultimately give way to an outright attack on the Chosen People.

The Prophecy: Russia to Invade Israel

Say, Thus saith the Lord God: Behold, I am against thee, O Gog, the chief prince of Meshech and Tubal; and I will turn thee back, and put hooks into thy jaws, and I will bring thee forth, and all thine army, horses, and horsemen, all of them clothed with all sorts of armor, even a company with bucklers and shields, all of them handling swords. . . .

Be thou prepared, and prepare for thyself, thou and all thy company that are assembled unto thee, and be thou a guard unto them. After many days thou shalt be visited: In the latter years thou shalt come into the land that is brought back from the sword, and is gathered out of many people, against the mountains of Israel, which have always been waste; but it is brought forth out of the nations, and they shall dwell safely all of them. Thou shalt ascend and come like a storm, thou shalt be like a cloud to cover the land, thou and all thy bands, and many people with thee . . .

Therefore, son of man, prophesy and say unto Gog, Thus saith the Lord God: In that day when my people of Israel dwelleth safely, shalt thou not know it? And thou shalt come from thy place out of the north parts, thou and many people with thee, all of them riding upon horses, a great company and a mighty army; and thou shalt come up against my people of Israel, as a cloud to cover the land; it shall be in the latter days, and I will bring thee against my land, that the heathen may know me, when I shall be sanctified in thee, O Gog, before their eyes (Ezekiel 38:3,4,7-9,14-16).

The Fulfillment

... if the Israelis threaten us, we will wipe them out within two days. I can assure you our plans are made for this eventuality (Soviet Ambassador Anatoly Dobrynin to Henry Kissinger).

Right-wing Russian nationalists are obsessed, as writings and conversations testify, with what they see as the excessive influence of Jews in Soviet society. Despite their denials, anti-Semitism lurks barely beneath the surface of the Russian Right (*The New Russians*).

I agree with Solzhenitsyn that without repentance, we cannot change ourselves or our society. We must feel responsibility for our history. Who was it who made Stalin's terror? It was we—our fathers—and we must now pay for our fathers. But this is repulsive to most people. They want to blame others. They accuse Jews or someone else. They do not want to accept responsibility (Andrei Smirnov, Film director in conversation with Hedrick Smith).

The Soviets continue to deny any interest in unilateral reduction of European conventional forces, but some U.S. experts say the Soviets are already secretly [and now since the U.N. speech openly] cutting troop numbers in central Europe, in a radical restructuring that could actually strengthen Soviet forces. "The Soviets are up to something," says conventional arms expert Philip Karber.

Hungary's army is the likely model; for two years it has received Moscow's most modern weapons. Larger military units have been downgraded and down-sized (personnel cuts up to 40%) but they have relatively more equipment. Tanks, artillery and infantry operate together in a leaner and tougher new fighting formation, the Operational Maneuver Group (OMG) Corps, designed for blitzkrieg (*Newsweek*).

Chapter 18

Spiritual Signs

There is no question that the key phrase of the last days is *religious deception*. In fact, when the disciples came to Jesus asking Him, "When shall these things be, and what shall be the sign of thy coming and of the end of the world?" (Matthew 24:3), the very first thing that Jesus warned was "Take heed that no man deceive you."

Jesus warned that we are to be very careful in watching for our souls. In Mark 13:23, after pointing out the specific deceptions of the last days, Jesus cautioned us with these words: "Take heed; behold, I have foretold you all things."

Just what are these specific deceptions that Jesus has warned of? And what is it that will make the ultimate deceptions so powerful that "if it were possible, they shall deceive the very elect" (Matthew 24:24)?

The Prophecy: Many False Christs

Many shall come in my name, saying, I am Christ, and shall deceive many (Matthew 24:5).

If any man shall say unto you, Lo, here is Christ, or there, believe it not. . . .

277

Wherefore if they shall say unto you, Behold, he is in the desert, go not forth; behold, he is in the secret chambers, believe it not. For as the lightning cometh out of the east and shineth even unto the west, so shall also the coming of the Son of man be (Matthew 24:23, 26,27).

The Fulfillment

As far back as 1981, Syracuse University Professor Agehananda Bharti concluded that "there are fully 2,000 practicing gurus posing as Christs." Likewise, Billy Graham noted that there are at least 400 Christ impostors in the Los Angeles area alone· But that was only the beginning:

Culminating in San Francisco, Benjamin Creme's latest media tour was remarkable. Sparked by The Sally Jesse Raphael Show in December, the field of television has reopened to his inspiring, thought-provoking message about the reappearance of Maitreya the Christ. . . . [Creme] indicated that the Christ is here as the world teacher for all humanity, not just a special-interest group, or a select few, to help us implement the virtues of all the religions and philosophies— in practical ways (*Network News*).

Sant Thakar Singh—He is Living . . . He is here. He is looking for souls who are looking for God. Learn the simple way to experience God for yourself. He has come to teach you how to connect with the inner light and sound (advertisement in *Time* magazine).

I am Jesus Christ. I am omnipotent. I announce the end of the world. The world will be destroyed (Mehmet Ali Agca at his trial for shooting Pope John Paul II).

I am God. You are God. We all are God (Shirley MacLaine and thousands of other New Agers).

Surrounding himself with an eclectic collection of swamis, scholars, lamas and imams, the Rev. Sun Myung Moon has declared himself the new world messiah.

Moon, the Korean founder of the Unification Church, made his pronouncement Aug. 17 at the opening session of his Assembly of World Religions.

Speaking before 500 conference participants, Moon said the world needs to find its "true parent" and free itself from Satan's influence.

"This person is the Messiah," said Moon. "To help fulfill this very purpose I have been called upon by God . . ." (*San Francisco Chronicle*).

The Prophecy: Great Signs and Wonders

There shall arise false Christs and false prophets, and shall show great signs and wonders, insomuch that, if it were possible, they shall deceive the very elect. Behold, I have told you before (Matthew 24:24, 25).

Him whose coming is after the working of Satan, with all power and signs and lying wonders (2 Thessalonians 2:9).

[He] deceiveth them that dwell on the earth by means of those miracles which he had power to do in the sight of the beast (Revelation 13:14).

As Jannes and Jambres withstood Moses, so do these also resist the truth—men of corrupt minds, reprobate concerning the faith (2 Timothy 3:8).

The Fulfillment

Forty-two percent of American adults believe they have been in contact with someone who has died, usually a dead spouse or sibling. Such paranormal experiences by definition, lying outside the normal, are generally viewed as hallucinations or symptoms of mental disorder. But if these experiences were signs of mental illness, our numbers would show the country is going nuts. What was paranormal is now normal. It's even happening to elite scientists and physicians who insist that such things cannot possibly happen.

In any case, other studies show that people who've tasted the paranormal, whether they accept it intellectually or not, are anything but religious nuts or psychiatric cases. They are, for the most part, ordinary Americans, somewhat above the norm in education and intelligence and somewhat less than average in religious involvement.

What's surprising is the vividness of the experiences. Of those who reported such contact, 78 percent said they saw the dead one, 50 percent heard, 21 percent touched, 32 percent felt the presence, 18 percent talked with the departed and 46 percent had some combination of the above.

It would be easier, certainly, to deny that these experiences exist. But the data show clearly that they do exist, that people experience them in great numbers—and that they could change the nature of our society.[1]

The signs of Maitreya's presence in the world will continue to increase. . . . The signs are for those who need them, to strengthen our faith and to give us the necessary courage and conviction to emerge from a state of complacency in order to take on, together, the myriad of necessary tasks to save the world (*Share Magazine*).

The last 15 years have witnessed an explosion of interest in psychic phenomena and parapsychology that is unprecedented in history. This fascination with things that are viewed as supernatural, or at least extra-natural, has permeated every level of our society. This is especially true in the academic community, where only 20 years ago such interests would have been considered absurd.

But now, after almost two centuries of general skepticism toward the miraculous, the secular world is being bombarded with growing evidence that there are indeed forces beyond the scope of the normal scientific process. Most major universities have added parapsychology departments that are not just studying the history of the occult, but exploring its mystery.

There is definite, validated evidence that unexplainable phenomena are taking place in various occultic practices. Medical doctors have verified many instances of supernatural physical cures performed by psychic surgeons . . . (Hal Lindsey).

. . . prominent men and women from such unlikely fields as theoretical physics, neuropsychology and anthropology have been looking seriously into such matters as . . . the always perplexing, yet well-documented capabilities of some people for mental activities ranging from telepathy and clairvoyance to precognition and telekinesis. What sort of scientists are daring to pursue these once "taboo" subject areas? Dr. Herbert Benson, Harvard University; Dr. Elmer Green, Menninger Clinic; Dr. Charles Tart, University of California; Dr. Stanley Krippner, President of Saybrook Institute; Dr. Daniel Goleman, Senior editor of *Psychology Today*; and Dr. Hal Puthoff of the Stanford Research Institute, to name just a few (Edgar Mitchell, astronaut and founder of Institute of Noetic Sciences).

The Prophecy: Strong Delusion

> For this cause God shall send them strong delusion,
> that they should believe a lie (2 Thessalonians 2:11).

The Fulfillment

In 2 Thessalonians we are told that those who will not receive the love of the truth will be allowed by God to come under strong delusion that will cause them to believe a lie. Already we see preparation for this delusion through the false prophets of these last days.

Part of this delusion will consist of the belief that science proves we are on the verge of a great evolutionary leap. This next step of evolution, we are told, will not be physical but spiritual. Spiritual entities will be able to play on such misguided beliefs to deceive millions.

> Western science is approaching a paradigm shift of unprecedented proportions, one that will change our concepts of reality and human nature, bridge the gap between ancient wisdom and modern science, and reconcile the difference between Eastern spirituality and Western pragmatism (Stanislav Grof in *Beyond the Brain*).

> In a feature called "The Search For Modern Humans" in the *National Geographic* magazine, October 1988, a physical anthropologist from the University of Witwatersrand, Johannesburg, Phillip Tobias, said:

> "From my lifetime of studying hominid fossils, I know we've hardly shown any anatomical changes in our bodies for 100,000 years. And I don't think we're suddenly going to start again showing anatomical change. I believe that our physical and anatomical evolution has become less and less significant, whilst our cultural, behavioral, linguistic

and spiritual evolution has become more and more important."

There are many signs of hope that a basic change in human consciousness is under way. These include the growing Green Movement around the world—gradually there is a heightening of awareness that this planet is the only home we have.

We need and are ready as a species to enter the third stage—the mystical awareness of the unity of all things, the interdependence and oneness of all humanity of the cosmos. Thankfully, this conceptual change has already begun (Tom Harpur in the *Toronto Star*).

A recent nationwide poll sponsored by the University of Chicago showed 67 percent of the public claiming psychic experiences (Dave Hunt in *America: The Sorcerer's New Apprentice*).

The Prophecy: Believing a Lie

For this cause God shall send them strong delusion, that they should believe a lie (2 Thessalonians 2:11).

The serpent said unto the woman, Ye shall not surely die; for God doth know that in the day ye eat thereof, then your eyes shall be opened, and ye shall be as gods (Genesis 3:4,5).

Who changed the truth of God into a lie, and worshiped and served the creature more than the Creator, who is blessed forever. Amen (Romans 1:25).

The Fulfillment

Many examples could be given here that millions of people around the world, including New Agers, are claiming to be God. Through practicing transcendental meditation, yoga, hypnosis, or many of the self-help techniques available on the market, scores of people all over the world now believe that they are indeed God and that they are all co-creators in our universe.

Man is an emerging God . . . my plan and my duty is to reveal to you a new way which will permit the divine in man to shine forth (Maitreya).

Be still and know that you are God (Maharishi Mahesh Yogi, founder of TM).

God and man are one. Man is an incarnate God (Sun Myung Moon).

All men are spiritually evolving . . . until each will fully express his divinity (Ernest Holmes, founder of the Church of Religious Science).

The devil told the truth [about godhood]. . . . I do not blame mother Eve. I would not have had her miss eating the forbidden fruit for anything (Brigham Young, former President, Mormon Church).

Just as dogs have puppies and cats have kittens, God has little gods. Until we can comprehend that we are little gods, and begin to act like little gods, we can't manifest the kingdom of God (Earl Paulk, Kingdom Dominion Leader).

You don't have a god in you. You are one (Kenneth Copeland).

I needed affirmations which would help reduce body pain. So I would affirm to myself (sometimes silently and sometimes audibly, depending on whether I would disturb someone else) a resolution such as: I am God in action. Or, I am God in health. Or, I am God with ease. Whatever came to my mind dictated my creative requirement (Shirley MacLaine in *Dancing in the Light*).

The Prophecy: Seducing Spirits

The Spirit speaketh expressly that in the latter times some shall depart from the faith, giving heed to seducing spirits (1 Timothy 4:1).

The Fulfillment

One of the most powerful tools used in the occult is the practice of visualization and guided imagery. Yet these same techniques are being adopted by the "scientific community" and are being incorporated into numerous stress-reducing and self-help programs. We are told that through these techniques, using the power of our mind, positive confession, and so forth, we can create our own reality.

In many of these stress-reducing and self-help programs being offered today, the user is also required to contact a spirit guide. Of course, the use of spirit guides is also a key element in the practice of shamanism and occultism. This spirit guide is referred to by different names, such as Higher Self, Wise Person, and so forth, depending on the program being used. However, we know from the Bible that they are indeed demons. And, through contacting these seducing spirits, mankind is falling into terrible deception:

The course Woman of Spirit and Power offers us the opportunity to travel deep into the treasures of our hearts' desire for compassion, clarity of purpose and harmony with all creation. Through Guided Imagery Meditation we will make our journey into the life of mystery. We will meet the Wise Women who live within and who are able to open for us the doors to our visions and dreams (United Church of Canada).

Mantra and meditation? Some form of transcendental meditation as preached by an Eastern guru? "That's a very frequent question," Elizabeth Parnis says. "The method is the same and, of course, Transcendental Meditation has its roots in Hinduism. But we look on this as a form of prayer and it's the whole theology that makes it different from Transcendental Meditation. It's rooted in the Christian faith. It's a method of meditation that comes to us from the desert fathers" (*Toronto Star*).

In her occult training Johanna Michaelsen [author of *The Beautiful Side of Evil*] chose "Jesus" as her spirit guide, which she contacted through meditation.... It was only after renouncing occultism and committing herself to Jesus Christ as her Lord and Savior that Johanna recognized it was not the real Jesus that she had been contacting through these occult techniques. In fact, those visualizing Mary, Napoleon, or Benjamin Franklin were all having the same powerful experiences that Johanna believed were from God.

Wise men of India for many centuries have trod the lofty peaks of spiritual powers and given birth to their oversouls.

Spirits of those [dead] for whom we have prayed on earth are working through us....

One conveys that healing force to the inner being [of the sick] through the law of suggestion (Agnes Sanford in *The Healing Light*).

The Prophecy: Focus on Prosperity

Go to now, ye rich men, weep and howl for your miseries that shall come upon you. Your riches are corrupted, and your garments are motheaten. Your gold and silver is cankered; and the rust of them shall be a witness against you, and shall eat your flesh as it were fire. Ye have heaped treasure together for the last days (James 5:1-3).

Thou sayest, I am rich and increased with goods, and have need of nothing, and knowest not that thou art wretched, and miserable, and poor, and blind, and naked; I counsel thee to buy of me gold tried in the fire, that thou mayest be rich, and white raiment, that thou mayest be clothed, and that the shame of thy nakedness do not appear; and anoint thy eyes with eyesalve, that thou mayest see (Revelation 3:17,18).

The grace of God that bringeth salvation hath appeared to all men, teaching us that, denying ungodliness and worldly lusts, we should live soberly, righteously, and godly in this present world; looking for that blessed hope and the glorious appearing of the great God and our Savior Jesus Christ (Titus 2:11-13).

The Fulfillment

These prophecies indicate very clearly that in the last days an unbalanced and unhealthy view of wealth would emerge in Christian circles. The Lord Himself tells us that the church of the last days would boast that it was successful because of its financial status. Jesus said, however, that this church will spiritually be "wretched, and miserable, and poor, and blind, and naked." Watching much of what is called Christian television today shows just how deeply this lie has infiltrated this last-days church.

Dr. Richard Halverson, during the 45th annual National Association of Evangelicals convention held in Buffalo, New York, during March 2-5, 1987, stated that "prosperity may be the greatest danger evangelicals face today." And yet the message of the prosperity gospel continues to spread through the church today.

[The Bible teaches] that when you give money to a

ministry, if you don't expect to reap a harvest of money you are mocking God! (Kenneth Copeland).

For every $1 you give you receive $100, which is a very good deal (Gloria Copeland).

We're a powerful group, and we're not going to go limping in [to the kingdom] barely making it. When God delivered the children of Israel they were laden down with silver and gold. . . .
He's given us power to create wealth and we're already seeing this happen, and I believe that in these last days the believer is not going to be at the back of the bus taking a back seat any longer! (Robert Tilton).

There is an evil wind blowing into God's house, deceiving multitudes of God's chosen people. It is a scriptural take-off on Napoleon Hill's book, *Think and Grow Rich*.
This perverted gospel seeks to make gods of people. They are told, "Your destiny is in the power of your mind. Whatever you can conceive is yours. Speak it into being. Create it by a positive mindset. Success, happiness, perfect health is all yours" (Dave Wilkerson as quoted in *The Seduction of Christianity*).

Another trait of Korean Christianity that disturbs some is the tendency, encouraged by prelates like Mr. Cho, to see Christianity as a path to material prosperity (*The Wall Street Journal*).

The Prophecy: A Coming World Religion

All that dwell upon the earth shall worship him, whose names are not written in the book of life of the Lamb, slain from the foundation of the world (Revelation 13:8).

The Fulfillment

In essence, this prophecy speaks for itself. All those who have not accepted the Lord Jesus Christ as their Savior will indeed become part of the world religion that will be established after the rapture of the church. And this world religion is forming right before us in these last days.

> Pope John Paul II urged all religions to work together against political, ideological and economic tensions that he said threaten the survival of mankind. . . . It's God's will that we work together . . . he said (Associated Press Story of Pope's message to Hindus, Moslems, Protestants, and Catholics).

> A sensitive, informed Christian can no longer either morally or intellectually disdain the faith of the great religious communities of our planet other than our own; can no longer dismiss it . . . as not divine . . . (Wilfred Smith, retired Director of the Center for the Study of World Religions at Harvard University).

> Religion taken as a whole benefited much from the variety in its different forms. All the centuries that the Spirit of God had been working in Christians, He must also have been working in Hindus, Buddhists, Muslims, and others . . . it takes humility and sincerity to concede that there is a certain incompleteness in each of our traditions. . . . This will mean that some claims about the exclusiveness of the church will have to be renounced (Robert Runcie, former Archbishop of Canterbury).

> We need a world or cosmic spirituality. . . . I hope that religious leaders will get together and define . . . the cosmic laws which are common to all their faiths. . . . They should tell the politicians what the cosmic laws are, what God, or the gods, or the cosmos are expecting from humans. . . .

We must also hope that the Pope will come before the year 2000 to the United Nations, speak for all the religions and spiritualities on this planet and give the world the religious view of how the third millenium should be a spiritual millennium (Robert Muller at the 1989 Global Gathering for Peace).

Every major religion of the world has similar ideals of love, the same goal of benefitting humanity through spiritual practice. The most important thing is to look at the purpose of religion and not at the details of theology or metaphysics. I believe that all the major religions of the world can contribute to world peace and work together for the benefit of humanity if we put aside subtle metaphysical differences, which are really the internal business of each religion. The undying faith in religion clearly demonstrates the potency of religion as such. This spiritual energy and power can be purposefully used to bring about the spiritual condition necessary for world peace (the Dalai Lama).

Chapter 19

Signs of the Times

The Prophecy: Mark-of-the-Beast Technology

> He causeth all, both small and great, rich and poor, free and bond, to receive a mark in their right hand or in their foreheads, and that no man might buy or sell save he that had the mark, or the name of the beast, or the number of his name (Revelation 13:16,17).

The Fulfillment

Again, like many of the other prophecies, the fulfillment of this prophecy will not ultimately take place until Antichrist has established his kingdom during the tribulation.

We know that during this time Antichrist will have established a worldwide economic system over which he has complete control. The monetary system of this economic order will require a mark in the right hand or in the forehead.

Today we can already see banking trends and technology falling into place which foreshadow the fulfillment of this prophecy of a worldwide economic system and the acceptance of the mark:

> Not quite yet, but sooner than many people think, a single plastic card could replace most cash and

checks . . . predict many of the cashless buying system's chief architects [who claim that] the majority of consumer purchases will be handled by machines.[1]

The first cashless society may soon be Singapore, which formally launched its latest move in that direction recently. No cash transactions are permitted in major department stores, supermarkets, gas stations, hospitals and government offices. The scheme, under which shoppers use their plastic automated teller machine cards to pay for goods and services, began weeks ago. . . . To promote the new system, the government closed all cash payment offices, leaving citizens little choice but to join Singapore's ceaseless drive toward a high-tech—but cashless—society.[2]

Consider how innovations [in microminiaturization of electronic components] might be employed to solve the age-old problem of providing positive identification of animals, equipment and people. That's what the design specialists at Identification Devices did. And here's the result: Fish biologists can now easily identify and track the movements of larger numbers of fish moving past a given point. A microminiature transponder implanted in the target fish transmits each fish's identification number upon command. . . . The implanted device has no adverse effect on the fish.[3]

A tiny homing device, implanted behind the ear, will help parents locate their missing children, says a plastic surgeon who developed the gadget using the same technology that led to cellular phones. "The device, which emits electronic signals, could also help law enforcement officials find parolees and aid in the search for victims of Alzheimer's disease who have wandered off," said the developer, Dr. Daniel Mann. "Private industry and government agencies have expressed interest in the mini beeper, which measures less than an inch in size." Mann was awarded a patent last month for the device . . . that could be monitored through a cellular system or possibly by satellite. . . . James A. Long, executive director of the Florida affiliate of the American Civil Liberties Union, said he would have no worries about the device as long as individuals agreed to have it implanted. But, he cautioned, "Somebody's bound to abuse it."[4]

With Europe coming together as the "United States of Europe," they are expressing concern that they will have to come up with a way to keep track of everyone in the new "open" world of the future. Amazingly, the very solution being proposed to keep track of everyone in the New World Order is exactly the one the Bible told us almost 2000 years ago would be embraced! On March 13-15, 1991, in Barcelona, Spain, "The First World Pragmatech Card Conference" took place. It was convened under the title "Borderless Borders." The promotional materials spelled out the prophetic agenda:

> Card technology applications are being affected radically by the dramatic changes in a Western Europe in the process of uniting with an emerging, new Eastern Europe. . . .
>
> Issues which must be addressed include:
>
> Identification: What information is necessary? Who are the keepers of the database? Will international passports be issued by individual nations or a central bureau, for example, the European Community (EC)?
>
> Security: How much identification is necessary to ensure a nation's security?
>
> Telecommunications: . . . Who will make the decisions—government, business or a worldwide entity?
>
> Banking/POS [Point of Sales]: Why should integrated Circuit/smart cards or debit cards replace cash? How

much will identification and social services requirements drive these card applications?

International Card Technology Institute President Arlen Lessin also made the following observations about the symposium:

> This is a very important conference—and not just because of the issues to be raised. The purpose of this conference is to formally and informally create a dialogue among the people who must make decisions about how we are going to live in an open world.

> We are not yet a global community. But that is clearly the direction in which we are heading. Borders will tend to blur and disappear on levels of economic, technological, political, military and even social activities. How can the integrity and security of a nation be maintained if people are free to cross from one nation to another? Of course, there must be some constraints, some means of knowing who is wishing to cross, some means of monitoring and/or identifying people from various nations.

The Prophecy: Earthquakes

> There shall be ... earthquakes in various places (Matthew 24:7; Mark 13:8; cf. Luke 21:11).

The Fulfillment

One of the most frequent arguments used against Bible prophecy is that there have always been earthquakes. However, Scripture seems to be indicating that the last-days sign will be the increasing intensity and frequency of these occurrences, and not just the simple fact that they are indeed occurring. Also, by saying that there will be earthquakes in various places, the Scriptures are also indicating that earthquakes will begin to occur in places which are not generally prone to earthquake activity. We have also been seeing this happen over the past few years.

There are now about 6000 earthquakes detected every year. Of these, 15 are serious. On the average, 20,000 people die annually as a direct result of earthquakes.

> A severe earthquake struck the Soviet republic of Armenia, Dec. 7. A government estimate put the death toll at 25,000, and some 500,000 persons were homeless. The city of Leninakan, population 290,000, was nearly leveled; at least 32 mountain villages were destroyed.[5]

> International aid began pouring in yesterday for victims of an earthquake that killed at least 74 people, injured more than 800 and left thousands homeless in Costa Rica and Panama.[6]

> MOSCOW—A powerful earthquake rocked the southern Soviet republic of Georgia yesterday, killing at least 30 people, destroying buildings and causing rockslides in mountain villages officials said.

> About five-and-one-half hours later, a second quake almost as strong struck the Georgian capital, Tbilisi, and its second city Kutaisi, officials said.

> The first quake measured about seven on the Richter scale, said Vladimir Strakhov, Soviet Earth Institute director.

> The quake caused rockslides in mountain villages.

> "The mountain fell on to the houses," said Marina Starostina, a Georgian government official in Moscow.

> "The extent of the damage or the number of victims [of the second quake] are not known," Tass reported. "Communications with those areas has been disrupted."[7]

The Prophecy: Pestilences

> There shall be ... pestilences (Matthew 24:7; cf. Luke 21:11).

The Fulfillment

In 1987, 14,000,000 children alone died from plagues, including diarrheal diseases, measles, tetanus, and malaria. As famine increases, these numbers will continue to rise.

> A Toronto doctor now working in Baltimore, Md., has found more than 5 percent of patients who came to a city hospital emergency department were infected with the AIDS virus, but most of them had no idea they were.
> Dr. Gabor Kelen, director of medical research in the Johns Hopkins Hospital emergency department, headed a study in which 2,300 patients treated in a six-week period were tested for the AIDS virus. Researchers found 119 infected people, of whom 92 were unaware of it.[8]

> GENEVA (AP)—The World Health Organization predicted Thursday that the AIDS virus will infect up to 30 million adults and 10 million children by the end of the century. That is 10 million higher than its estimate a year ago.[9]

> One in 100 19-year-old women giving birth statewide [New York state] is infected with the AIDS virus, as are 1 in 1,000 15-year-olds.
> Half of the city's teen-age girls with AIDS say they got infected by having sex with males.
> State researchers found about 6 percent of homeless boys and girls at one city shelter were infected.

One city health clinic found 26 percent of sexually active teen-age girls had tried anal sex—the most risky sexual practice for males and females.[10]

GENEVA (Reuters)—Nearly 6 million Africans are believed infected with the HIV virus which causes AIDS, the World Health Organization said Tuesday.

By early 1991 more than 1 million men, women and children living in countries south of the Sahara were estimated to have contracted the fatal disease produced by the virus, WHO said.

AIDS cases officially reported by African governments totaled 85,728 by March 31, but the health body says many countries under-report cases or are slow to notify them.[11]

GENEVA (AP)—Latin America's cholera epidemic threatens up to 120 million people in the region, and providing safe water and sanitation to stop its spread could cost $50 billion, the World Health Organization said yesterday.

The epidemic, which appeared on Peru's northern coast in January, has spread to neighboring Ecuador, Colombia, Chile and Brazil.[12]

QUITO—A Cholera epidemic that spread to Ecuador from neighboring Peru has killed 100 people and infected 5,000, the head of the Ecuadoran Medical Federation says.

"We will see the epidemic peak in May," Francisco Plaza [President of EMF] said in a televised interview. "Cholera will remain in Ecuador for about 15 years and the disease will become epidemic."[13]

The war is still going on in Iraq, where innocent civilians suffer from lack of food and medicine and must live in squalor, says a Canadian doctor who just spent 10 days in Baghdad.

Dr. Eric Hoskins says he found the residents of the war-torn city devastated by the lack of emergency help in the aftermath of the Persian Gulf war.

Hoskins, a physician from Simcoe, Ont., was most affected by the plight of the children, who are getting sick because they are forced to live in filth.

Hoskins witnessed raw sewage flowing out into the street and backed up in the basement of the hospital.[14]

DHAKA, Bangladesh—Rough weather slowed efforts yesterday to get emergency aid to millions of survivors of last week's devastating cyclone, who now face new dangers from hunger, disease and poisonous snakes.

As the official death toll rose above 125,000, aid officials reported that people are dying from snake bites and cholera, and warned of epidemics in overcrowded relief camps, where water, food and medicine are scarce.[15]

The Prophecy: Hatred of Christians

Then shall they deliver you up to be afflicted, and shall kill you; and ye shall be hated of all nations for my name's sake (Matthew 24:9).

And ye shall be hated of all men for my name's sake (Luke 21:17).

He [the Antichrist] shall speak great words against the Most High, and shall wear out the saints of the Most High (Daniel 7:25).

The Fulfillment

Today, in the rush to build a New World Order based on the principles of unity and tolerance, the only group that is not being tolerated are those who believe that Jesus Christ is the only way of salvation. Such thinking is too narrow, we are being told. It is true that there has always been persecution against true believers, but it will intensify in the last days until it becomes one of the foundation stones of the New World Order ruled by the Antichrist. Today an increasing anti-Christian fervor, the emergence of "hate-literature laws," and the Genocide Convention foreshadow such a day.

> We have no problem at all if religion does not claim to involve knowledge and is not concerned with what is true and what is false.
>
> If, however, it claims to involve knowledge [and claims that] it alone has its source in divine revelation, accepted by an act of faith that is in itself divinely caused [and if] religion claims to be supernatural knowledge—that man has only as a gift from God... then we are confronted with a special problem....I submit that cultural diversity should be tolerated only in those areas in which the criteria of truth and falsity do not apply.[16]

> If the future is not for the fainthearted, it is even more certainly not for the cowardly...Those who insist theirs is the only correct government or economic system deserve the same contempt as those who insist that they have the only true God.[17]

> Reaching an estimated 60 million Americans, charismatic war-minded evangelists insist that they have the right and power to help orchestrate not only their End of Times, but doomsday for all the rest of the species. As rising stars of the New Christian Right and the Republican Party, these militant conservatives seemingly have unlimited financial resources, a site in Israel for the "last great battle" and a line of reasoning for a nuclear war—because God wills it. They preach,

promote and actually sell Americans on the idea of building more bombs and then using them to destroy planet earth.[18]

The attacks by "People for the American Way" on the leaders and organizations of Orthodox Christianity parallel the Brown Shirts' pointed attacks upon the Jewish community in Germany during the '30s. Left unchecked, the momentum created by that hatred, presented as love of country, resulted in the death of millions of Jews, Christians, and others who tried, too late, to help the persecuted minority.[19]

NOTES

Chapter 1—A Way That Seems Right

1. Evangelical Fellowship of Canada, *Discerning the Times Seminar Workbook*.
2. *Harvest Time*, June 1984, p. 2.
3. Revelation 1:3.
4. Luke 21:26.
5. Matthew 24:6; Mark 13:7; Luke 21:9.
6. John Randolph Price, *The Planetary Commission* (Quartus Foundation, 1984).
7. Planetary Initiative brochure, Planetary Citizens, P.O. Box 426, Menlo Park, CA 94026.
8. Thomas Berry, *Toronto Star*, September 7, 1986.
9. M. Scott Peck, *The Different Drum* (New York: Simon and Schuster, 1987), p. 19.
10. *New York Times*, October 12, 1989.
11. *New York Times*, October 12, 1989.
12. *New York Times*, February 14, 1988.
13. *New York Times*, February 14, 1988.
14. Mikhail Gorbachev, *Perestroika: New Thinking for Our Country and the World* (New York: Harper and Row, 1987).
15. George Bush, "Address to the Nation," September 16, 1990.
16. *Westchester Newspapers* (Westchester County, NY), January 23, 1988.
17. *Herald Statesman* (Westchester County, NY), January 9, 1988.
18. *Catholic World*, May/June 1989, p. 140.

Chapter 2—The Fake Messiah

1. Ezekiel 38:8.
2. Isaiah 11:11-12; Ezekiel 36:24.
3. Deuteronomy 28:67; Luke 21:24.
4. Dave Hunt, "Discerning the Times, '90 Prophecy Conference," Niagara Falls, Canada, October 21-24, 1990 (available from the Omega-Letter Publishing Group, P.O. Box 1440, Niagara Falls, NY 14305).
5. *Jewish Press* (newspaper), August 10, 1990.
6. *New York Times*, January 5, 1991.

Chapter 3—The Democratic Kingdom of Antichrist

1. In America, the political connotations of this nursery rhyme are not generally known. For Europeans, however, there is a double meaning.
2. Daniel 9:26.
3. J. Dwight Pentecost, *Things to Come* (Grand Rapids, MI: Zondervan, 1958), p. 325.
4. Ibid., p. 319.
5. *Europe Magazine*, November 1989.
6. *New York Times*, June 8, 1990.
7. *World Press Review*, March 1990.
8. *New York Times*, August 6, 1990.
9. *New York Times*, March 12, 1990.
10. U.S. Secretary of State James Baker, speech in Berlin, December 1989.
11. *Europe* magazine, July/August 1989.
12. *The European*, September 19, 1990.
13. Ibid.

14. Canadian Prime Minister Brian Mulroney, May 1990.
15. Canadian External Affairs Minister Joe Clark, May 1990.
16. Mikhail Gorbachev, address to the U.N. General Assembly, December 7, 1988.
17. *Reuters*, November 15, 1989.
18. As quoted in Malachi Martin, *Keys of This Blood* (New York: Simon and Schuster, 1990).

Chapter 4—The Great Whore
1. John F. Walvoord, *The Revelation of Jesus Christ* (Chicago: Moody Bible Institute, 1966), p. 244.
2. F.C. Jennings, *Our Hope Magazine*, December 1940.
3. Cardinal Alphonsus de'Liguor, *The Glories of Mary* (Rockford, IL: Tan Books, 1977), p. 94.
4. Ibid., p. 136.
5. Ibid., p. 137, 141, 143.
6. Ibid., p. 180, 181.
7. Archbishop of Canterbury Robert Runcie, September 31, 1989.
8. Malachi Martin, *Keys of this Blood* (New York: Simon and Schuster, 1990), p. 354.
9. Ibid., p. 311.
10. Ibid., p. 109-110.
11. *Europe Magazine*, July/August 1990.
12. Redemptor Homis, as paraphrased in Martin, *Keys of This Blood*, p. 74.
13. Gorbachev, address to the U.N., December 7, 1988.
14. Martin, *Keys of This Blood*, p. 15, 17.
15. Ibid., p. 134.
16. Ibid., p. 132.
17. Ibid., p. 132.
18. Ibid., p. 111.
19. Ibid., p. 143.
20. Pat Robertson, *The New Millennium* (Dallas: Word, 1990).
21. *The Contender* (newspaper), November 15, 1987.
22. CIB Bulletin, as quoted in *The Omega-Letter*, January 1990.
23. *New York Times*, May 10, 1988.

Chapter 5—The Whore and the Beast
1. Malachi Martin, *The Keys of This Blood* (New York: Simon and Schuster, 1990), p. 259.
2. *Religious Herald*, January 25, 1990.
3. James Baker, at National Prayer Breakfast, 1990.
4. Kim Miller, Concerned Christians, Denver, CO.
5. John Walvoord, *The Revelation of Jesus Christ* (Chicago: Moody Press, 1986), p. 248.
6. *International Herald Tribune* (New York), October 17, 1990.
7. Robert Muller, "Global Gathering for Peace," speech before the Global Gathering for Peace.
8. Ibid.
9. Ecumenical Press Service of the World Council of Churches, September 18-24, 1988.
10. Manifesto of the Global Forum of Spiritual and Parlimentary Leaders on Human Survival (available from Global Forum, 304 E. 45th St., New York, NY 10017).

Chapter 6—Toward the New World Order
1. Paul Johnson, *World Press Review*, March 1990.
2. *New York Times*, November 22, 1989.
3. Associated Press release, June 8, 1990.
4. *USA Today*, December 26, 1989.
5. Malachi Martin, *The Keys of This Blood* (New York: Simon and Schuster, 1990), p. 15.
6. Ibid., p. 17.
7. Ibid., p. 89.
8. Ibid., p. 377.
9. Ibid., p. 392.

10. *Time Magazine*, September 17, 1990.
11. *Jewish Press*, December 7, 1990.
12. Paul Mazur, "Unfinished Business," as quoted in Martin, *Keys of This Blood*, p. 343.
13. *International Herald Tribune*, June 16, 1990.
14. *The Toronto Star*, September 17, 1987.
15. *The Toronto Star*, October 5, 1987.
16. Martin, *Keys of This Blood*, p. 36.
17. Associated Press, June 8, 1990.
18. Martin, *Keys of This Blood*, p. 209.
19. Ibid., p. 16.

Chapter 7—The Blueprint

1. Karen Hoyt, *The New Age Rage* (Old Tappan, NJ: Fleming H. Revell, 1987), p. 198-200.
2. Barry Goldwater, *With No Apologies* (New York: Berkeley Books, 1979) p. 292.
3. Ibid., p. 4.
4. Ibid., p. 293, 297, 299.
5. Speech before the U.S. Senate as quoted in the *Independent American*, September/October, 1988.
6. As quoted in Gary Allen, *None Dare Call It Conspiracy* (San Francisco: Concord Press, 1971).
7. Carol Quigley, *Tragedy and Hope*, as quoted in Gary Allen, *None Dare Call It Conspiracy*.
8. Editorial in *Saturday Review*, March 23, 1953.
9. *New York Times*, September 11, 1989.
10. Ibid.
11. Ibid.
12. *Daily News*, July 19, 1989.
13. *Daily Variety*, November 5, 1986.
14. "Pope's Message to Medical Leaders," as quoted in *The Pope Speaks*, May 31, 1987.
15. *Insight*, June 19, 1989.

Chapter 8—A Political Transformation

1. *Straight Talk*, August 9, 1990.
2. *Times* magazine, July 9, 1990.
3. Ibid.
4. "Seattle Public School Memorandum," April 19, 1985 (see *The Omega-Letter*, October 1986).
5. Summary Report of the NEA Bicentennial Program, National Education Association.
6. Leonard Kenworthy, U.N. Association of USA (a non-government organization affiliated with the United Nations), 1978.
7. Conclusion of the Cunningham Report, Department of Education's Denver Regional Office.
8. *New York Times*, December 11, 1988.
9. Bob Guccione, *USA Today*, December 27, 1988.
10. *The Toronto Star*, June 12, 1988.
11. Ibid.
12. Harry Belafonte, in *Billboard* magazine as quoted in *The Omega-Letter*, September 1986.
13. Peter Russell, *The Awakening Earth* (Ark Paperbacks, 1982) p. 3, quoting Fred Hoyle (in 1948).
14. *Shared Vision*, Vol. 3, 1989.
15. Senator Jesse Helms, as quoted by an American Educational League brochure.
16. *TV Guide*, October 3, 1987.

Chapter 9—The Pied Pipers

1. Zbigniew Brzezinski, *Between Two Ages* (New York: Viking, 1970).
2. Mark Satin, *New Age Politics: Healing Self and Society* (New York: Dell Publishing Co., 1978).
3. Pacem in Teris III Conference in Washington, 1973.
4. *The Evangelist*, July 1987.
5. *USA Today*, November 6, 1987.
6. *New York Times*, October 28, 1987.

7. *New York Times*, November 1, 1987.
8. Global Economy Conference, "The World Future Society," 1985, World Future Society, Betheseda, MD.
9. *Foreign Affairs Magazine*, Fall 1984.
10. *New York Times*, August 5, 1987.
11. *Newsweek*, August 8, 1988.
12. *New York Times*, December 25, 1988.
13. *Gannett Westchester Newspapers* (Westchester County, NY), December 5, 1988.
14. *New York Times*, November 27, 1988.
15. *Angus Reid* (Canadian polling organization), October 22, 1989.
16. Ibid.
17. "Our Common Future Television Special," MTV, June 3, 1989.
18. World Commission on Environment and Development Public Hearings, May 1988.
19. "Our Common Future Television Special."
20. Ervin Lazlo, presentation to Worldview '84 Congress, 1978.
21. Ibid.
22. Ibid.
23. Willis Harman, *An Alternative Guide to the Future* (New York: Norton, 1979).
24. Lazlo, "Presentation to Worldview."
25. At the Crossroads Communications Era Task Force, 1983, distributed at Worldview 14, The World Future Society, Betheseda, MD.
26. Lazlo, presentation to Worldview.
27. *Canadian World Federalist*, February 1985.
28. Betty Lynn, *The Omega-Letter*, July 1990, Niagara Falls, NY.
29. *Canadian World Federalist*, February 1985.
30. Lewis Mumford, as quoted in Willis Harmon, *An Incomplete Guide to the Future* (New York: Norton, 1979).

Chapter 10—The Gospel of Antichrist

1. *The Oregonian* (Portland, OR), March 21, 1990.
2. *Cleveland Plain Dealer*, December 30, 1989.
3. *Des Moines Register*, April 4, 1990.
4. *American Health Magazine*, January/February 1987, p. 47.
5. *New York Times*, September 29, 1986.
6. *U.S. News and World Report*, December 5, 1988.
7. *Newsweek*, June 26, 1989.
8. "Desert News Church Section," June 18, 1873, p. 308, as cited in Ed Decker and Dave Hunt, *The God Makers* (Eugene, OR: Harvest House, 1984) p. 30.
9. Shirley MacLaine, *Out on a Limb* (New York: Bantam Books, 1983).
10. Fred Polak, *The Image of the Future*, as cited in Willis Harman, *An Incomplete Guide to the Future* (New York: Norton, 1976), p. 114.
11. Willis Harman, *An Incomplete Guide to the Future* (New York: Norton, 1976), p. 33.
12. *Canadian World Federalist*, February 1985.
13. Introduction to the He-Man Cartoon Series.
14. *The Incredible Shrinking Turtles*, a cartoon version video of the Teenage Mutant Ninja Turtles.
15. Shirley MacLaine, *It's All in the Playing* (New York: Bantam Books, 1988).
16. Maria Monetta at the "Through Crisis to Transformation Conference," June 19-21, 1987, as cited in Johanna Michaelsen, *Like Lambs to the Slaughter* (Eugene, OR: Harvest House, 1989), p. 46.
17. Larry and Les Ann Ciglen, *News*, October 1989, Vol. 4, No. 1, a publication of the Ontario Public School Teachers' Federation, Ontario, Canada.
18. *OMNI*, November 1989.
19. Mary Bell, "Psychic Children Playing with the Spirit," *Psychic Life*, Vol. 5, No. 2., 1985.
20. Dick Sutphen, "Infiltrating the New Age into Society," *What Is?*, Summer 1986, p. 14.
21. Meditation tape (Tape #1, side 2) used by the Quieting Reflex and Success Imagery program, Pinnelas County, Florida, developed in 1974 by Dr. Charles Stroebel.

22. The Society for Accelerated Education, "New Dimensions in Education, Confluent Learning," April 25, 1980, Los Angeles, CA.

Chapter 11—Signs, Wonders, and the Rise of Antichrist
1. Hal Lindsey, *The 1980s: Countdown to Armageddon* (New York: Bantam Books, 1981), p. 32-33.
2. Geneva Summit, December 5, 1985.
3. Jacques Vallee, *Messengers of Deception* (Berkeley, 1979), pp. 204-5.
4. Dave Hunt, *The Cult Explosion* (Eugene, OR: Harvest House Publishers, 1978), pp. 19-20.
5. Whitley Strieher, *Transformation* (New York: Beech Tree Books, 1988), p. 44.
6. Benjamin Creme, Q107 Radio Toronto, Interview by Jane Hawtin, May 30, 1984.
7. *National Geographic*, October 1988.
8. *Detroit Free Press*, December 31, 1986.
9. *The Omega-Letter*, October 1986.
10. Shirley MacLaine, *Dancing in the Light* (New York: Bantam Books, 1985), p. 347-48.
11. Barbara Marx Hubbard, *The Book of Co-Creation: An Evolutionary Interpretation of the New Testament*, a three part unpublished manuscript dated 1980.
12. World Healing Day flyer, December 1986, Quartus Foundation, Austin, TX.
13. Hubbard, *The Book of Co-Creation*.
14. Ibid.
15. Ruth Montgomery, "Threshold to Tomorrow," *Magical Blend*, Issue 113, 1986, p. 206.

Chapter 12—A Deceptive Christ
1. Malachi Martin, *Keys of This Blood* (New York: Simon and Schuster, 1990), p. 48.
2. Ibid., p. 456.
3. Ibid., p. 649.
4. Quoted on World Pope, Steel on Steel radio program, tape 4, Denver, CO.
5. Ibid.
6. Martin, *Keys of This Blood*, p. 657.
7. Ibid., p. 483, 639.

Chapter 13—If They Hated Me . . .
1. *Time*, January 2, 1989.
2. "Planet in Peril," *Southam Newspapers*, Fall 1989.
3. Mortimer J. Adler, "World Peace in Truth," *Center Magazine*, March/April 1978.
4. Ibid.
5. Gene Roddenberry, *Time* magazine, April 18, 1988.
6. The Genocide Convention (treaty), approved in December 1948, was in reaction to the persecution that Jews faced in the hands of Hitler; however, today this treaty is being used for much less noble purposes.
7. Ibid., many critics of this treaty are convinced that such power now exists in the treaty with no further modification needed.
8. Barry Goldwater, *With No Apologies* (Berkeley 1979), p. 293, 297.
9. Tom Harper, *Toronto Star*, July 28, 1985.
10. *Calgary Sun*, as cited in *The Omega-Letter*, May 1986.
11. House of Commons debates, March 26, 1985.
12. Paul Gibson, "Health and Human Services Task Force," quoted in *Christian World Report*, July 1990.
13. As quoted in *The Straight Talk* newsletter.
14. As quoted in *Christian World Report*, July 1990.
15. See *The Christian World Report*, March 1990, for additional examples.
16. Ibid.
17. *Christian Herald*, May 1988.
18. *The Republic*, North Vernon, Ohio.
19. *National International Religion Report*, 5/8/89.

20. Patrick Buchanan as quoted in *The Christian World Report*, August 1989.
21. UPI press release, 9/23/89.
22. *Toronto Star*, 4/29/59.
23. Wire Dispatcher, 7/8/90.
24. *The Christian World Report*, August 1989.
25. Ibid., March 1990.
26. Save the Family Foundation brochure, 1987.
27. Andrew Lang, The Christic Institute, *Cleveland Plain Dealer* (Cleveland, OH), 1/4/89.
28. Global Forum Conference, Oxford University, April 11-15, 1988.

Chapter 14—The Sleeping Bear
1. Michael Dobbs, *Washington Post*, 4/21/88.
2. Message to the Supreme Soviet, November 2, 1987.
3. Mikhail Gorbachev, November 89, as quoted by Malachi Martin, *Keys of This Blood* (New York: Simon and Schuster, 1990), p. 32.
4. Student Forum, November 5, 1989, Moscow.
5. Mikhail Gorbachev, *Perestroika* (New York: Harper and Row, 1987).
6. As quoted in *The Omega-Letter*, February 1989.
7. *America's Future* newsletter, November 1989.
8. Richard Pipers, *New York Times*, 01/09/89.
9. According to Communist theory, all events will eventually work together to push the world into the utopian workers state.
10. Martin, *Keys of This Blood*, p. 251.
11. Hedrick Smith, *The New Russians* (New York: Random House, 1990), p. 404.
12. Assistant Prof. Raymond Puch and Prof. James Gibson, *Jewish Press*, April 6-12, 1990.
13. Smith, *The New Russians*, p. 121.
14. *Herald Statesman*, 9/5/90.
15. *International Herald Tribune*, 7/29/90.

Chapter 15—Testing the Mark of the Beast
1. *USA Today*, Weekend Edition, 6/24-26/88.
2. *Insight*, 8/21/89.
3. Programs like this one are being run by both MasterCard and VISA all across the nation.
4. Terry Galanoy, *Charge It* (New York: Putnam Publishers, 1980).
5. George E. Word, *Time* magazine, December 26, 1988.
6. *Journal-Lorain* (newspaper), 7/12/89.
7. *U.S. News and World Report*, 12/17/84.
8. "Federal Reserve Bank of Atlanta," *Economic Review*, March 1983.
9. *Cat Fancy*, October 1984.
10. Undated promotional brochure, Identification Devices, Denver, CO.
11. AP press release, 7/19/89.
12. Gannett News Services, as quoted in *The Omega-Letter*, October 1986.
13. *Journal Record* (New York), 8/21/87.
14. *Omni*, March 1987.
15. Identification Devices Promotional Packet, Denver, CO.
16. *USA Today*, 1/22/88.
17. *USA Today*, 6/28/89.
18. *Herald Statesman* (Westchester County, NY), 6/7/89.
19. Borderless Borders: The First World Pragmatech Card Conference, Barcelona Spain, March 13-15, 1991.
20. Ibid.
21. Gannett News Service, 4/16/89.
22. *New York Times*, 12/19/88.

23. *USA Today*, 6/20/89.
24. *International Herald Tribune*, 7/17/90.

Chapter 17—Geopolitical Signs
1. *New York Times*, May 14, 1948.
2. Ibid., June 7, 1967.
3. Associated Press as cited in *End-Time News Digest*, July, 1989.
4. Ibid.
5. Hulmut Kohl, Associated Press release, June 8, 1990.
6. George Bush, "Address to the Nation," September 16, 1990.
7. Mikhail Gorbachev, *Perestroika: New Thinking for Our Country and the World* (New York: Harper and Row, 1987).
8. J. Dwight Pentecost, *Things to Come* (Grand Rapids, MI: Zondervan, 1958).
9. *Foreign Affairs* magazine, Fall 1984.

Chapter 18—Spiritual Signs
1. Andrew Greely, "Mysticism Goes Mainstream," *American Health*, January/February 1987.

Chapter 19—Signs of the Times
1. *U.S. News and World Report*, December, 1983.
2. *Insight* magazine, March 10, 1986.
3. Promotional brochure, Identification Devices, Denver, CO.
4. Associated Press release, July 19, 1989.
5. Independent News Service, 5/8/91.
6. *The World Almanac* (New York: Pharos Books, 1990).
7. Canadian Press, 4/3/91.
8. *Toronto Star*, 6/23/88.
9. *Buffalo News*, 5/3/91.
10. *USA Today*, July 20, 1989.
11. *Reuters*, 5/1/91.
12. *Toronto Star*, April 26, 1991.
13. *Reuters*, 4/16/91.
14. *Toronto Star*, 3/21/91.
15. Associated Press release, 5/5/91.
16. Mortimer J. Adler, "World Peace in Truth," *Center* magazine, March/April 1978.
17. Gene Roddenberry, *Time* magazine, April 18, 1988.
18. Grace Halsell, *Prophecy and Politics* (Westport, CT: Laurence Hill and Co., 1986).
19. Save the Family Foundation brochure.

Omega-Letter
Video Productions Presents:

☐ *The Games Children Play*: In this video documentary you will study with Peter Lalonde the incredible flood of New Age poison that is invading the everyday lives of our children. Toys, games, music and even the public schools are pushing the New Age theme on our children. It is must viewing for every parent or grandparent . . . or anyone who deals with young people in any way. **56 minutes, VHS, documentary**

☐ *The Mark of the Beast*: Join Omega-Letter editor Peter Lalonde as he cuts through all the stories and gives you the facts. From the development of the cashless society, to hand scanners, eye-scanners and actual microchip implants—you will see the latest technology explained in one of the most dramatic, prophetic videos every produced.
59 minutes, VHS, documentary

☐ *New World Order:* This comprehensive report not only explains the coming World Government, but also the World Religion that will accompany it. Also discussed are the various possibilities of how such a New World Order could come about. Just how close are we? This video will show you that although we don't know the day or the hour, we can understand just how soon Jesus may return. **58 minutes, VHS**

☐ *Why We Believe We're Living in the Last Days:* Examining dozens of prophecies from the pages of the Bible, this important video documentary will bring those prophecies to life like never before. The Mark of the Beast, the coming world religion, the rise of the Antichrist, the New Age Movement, the Persian Gulf war, the Whore and the Beast . . . these are just a few of the prophecies that will be explained, documented and analyzed by Omega-Letter editor Peter Lalonde.
59 minutes, VHS, documentary

☐ *Unlocking the New Age Lie:* America is being invaded by a new mystical gospel. *The New York Times* reports that new age/occult training is now often assigned to employees of most of the nation's major corporations, including IBM, Ford, General Motors and Westinghouse. Join Peter Lalonde as he unlocks the secrets of the New Age.

59 minutes, VHS, documentary

For more information on these and other resources...

Peter Lalonde and The Omega-Letter Publishing Group offer a newsletter on Bible prophecy called *The Omega-Letter*.

If you would like to receive a free copy of this newsletter or wish to have information about other publications, tapes, or videos by Peter Lalonde, write to:

> *The Omega-Letter*
> P.O. Box 1440
> Niagara Falls, NY 14302
>
> 4429 Queen St.
> Niagara Falls, ON L2E 2L2
> Canada

> *For faster service call toll-free:*
> **1-800-PROPHECY (776-7432)**

For More Information:

Peter Lalonde and The Omega-Letter Publishing Group offer a newsletter on Bible prophecy called *The Omega-Letter*.

If you would like to receive a free copy of this newsletter or wish to have information about other publications, tapes, or videos by Peter Lalonde, write to:

The Omega-Letter
P.O. Box 1440
Niagara Falls, NY 14302

4429 Queen St.
Niagara Falls, ON L2E 2L2
Canada

For faster service call toll-free:
1-800-PROPHECY   (776-7432)